YOUR FIRST YEAR IN SALES

2ND EDITION

THREE RIVERS PRESS
NEW YORK

YOUR FIRST YEAR IN

SALES

2ND EDITION

MAKING THE TRANSITION FROM TOTAL NOVICE TO SUCCESSFUL PROFESSIONAL

TIM CONNOR, CSP

Copyright © 2010 by Three Rivers Press,
an imprint of the Crown Publishing Group,
a division of Random House, Inc.

Published in the United States by Three Rivers Press,
an imprint of the Crown Publishing Group,
a division of Random House, Inc., New York.
www.crownpublishing.com

Three Rivers Press and the Tugboat design are registered trademarks of Random House, Inc.

A previous edition of this work was originally published in the United States by Prima Publishing,
California, in 2001.

Library of Congress Cataloging-in-Publication Data
Connor, Tim 1942–
  Your first year in sales : making the transition from total novice to successful
  professional / Tim Connor—2nd ed.
    p. cm.
  Includes index.
  1. Selling.   I. Title.
  HF5438.25.C6553 2009
  658.85—dc22
                                                                              2009029421

ISBN 978–0–307–45152–1

Printed in the United States of America

10 9 8 7 6 5 4 3 2 1

Second Edition

To Dad.

Your example, support, inspiration, and insight stand

as a beacon in my life as I share my lessons with the world.

CONTENTS

ACKNOWLEDGMENTS

There are hundreds of people who have touched my life and contributed to my knowledge, including clients, audience members, peers, and friends. Thank you all.

PREFACE TO THE 2ND EDITION

SELLING DEFINED

If you were to ask one thousand people to define "selling," I guarantee that you would get one thousand different answers. Some might say it's one of the following:

- persuading others to buy
- moving products and services
- closing the deal
- helping others get what they want
- selling ice cream to Eskimos
- convincing people that what you have to offer is the best there is

But finding a narrow definition of selling isn't as important as understanding the bigger picture—after all, most of these definitions are in some way right. A more important question might be, do you think selling has changed in the past ten years? One hundred years? One thousand years? Before you spend too much time coming up with a clever answer, let me tell you that this is a trick question—the answer is of course yes *and* no. There are any number of factors that have influenced the sales profession for thousands (yes, thousands) of years. Let's go back just a few hundred.

A few hundred years ago, selling was about relationships, friends buying from friends. People buying because they trusted that their neighbor wouldn't cheat them. Was this trust always merited? Of course not. In every age there are crooks, scoundrels, and people without an ethical bone in their body. But generally speaking, selling in its earliest days was about relationships grounded in trust and respect.

Flash forward to the year 2000, and you can see how many variables have affected the selling profession. For starters, there's the Internet, cell phones, webinars, and countless other technology-based selling strategies and approaches. Have these helped organizations increase their sales? Again, this is a tricky question—and again, the answer is yes and no. Yes, because it's often easier for buyers when they have unlimited access to information about products and services, even before they have contact with a salesperson. No, because this information overload in many ways undermines the trust and respect that were originally parts of the sales relationship—which now becomes about the product or service only.

At the writing of this preface, the year is 2009, and for the past several months the world has been in an economic situation (I hate using the words "dire" and "crisis," as I have heard them enough in the past few months to last me a lifetime) that has challenged both buyers and sellers. Buyers have to make better and wiser choices, and sellers have to help maintain respectable sales results in a climate where people have more choices but are more discriminate and are buying less.

Is there any way to define a type of selling that would have worked a thousand years ago, would work today, and will work a thousand years from now? Well, it's a challenge, but here I go: Selling is persuading and influencing people to take action. Whether you're selling a product, a service, an idea, or a concept. Whether you're selling to your children, your employees, your church members, or your customers. Whether it's Tuesday afternoon or Saturday morning or the end of the month or the beginning of the week. Whether you're dealing with a first-time customer or a long-term client. Whether you're selling to someone who is wealthy or someone who is living on the street. Whether you're selling to someone who is retired or a child who is making his or her very first purchase.

What is the common thread here? *People sell to people,* and *people buy from people.* I will even go a step further: *successful* selling is about building and maintaining trust and respect in a sales relationship. If your employees don't trust you, it's unlikely they will buy your ideas. If your children don't trust you, I'll bet you will have some trouble selling them on their curfew. If your customers don't trust you, I'll wager that they will resist buying the latest version of your product.

So, selling is influencing and persuading others to take action in a relationship that is grounded in trust and respect. This definition has been proven throughout the ages, and it will be the bedrock of selling in years to come.

There are no fewer than one thousand sales books on the market today—I know many of their authors—and I'll bet that if you asked them to define selling you'd get a different answer from each. Here's what I suggest. After you finish this book, you decide for yourself what selling is and how you will best function in the industry.

THE BASICS

Many salespeople tend to embrace the latest fad, technique, or technology as the greatest way to sell quickly and easily. I have been selling for more than fifty years, and I can tell you that I have seen it all. I have read the latest books, surfed the Internet, and attended more sales seminars than I care to admit. Having said this, I can also tell you that these "latest and greatest" sales fads are all myths. If we keep going on like this, working up to a point where selling no longer involves any human interaction at all and just uses technology instead, selling will no longer be the great profession that it is. I firmly believe that selling is one of the greatest professions of all time. After all, nothing happens until somebody sells something to someone.

This book is grounded in the fundamentals, the basics that have stood the test of time and, I believe, will stand the test of time for years to come. Selling is a noble profession, but only when the seller has a mind-set of integrity, service, and knowledge. Many things have changed over the years in the sales profession, but one has not: Salespeople who routinely embrace the basics outsell their counterparts again and again.

In times of challenge, uncertainty, and unrest it is particularly important to get back to the basics—that is to say, the techniques, concepts, and approaches that will always be more effective than the latest fad.

Just what are the basics?

Let me ask you. Can you manufacture antiques? Can you reinvent water or air? You might ask, what do water and air have to do with selling or the basics? Well, they are fundamentals required for life. Eliminate either of them and life will cease to exist. Yes, many things can be reinvented, improved, or modified, but does this always make them better? No. Yes, some things can be improved with age, research, and rethinking—but some things should just stay untouched.

There's a story about Vince Lombardi that I love and think helps explain the point I'm trying to make here. Every year he would start the first practice with a group of seasoned professional football players with the simple words, "Gentlemen, this is a football." He would go on to say that if they mastered the basics of blocking, kicking, and tackling, they would win the day. Did they experiment with new plays, approaches, and strategies? Of course, but the testimony to his success as a coach was simple. He insisted that each player master the basics.

This book's goal is to illustrate and explain many of the basics, but I'll get ahead of myself for a minute and list some of the simplest and most straightforward now:

- maintaining attitudes that contribute to your enduring success
- prospecting for new business in ways that are effective
- having a sales process that is grounded in getting accurate information throughout the relationship
- giving customer-focused sales presentations
- maintaining your passion, belief, and persistence
- communicating with clarity and honesty
- creating trusting and respectful relationships
- managing the prospect's buying tension level
- promising a lot and delivering more
- asking for the business
- serving customers with integrity and commitment

If you want to consistently sell more each year, you must master the basics. Yes, you can experiment with all of the latest techniques and approaches, but to ensure that you can weather any situation or economic circumstance, the only thing that will guarantee that you last is your mastery of the fundamentals, the basics.

ALWAYS REMEMBER, YOU ARE SELF-EMPLOYED

Many people who work for a living think of themselves as employees. Yes, you may have a supervisor, fellow workers, an office or cubicle, a telephone and computer; yes, you may get a paycheck every week or month. But even if you go to the same job five or six days a week, you are more than just an employee.

If you have ever been laid off, terminated, or had your hours cut back, you understand that you are not really an employee; you are self-employed.

Let me explain.

As an independent businessperson I sell my services to my clients. They can hire me or not. If they do, I perform a service and I get paid. If they don't hire me, well, it's fairly simple: I don't get paid for doing nothing for them. There are no promotions, benefits, offices, or regular paychecks. The overall health of their businesses is determined by my performance, and my performance determines whether or not I get a raise or am successful.

If I don't improve my ability to deliver better services or information, I will most likely never get a raise or have any guarantee of continuing business. You are no different.

You have chosen to sell your time, experience, ability, talent, and motivation to your employer for a certain amount of money each year. If you don't improve in your roles and responsibilities, it's unlikely you will ever get a raise or have any degree of security. (By the way, there is almost never security in a job or career. Some of you reading this may have already learned this the hard way; some of you may be hoping to retire from your current position only when you are ready. But rest assured—this type of security doesn't really exist.)

Let's assume that you believe your talent, time, experience, and ability are worth more than your employer is willing to pay you. What do you do? Either you stay and receive less than you think you are worth, or you decide to sell your time, experience, talent, and ability to some other organization that is willing to pay you what you feel you are worth. Throughout your career, you will be making decisions like these—and the only real reason to stay where you are is if you in some way feel that you are being compensated for your value.

You always have the option, and the right, to sell "you" (and your talent, time, experience, and ability) to any other organization at any time. Conversely, your company generally has the right to decide that you are no longer needed or desired as an employee for any number of reasons and at any time.

With the frequency of mergers, acquisitions, and downsizing going on in business every day, it's easy to see that you may need to sell "you" to another company sooner or later. With this in mind, it's important to think of yourself not as an employee but as a *contractor* who has chosen at this particular moment to sell "you" to your current employer.

One of the reasons so many people get stressed out when they lose a position is that they were living in a fantasy where they were valuable "employees." From now on, I would like you to see yourself as a "self-employed person" who has chosen to sell your services, time, talent, and experience to this employer. But you always have the option to sell "you" to some other organization for any reasons you choose.

Bottom line—if you want to be able to sell yourself for higher wages to either your current employer or your next employer, you'd better keep getting better, smarter, more effective, and more creative in your roles and responsibilities.

I will say that even during challenging times, when thousands upon thousands of people are let go, the easiest way to ensure that you *won't* secure a new position is to give up on self-improvement. I know some of you may take issue with this, especially people who have been trying to find work but can't. Nevertheless, I am convinced that if you are good—no, if you are one of the *best* at what you do, you will land on your feet sooner rather than later.

WHAT'S DRIVING YOU—YOUR VALUES OR YOUR CIRCUMSTANCES?

Behavior is a function of many factors: Goals, beliefs, integrity, attitudes, values, expectations, circumstances, experience, and knowledge are just a few of the dominant ones. Eventually everyone who sells will face any number of these driving forces, especially when making life, career, or business choices and decisions.

Let's take a brief look at two aspects of behavior that often overshadow some of the others: circumstances and values. But before we begin, a quick question. If you are confronted with a serious challenge, which of these two do you believe will have the greatest impact on your behavior and your outcomes—your values or your circumstances?

Circumstances are present situations or events that influence our responses, attitudes, and behavior. These can be either negative or positive. Let's say you need to make a sale to pay your important bills this week. Your creditors are breathing down your neck and your spouse is over the edge. You have a good prospect who is stalling, but you believe the sale will go through. You have a personal rule (value) not to lower price just to get a sale, but your circumstances are creating tremendous stress and pressure. What do you do? Lower the price as an incentive to speed up your prospect or stand by your values and let nature take its course? (I am assuming here that you have done everything possible from a professional sales standpoint to close this deal—such as prospecting, presenting, and disarming objections.) Do you give in to circumstances and let them override your values or do you stand by your values and accept the outcome with dignity?

Your values are your fundamental life philosophies, standards, benchmarks, or natural behaviors when your stressors are under control. Your values may include a need for organization, control, or power; a communication style that is grounded in your self-image; or your approach to decision making and conflict. They can also include things like your opinions, your need for creative expression, and your strategic acumen. There are literally hundreds of personal values and degrees of each. So let's go back to the previous example.

You need the sale. You need the money now, but you hate giving in to pressure to deviate from your values. Nevertheless, you tell yourself that this circumstance is an exception; you need to pay certain bills. You begin to waver on your fundamental values and allow yourself the privilege of seeing this situation in degrees:

- This is a one-time exception.
- You have no other options.
- The consequences of not paying these bills could create even more stress and uncertainty.

- These unpaid bills are a distraction that is preventing you from making other sales.

This is just one example of where your values can collide with your circumstances, but there are many other values that can determine your ultimate action, decision, or behavior. There is no right or wrong answer to the above scenario, but you have to live with the consequences either way. What I'm asking you to consider here is, do you generally let your circumstances or your values drive your decisions, actions, and behavior? Every person has a different answer, but it is important to know where you stand on this issue.

THE EVOLUTION OF SELLING

There are many factors that affect the state of the sales profession and selling in general. I have already mentioned a few. Selling, like any other profession, is in a constant state of evolution as a result of technology, the global economy, and the variety of major buying groups (e.g., baby boomers or seniors).

People generally want four things in life: safety, security, health, and happiness. This has been true for centuries. But even if what people want stays the same over time, the products and services that meet these needs change dramatically over time. Take a look at any industry and this becomes immediately evident: automobiles or pharmaceuticals, cell phones or organic foods. The story is the same—some products and services change in order to satisfy buyers' basic desires, but these changes don't necessarily benefit society as a whole. Yes, the latest cell phone might at first seem to be progress, but I ask you, do we all need to be able to take photos with our phones—and, more to the point, do we all need camera phones if it means that we'll be dumping our old phones into landfills? What price (exacted from the environment, from our safety, from the future) are we willing to pay for "progress"?

While some aspects of selling haven't changed over the years, one fundamental shift is taking place: The philosophy of selling is evolving toward mere order taking. In other words, many transactions today don't involve any "selling" at all—buyers browse the latest catalogue, go online, place their orders, and then wait. Salespeople as we traditionally understand them are out of the picture. And just as the role of salespeople has changed, so has the role of buyers. In fact, today there are three different categories of buyers: shoppers, buyers, and customers. Shoppers do not want human interaction and want to control the entire buying process. Buyers want their purchases to solve their problems in an easy and seamless way. Customers want relationships that will serve their best long-term interests. Selling today is really about the third group. However, people in the first two groups are the first to complain when they have a problem with a purchase and have no recourse beyond a website or call center. This book is about creating successful relationships with customers—who will be your greatest assets as you continue your sales career.

ECONOMIC TRENDS—THE HIGHS AND THE LOWS

During challenging economic times, many salespeople tend to let their stress dictate their attitudes and approaches. They lower prices without being asked, they act desperate, and they often even grovel for the business. During these times it is vital that you maintain your composure, confidence, and commitment. Acting like you need the business will not further your cause or gain you respect from your customers and prospects.

This doesn't mean that you can't get creative with financing and other sales strategies, but it is imperative, if you do deviate from your normal philosophy, that your customers and prospects know that this is not a knee-jerk reaction but a planned approach to maintaining customer loyalty.

Over the years I have weathered four recessions, and I can tell you from personal experience that the only way out of these difficult times is that you must tap into your creative powers and be willing to reinvent yourself without sacrificing your values. There are three ways people emerge from difficult times—either they fail, survive, or prosper. In which group will you find yourself as the days, months, and years ahead unfold? And what are the characteristics, behaviors, and attitudes of each group? Let's start with those who will survive.

Just what is survival? And no, I'm not looking for the dictionary definition. To me, survival is the status quo—same stuff, different day. It's when you have nothing better to look forward to than the same experiences, setbacks, and outcomes that you have had so far. How do people behave who are in survival mode? They do only what is necessary to maintain some semblance of their lives. They are outwardly complacent, but inside they are often in turmoil. I've been in survival mode myself, and I know it's not fun wishing and hoping for something better but not knowing what to change or how to do it. The main problem with the survival people is that they really don't believe that they deserve more, so they will continue on through life focused only on "staying the course," no matter what is happening around them. They will survive.

The next group is those who will fail. Been there too, folks. Last year I had five client businesses fail; they ranged in sales from $5 million to $400 million. That money was gone, history, no more! Why? Well, in my opinion, these organizations were stuck in the past and unwilling to reinvent themselves to fit a dynamic world. People do the same thing.

Millions of people have been laid off and are not sure where their next paycheck or meal is coming from. What are the mind-sets of these people? They are stuck. Often they are too stuck to change or let whatever is holding them back go; they are too stuck to reinvent themselves. "Reinvention" is a scary word for some people, but it doesn't have to mean that you completely start from scratch. When you reinvent yourself, you take lessons from your experiences, but you don't have to let them dictate your present behavior, attitudes, decisions, or actions. They don't have to change your core values. Even so, it's a new world, and you are either on the bus, headed toward an unknown and uncertain future, or you are sitting on the curb, hoping that what you have done and who you have been will still suffice. Sorry, but sitting on the curb won't work. This is why last year I changed my mantra to "I'm just getting warmed up."

The last group of people are those who will prosper. How do these people behave, and what are their mind-sets or attitudes? First of all, let me be clear that past financial success has nothing to do with future prosperity. Just follow the stock market for a few weeks, paying special attention to the traders' hypersensitive reactions or the ever-fluctuating real estate market, and you'll see that there is no guarantee that the wealth or financial security you have enjoyed in the past will be there tomorrow. Prosperity is not about money, but about attitudes. So how do the people who will prosper in the future think or behave?

They believe in themselves and their goals. They have passion and they don't let the latest news or economic report dominate their thinking. They charge ahead with new vision and renewed strength, and they know that if they keep control of their thinking and attitudes, they will prevail, one way or another. They reinvent themselves every day, if necessary.

Which group are you in?

SELF-IMPROVEMENT

Are you investing enough in yourself?

There are a number of places where you and I can put our money, including:

1. Toys
2. Education
3. Travel
4. Looking younger
5. Looking more successful
6. Things that we hope will impress others
7. Savings
8. Investments
9. Bills
10. Food, either at home or out

Obviously, there are others, but I just want to get you thinking. Which ones in the above list do you believe will contribute to your ability to improve your success, happiness, income, and lifestyle as you pass from one year to the next? They are savings, investments, and education—and not necessarily in that order. Which two will help your chances of improving the other? Education and investments.

Sure, looking younger may make you feel temporarily better about yourself, but in the end what really matters is what you know and what you can do—not how you look, the car you drive, or the color of your hair.

Many people don't think twice about spending thousands of dollars a year on clothes, cars, meals, entertainment, their hair, their toys, and so on. Many of these same people would like to be able to afford better restaurants, nicer clothes, and fancier gadgets, but they forget that the only way to realize these goals is to cultivate their minds.

Any investment you make in yourself—in your skills or attitudes—will return itself a hundredfold, or even a thousandfold, over time. Last night's meal is gone, history. We only get to rent food temporarily. Ideas we get to keep and use again and again. Why not keep a log this year of how much you invest in your skills and abilities and how much you invest in going out to eat? Review the log once a month to see if your priorities are in line with your goals.

More than fifty years ago, when I was fired by a major insurance company for poor performance, I made a decision that for the rest of my life I would invest 10 percent of my time and 10 percent of my income every year in personal development. To this end, each year I read around one hundred books, attend two or three development retreats, and participate in a variety of seminars. With the help of various coaches, mentors, and programs, I have met my 10 percent goal each year, and friends, I can tell you this simple formula works.

YOUR DESTINY

Yesterday, be it full of mistakes, failures, and poor decisions or achievements, successes, and accomplishments, is gone. You may be left with regrets or wonderful memories, but your tomorrows have yet to come. Today is where your future memories are logged—your adventures wait patiently to be written and fulfilled. Too many people carry far too much emotional baggage into their futures, limiting the joy, happiness, peace, and success that awaits them. We all make mistakes. Sooner or later we all fail at something. A basic premise of this book is that there are no mistakes in life, only lessons to be learned or not learned. When we learn them, we can move on to new lessons. When we don't, there will always be another opportunity to learn the lessons necessary to move to a higher ground.

No one is immune to the poor choices and uncertainty that await us all as life unfolds. No one can guarantee that the past will lead to a successful future. No one can sit idly by and disconnect from life's curves, roadblocks, detours, and unknowns.

As I am writing this, millions of people have had years of savings and hard work swept away in a heartbeat because of economic challenges and changes.

People have lost their savings, investments, homes, and the very lives that they had planned and hoped for. This is life. There is no such thing as a contract that says you will make it from birth to death without disappointment, frustration, failure, discouragement, or uncertainty.

Life is uncertain. It is, always has been, and always will be. Goals are important, but in the end many of the things that will determine your life are totally beyond your control.

A hurricane, a flood, a stock market crash, a sudden divorce, or the untimely death of someone close—these are unforeseen and irrevocable circumstances. Again, this is life. By saying this, I do not mean to make light of people's struggles, adversity, or pain. I have had my share of failure, disappointment, despair, and stress. But my point is that there are two ways and only two ways to look at life: to take responsibility for yourself and your actions or to sit around feeling like a victim. None of us can control what comes into our lives, but each of us can control our responses. Don't let your history become your destiny.

SELF-MANAGEMENT

During the past several months I have been researching the defining differences between people who are struggling through life and people who appear to sail though with apparent ease. The one thing that both groups have in common is that they face adversity, challenges, and failures. The main difference between the two groups is the effectiveness of their self-management.

Exactly what is self-management and how can a person improve in this vital area of life? Let me break the subject down into five critical areas.

1. **Life outlook.** Either the glass is half full, half empty, filling up, or emptying out. If you have a positive life outlook, you don't let others' feelings, attitudes, prejudices, or opinions influence your life journey; you live life your own way (assuming that your choices don't cause harm to others, of course). You understand that your destiny and legacy are in your hands and not the hands of a government, a spouse,

an employer, or any other entity. You are optimistic about your future, rather than filled with remorse, fear, and dread.

2. **Mind-set control.** You accept with dignity and poise that some things are beyond your control, and you let go of the mistakes, the failures, or the poor judgments that you believe in hindsight could have or should have been avoided. You don't let other people's emotional baggage dominate your thinking, decisions, behaviors, or actions. You live in the present moment, embracing each experience and circumstance as a part of the unfolding life process. You understand the simple concept that you are responsible to people but not for them.

3. **Growth direction.** You believe that your life outcomes and rewards are the direct result of your willingness to continuously grow, learn, and modify your attitudes as new experiences enter your life. You are on a constant path of self-discovery—one that you have chosen, not one that has been selected for you by someone else. You consistently invest in your current skills, new skill development, and attitude improvement and modification as situations warrant.

4. **Adaptation intention.** You refuse to let current circumstances become your destiny. Your mantra is to continue to adapt to, understand, embrace, and make the best of whatever obstacles life throws in your path, be they changes in your relationships, career, health, or finances. You accept that life is a work in progress, that yesterday's decisions and choices were just that—yesterday's. Those decisions were based on the knowledge and experience you had at the time, and now that you have newer and greater experience, you are not destined to fall prey to the same mistakes.

5. **Reinvention attitudes.** You continuously look for new ways to create, become, and change rather than let your history become your destiny. You can let go of old emotional baggage, expectations, beliefs, and attitudes that are no longer in your best interests for your career, relationships, or life in general.

That's it. So how would you rate yourself, your life, and your future based on these five simple yet straightforward self-management principles?

THE APPROACH TO THIS BOOK

This is not your typical sales book. It was written and designed to be a learning tool—something you study instead of just read.

If we were to break down learning into its stages, they would look something like this:

- exposure to new material and ideas
- study of the material
- practice
- review
- integration
- mastery

Here is the process I recommend if you want to get the most from this learning tool:

1. Spend a few hours just getting familiar with the content and its flow.
2. Now go back and read a chapter a day.
3. When you're finished reading, spend a week on each chapter, taking notes and personalizing the content as you go.
4. When you've again reached the end, go back through the book one more time and come up with action steps or plans (in a journal) to implement and integrate the material into your own life.
5. Now go through your journal and prioritize your actions based on their relevance to your career and your ability, resources, and time.
6. This is the easy step—start executing your plans.
7. Each week take a few minutes to update your experiences and learning in your journal. The goal here is to totally integrate and customize the content of *Your First Year in Sales* into your personal journal. I guarantee that if you follow this process, you will be amazed at how quickly you master the ideas, techniques, and approaches contained in this book.

Now, let's get selling!

INTRODUCTION

In sales as in life, sometimes it is best to get right to the point. Thus, I will keep my introduction short and allow us to get to the great material that follows.

The average cost of a sales call today is more than $500, regardless of whether you close the sale. Can you imagine the yearly investment for your company, even if it has only twenty-five salespeople making an average of four calls a day? That's $8 million a year! And that doesn't include extra compensation such as bonuses or commissions, special training, attending sales meetings, and anything and everything else.

Now I ask you, why should a company invest that much of its income in a sales force that is less than professional, poorly trained, or generally has a negative attitude? I don't have an answer to that one, but I can tell you that if sooner or later they don't recoup that investment, you will be looking for a new employer.

During my forty-five-year sales career, I have done some research on the amount of time salespeople spend actually selling. What I have learned is that the average salesperson spends less than 10 to 20 percent of total work time selling and more than 80 percent doing everything else, like traveling, attending meetings, managing paperwork, serving customers, handling after-sales problems, and the many other tasks that come with being in sales. Can you imagine for a moment, a company paying salespeople over $50,000 a year to do paperwork? For windshield time? For after-sales service? Don't fool yourself. You are paid to sell—period. Yes, your position has other requirements, but in the end, how much you have sold will determine your income, status, success, and lifestyle.

There are numerous advantages to a career in sales, and I will cover many of these in the first chapter. But for now I'll assume that you are reading this book because you want to succeed *now* in your new career. Your sales success—immediate and ongoing—will be a function of many skills and attitudes. In the pages that follow, you will learn the essentials as well as the strategies that will put you over the top and turn you into a sales leader.

First, you need to answer a serious question: Why have you selected a career in sales? Did it happen by accident? Did you assume that since you couldn't make it in another career, you could always sell for a living? (Any reader affected by the economic downturn of the late 2000s probably understands the folly of this attitude.) Was it for the money? Freedom? Glamour? Or something else? Your honest answer to this question, before you settle into a career in selling, may well determine your success. Many people who could have done really well in sales quit because they never answered this question. They had no clear expectation of what they wanted to get out of sales.

Second, ask yourself what you are willing to give up to enjoy the success you say you want. Earning success takes sacrifice. That's why you *earn* success.

And finally, ask yourself what motivates you to continue anything when life throws you for a loop. There will be ups and downs in this profession, like any other, and the more you have thought about how you will deal with the downs, the better prepared you will be to overcome unexpected obstacles.

I have been in sales, as a salesperson and as a trainer, for forty-five years. Obviously, I am doing something right, or I wouldn't have lasted this long. I can tell you that a successful sales career is worth the effort, price, commitment, and time. Many people want to take the easy road. The easy road goes nowhere; trust me. Sooner or later, your resolve, goals, commitment, will, and desire will be tested. Whether you pass the test is up to you and no one else. Be prepared to be tested over and over. If you have a weak spirit, a shallow resolve, and a tendency to quit or give up early, commit yourself to toughening up and take the appropriate steps to do so, or save yourself the trouble. While it may sound strange to discourage you before you even begin, my purpose in writing this book is to contribute to your success and the satisfaction of your customers, *not* to give excuses to the weakhearted.

I love this profession. It has given me the ability to live as I want. It can give that to you, too. But you will have to do the work. You will have to study, practice, learn, try, fail, and get up again and again. And if you do, you will look back with pride, satisfaction, gratitude, and a smile.

CHAPTER 1

IT'S YOUR MOVE

Welcome to the exciting profession of sales. You deserve to be congratulated for choosing sales and thus making the decision to determine your destiny, lifestyle, and personal freedom. Approached with the proper attitude, skills, determination, and knowledge, the field of sales can be an exciting career. Reading this book is the perfect start to that career.

I have been selling for more than forty-five years and teaching people to sell for thirty-seven years. I have seen and taught people of both genders and from all backgrounds, nationalities, education levels, and ethnicities.

Whether you succeed has absolutely nothing to do with any of those characteristics. Your prime needs are the will to succeed; a commitment to excellence; effort; a willingness to learn, grow, and change; a desire to serve others; persistence in difficult times and situations; and staying power.

Sales is not an easy profession, but the harder you work, the greater your rewards. The sales profession is full of obstacles: difficult people, difficult situations, and seemingly impassable dead ends. But it is also the source of a lot of fun, a great deal of satisfaction, personal security, excitement, tremendous earning potential, and daily opportunities to meet wonderful people from different walks of life.

I'll let you in on a secret: I was fired from my first sales position. But with time, patience, and a lot of effort and study, years later I sold *that same company*

> ### Think About It
>
> There is only one reason not to go into sales: if you are uncomfortable controlling your personal and financial destiny.

some sales training. Yes! Cha-ching. All it took was belief in myself, persistence, and a lot of hard work. Believe me when I say it was well worth it.

Throughout this book are the hints, tips, secrets, and rules for success. Together, they create a formula that will lead you to succeed during your first year as a salesperson. *Your First Year in Sales* describes in detail the attitudes you need to develop, the skills you must master, and the philosophy you should adopt.

OUR OWN QUICK START

This profession will change you as well as challenge you to grow personally and professionally. You are the only one who can determine your success and what you give to and take from your sales career as it unfolds in the months and years ahead.

For me, getting into this wonderful profession was one of the best decisions I ever made. I have met all of my friends during the course of this career. Everything I have learned was because of this profession. And all of the satisfaction I have gained and any contribution I have made to society was made possible by my occupation as a salesperson. My goal here is to give you everything you need to be able to look back years from now and say the same things.

The Quick-Start Concept

In sports, there is a concept called the quick start. It means that the first team to score in any game has a greater chance of winning than does its opponent. The same can be said for sales, where the quick-start concept means you must

- come out of the gate each year on January 1 at a dead run
- begin each new week with a good sale
- start each month with a positive outlook and expectations

- start the day early with a positive plan for success
- jump-start your new career and quickly move into the fast lane

This book will give you the tools to do just that. If you read this book, study it, live it, and breathe it, I guarantee that you will be ahead of the pack before you've even finished your first year as a salesperson. You will set sales records, position yourself for long-term success, and immediately earn the respect of your customers, peers, friends, and supervisor.

WHAT IS A PROFESSIONAL SALESPERSON?

For years I have heard people use the word "professional," especially when they refer to salespeople. How would you define a professional? I have been asking my audiences for years to describe a sales professional. The consensus is that a professional salesperson is

- well groomed
- punctual
- well dressed
- honest
- knowledgeable
- positive, with a good attitude
- courteous and doesn't bad-mouth the competition
- customer focused
- dependable
- caring
- a creative problem solver
- good at sales follow-up

This list could go on for several pages. Again, I ask you, how would you define a professional? To me, being a professional is not about what you sell, but how you sell. Let me explain. Some people selling high-priced and highly regarded products are far from professional. I have met some pretty sleazy salespeople selling very expensive products and services, and I have had the pleasure of doing business with some really great people selling appropriately priced products and services.

Salespeople Are Not Becoming Obsolete

Will the continual advances in technology replace the profession of selling in the foreseeable future? I am not a fortune-teller or a mystic, but I do believe that we will see dramatic changes in the roles salespeople play within their organizations and the economy in general. During the next several years, even the next few decades, we will see dramatic and all-encompassing change in every industry, field, and profession.

We are rapidly becoming a society that no longer talks face-to-face. We communicate by e-mail and the Internet using cell phones and a variety of other electronic devices. We are losing the human touch. But as salespeople, we bridge the gap between this impersonal electronic world and our human customers: one of several reasons why the sales profession is alive and well and will continue to play a vital role in a growing economy for years. Salespeople are charged with any or all of the following:

- They present new ideas, concepts, products, and services to present and potential clients.
- They assess the marketplace and gauge customer satisfaction levels and perceptions, general market attitudes, competitors' strengths and weaknesses, and consumer interest trends.
- They witness and report on the emergence of grassroots market shifts, trends, and interests.
- They soothe the ruffled egos of disappointed, frustrated, and angry customers.
- They provide bottom-up feedback to the management of their organization on any number of opportunities, problems, and issues.
- They are the front line of attack for any number of corporate marketing strategies and programs.
- They work the trade show booths (a grueling task, if you have never done it) in thousands of trade shows each year.

- They are on the lookout for new product or service opportunities that a corporate person would never see.
- They are ambassadors for management, building positive ongoing relationships that can increase business and profits.

I challenge you to find a software program, customer service representative, or marketing person who can do all of this with the courage of a mountain climber; the patience of Job; the sense of sacrifice of a humanitarian; the energy of a two-year-old; the creativity of Frank Lloyd Wright; the dedication of a mother; the wisdom of Confucius; the enthusiasm of a cheerleader; the commitment of an Olympic athlete; and the persistence of a toddler trying to reach the cookie jar. The role of the sales professional will continue to shift and change, but the fundamental mission will remain intact.

So, selling is not what you sell, but how you sell what you sell. Ask yourself: How am I doing when it comes to being a professional? How do I want my clients or customers to think of me? How do I want my competitors to think about me? How do I want the marketplace to view my activity? Don't wait for the results to come in from these sources. Ask yourself and adapt your style and attitude to match your desired result.

ATTITUDES FOR SALES SUCCESS

The way you prepare for each day, each sale, and how you respond to your successes and failures will ultimately determine just how enjoyable and lucrative your career in sales will be. Let's touch on a few of the critical attitudes and behaviors you must develop if you are to succeed.

- **Persistence.** You must have persistence. More often than not, people will put off saying yes to your presentation. The key is knowing how to discover the prospect's critical sense of urgency and when the best times to persevere and follow up with that potential customer are.

Equally important is the ability to not be discouraged when you are rejected or unsuccessful.

- **Resilience.** People will say no, with that being their final answer. Whether you have the fortitude to march on, even with such rejections, will play a large part in determining your success.

- **Interest in self-improvement.** Be willing to learn new skills and attitudes. There are *always* new things you can learn and attitudes you can acquire. Those who stay knowledgeable about new trends and corporate thinking remain on top of the sales leaderboard.

- **Confidence yet modesty.** Keep your ego in check. Today may have been great; tomorrow could be just the opposite. Keep a level head. The ups and downs of sales can be frequent, and the higher you let your ego float, the harder and farther it can fall.

- **Flexibility.** The ability to work effectively in a less-than-ideal business environment is essential. No company is perfect. Few sales situations are ideal. The key is to be able to take a difficult situation and turn it into a positive outcome. For example: I can recall, in my second sales position, that my work space was about five square feet with a school-size desk to work from. The telephone was on a windowsill behind me. Not ideal circumstances by any stretch of the imagination. But I had to sell regardless of my environment. I quickly figured out that if I let the circumstances dictate my attitude, I was in big trouble. So, I simply looked at it as only a temporary situation. I kept telling myself that if I could be successful under those circumstances, I could sell anywhere, anytime. And when I proved my success to my supervisors, I could count on the fact that my environment would change.

> *Think About It*
> Your ability to direct and guide a prospect's thinking is directly related to your ability to control your own thoughts.

- **Professionalism.** Be adept at cultivating positive working relationships, even with those who can be difficult to work with. Not everyone has to be your best friend. Be open to developing a positive business relationship with *anyone*. Business is business, friendship is friendship, but here, business is the name of the game.

- **Motivation.** Keep yourself motivated. Again, business is business. No matter what distractions you have in your personal life, you must be able to put on your game face every day and get the job done.
- **Self-control.** Control your attitudes and emotions. Keeping your attitudes and emotions at the appropriate level for the situation is a must. Knowing when and how to react will help you enormously in your career.

Each of these attitudes and behaviors is something you must develop to ensure your success.

WHAT TO EXPECT

Selling is fun and rewarding. You help people solve problems, overcome challenges, improve their sales or results, or maybe help them sleep better at night because of your creative solutions. The average professional salesperson keeps at least thirty other people employed in our economy. That, my friend, is a worthy professional accomplishment. This success, however, does not come cheap. You'll face hurdles, challenges, problems, risks, and potential failures that will frustrate you. And there are always many other things to turn your attention to if the frustration gets the best of you. However, you'll experience an overflowing feeling of satisfaction with each obstacle cleared. If you prepare to experience all of the following, then you will be better prepared to endure the challenging times and manage the prosperous periods.

Here's what you can expect, good and bad:

- long days
- a sense of satisfaction
- early-morning risings
- controlling your destiny
- late nights
- lots of new friends
- evening appointments
- opportunities for personal growth

- time away from friends and family
- a chance to make more money than you ever dreamed possible
- stress, pressure, and deadlines
- the ability to contribute to the success of others
- upset customers
- being paid what you are worth
- demanding bosses
- travel
- unethical competitors

If you approach your new career with a chin-up attitude, you will certainly enjoy your share of the good times. Inevitably, though, some of the negative elements will also creep into your career. Just remember that it is natural to want to quit something when it is new and difficult. It is human nature to want everything to be easy. Problem is, if everything were easy, you wouldn't get the same sense of satisfaction and joy. Struggle, once overcome, is the source of all of our good feelings about ourselves. No challenge? Well, sure, you may get the prize, but I guarantee you won't enjoy it as much. This comes from someone who has failed far more often than he has ever succeeded.

I am not a pessimist. I am not a realist. I have found there is no value in anything less than pure optimism. I grew up failing. Most of us endure many, many failures over our lifetimes. I'll just say that sooner or later, your worth will be tested, not by your successes but by your failures. There is nothing wrong with wanting to quit. Just don't do it. Give yourself the benefit of the doubt when life throws up obstacles. The light is always at the end of the tunnel, but you have to keep on driving to reach it. If you can both weather these difficulties and not let success make you arrogant, believe me, the journey will be well worth it.

The light is always at the end of the tunnel, but you have to keep on driving to reach it.

TRAPS TO AVOID

New salespeople are vulnerable to falling into any number of traps or going in directions that lead to dead ends. Some of these may seem insignificant at first, but do not be lulled into a false sense of security. Remember that you are in the formative months of a new profession and learning both good and bad habits that will be with you for years. Don't risk starting something that you can't stop. The price of failure is far too high. Your customers will set some of these traps; others may be set by your fellow salespeople or support staff. Even your supervisor may set you some traps.

One of the biggest traps is developing the habit of comparing yourself with other salespeople and your successes with theirs. Whether they are on your sales team or are your competitors, your success has nothing to do with theirs. The only thing that matters is what you are doing and what you *could* be doing; that is the only way to truly take stock of your accomplishments.

In my first sales position, I was discouraged because I was always on the bottom of the list of salespeople when the results were tallied at the end of the month. I became anxious, frustrated, and began to focus on not doing things wrong rather than on doing them right and paying attention to what I was learning and how I was progressing. Avoid this trap—even if you finish on the bottom of the list, you have the opportunity to learn invaluable lessons if you are self-aware and always think about the factors contributing to your performance.

Years later, when I was a veteran, one of my fellow salespeople who was doing better than I kept trying to manipulate me by telling me that even though I was doing well, I would never really hit the big time in sales. Fortunately, I had enough belief in myself that his words had no long-term negative impact on me.

The traps are out there. Keep your eyes out for them, and stay confident in yourself and your abilities.

WHAT YOU NEED TO LEARN

Any new career requires you to develop new skills, attitudes, and knowledge of the job itself.

You will need time, patience, an open mind, a willingness to learn, flexibility, and the ability to let go of the old baggage from your previous career. This baggage can take the form of previous slights, failures, relationship challenges, company policies or procedures that you didn't like or agree with, and numerous other issues.

Sales is not like any other career. To be successful in sales requires a unique set of people skills, sales techniques, relationship skills, attitude management skills, and effective time and territory management. You have a great deal to learn. Be patient with yourself as you develop these new habits, attitudes, and techniques. This does not mean that you should not throw yourself into your new position with everything you have. It only implies that learning new skills and techniques requires time. You must learn how to

- manage and overcome the fear of rejection
- cultivate positive relationships with support staff
- meet the expectations of your supervisor
- balance your time between selling, learning, and personal and family time
- determine which prospects are worthy of your time
- keep yourself motivated when things go wrong
- keep personal challenges, issues, and negatives out of your mind while selling
- not beat yourself to a pulp when things go wrong

Patience is your biggest virtue while you are learning your new trade. With patience, you will learn faster and enjoy the ride toward success. Without patience, you will have a tough time learning the right way to do anything. Be aggressive, but also thoughtful, as you move along.

ONE WORD—*ASK*—IS ALL IT TAKES

This three-letter word is at the root of more failures and successes in sales than any other I know. People who consistently succeed in sales, whatever success means to them, do so because they *ask* for what they want. Salespeople who fail tend to do so because they either don't know what they want or don't know how to ask for it. If you ask the right people the right questions and learn everything you can, you will undoubtedly reap the benefits in many areas of your career. Figure 1 shows you how.

Knowledge

↓

Belief

↓

Confidence

↓

Professionalism

↓

Improved Performance

↓

Success

Figure 1 | **KNOWLEDGE IS KING**

Ask, Ask, Ask

You must ask your customers many things:

- Ask for the order (the obvious one).
- Ask for referrals, each and every time.
- Ask for letters of testimony (every contact).
- Ask questions, a lot of them, and keep asking them.
- Ask if you may use them as references (this can get you more business).
- Find out why they did business with you. You need to know.
- Find out why they *didn't* do business with you (every lost sale).
- Ask for the right to use third-party influence.
- Ask how you can best serve them.

There are many more. In fact, you should constantly be updating your list of questions as you gain experience. You can then tailor your list to your particular position as you start to understand what it takes to be successful.

Years ago I made a cold call to the president of a Fortune 500 company. I'll never forget it. He actually saw me, and he taught me a valuable lesson. At the conclusion of the call, I asked him why he was willing to see me. He said, "No one has ever tried to see me as president without an appointment. I wanted to meet the person who had the guts to ask."

So don't miss another opportunity to achieve your dreams. Ask for what you want. There are only two outcomes when you do: You will get what you want or you won't. If you don't, you have lost nothing by asking. When in doubt, ask for it. Guess what? You might just get it. Failure is not about missing the mark, but rather about not taking the first step.

GETTING ORGANIZED

Getting organized means many things in the sales profession. You must coordinate your materials, time, learning, territory, attitudes, and sales approaches. The foundation for becoming highly organized is an effective planning philosophy and strategy. Here are a few things to consider:

- Get up an hour earlier every day than you are accustomed to.
- Make an appointment with yourself every evening to plan your goals, activities, and objectives for the next day.
- Spend time preparing for each week and month.
- Schedule time every day for learning about your product, polishing your sales skills, and perfecting the strategies you use to manage your relationships.
- Develop positive work habits.
- Keep track of your time wasters.
- Keep a time-and-activity log for your first three months on the job.
- Spend time each week with seasoned salespeople and think of specific questions to ask them.
- Spend time regularly with your supervisor. Seek feedback on specific questions.

- Develop the habit of asking lots of questions.
- Start a success journal. Keep track of your successes no matter how small you think they are.
- Set deadlines for yourself to master new skills or learn new information.
- Read, read, read. Keep your TV off for three months.
- Evaluate your time-use rituals, that is, reading the newspaper, watching TV, and the like.

Add to this list as you progress through your new career.

All of these things will pave the road for success—and you need them all. But what other traits do successful salespeople share?

> **Think About It**
> Being a professional is not about what you sell, but how you sell.

TRAITS OF SUCCESSFUL SALESPEOPLE

Successful salespeople have developed certain traits and attitudes that contribute to their success. I have been observing salespeople for a long time, and I can tell you that they don't all have each of the characteristics or abilities listed below. They are, however, able to master those traits that are critical for their particular product or service, their organizational culture, and their customers' needs and expectations, as well as learn competitors' strengths and weaknesses. The following list is in no particular order, but it does give you an idea of the profile of success in the selling profession.

- Successful salespeople manage their attitudes from the inside out, not from the outside in. They are proactive, not reactive.
- They are on fire with passion and desire.
- They are a resource for their clients. They go the extra mile.
- They are excellent communicators.
- They are focused and concentrate on the task at hand.
- They are able to win the goodwill of all inside support staff.
- They spend more time digesting information than giving it.

- They are masters at asking the right questions, in the right way and at the right time.
- They sell value, not price. They know that, over time, this is the most important issue to the customer.
- They manage their time, as well as company resources, money, and people.
- They keep in touch with their clients and prospective clients regularly.
- They have high-quality service and customer loyalty as their primary goals.
- They honor their commitments.
- They give something back to their community and profession.
- They are everywhere at once. They network and understand the value of good contacts.
- They have lofty goals. They don't always reach them, but they aim for the stars.
- They promise a lot and deliver more.
- They understand the importance of knowledge of customers, competitors, and the marketplace.
- They give their word as their bond.
- They work hard and smart.
- They don't try only for the home runs. They know that if they just keep hitting singles consistently, sooner or later they will hit a home run.

A long list, I know, but if you want to separate yourself from the also-rans in this profession, mastering most of this list is vital. Even if it takes you your entire career to do so, if you integrate these concepts into your selling behavior early, little by little, in time you'll become a superstar.

Why not measure yourself against this list and then, over time, ask your clients to do the same? You might find out some interesting and valuable information about how you are progressing.

CREATING A TRUSTWORTHY AND FAVORABLE IMPRESSION

There is an old saying: You never get a second chance to make a first impression. I don't really know whether it is true or not. Many clichés have a way of hanging around, and no one ever questions them. Regardless, first impressions certainly are important, especially in business.

In your personal life, if you make a poor first impression on someone new, it probably won't cost you your job or suddenly put you in the ranks of the unemployed. However, if you consistently make poor first impressions in business, it can create a stigma that can be hard to shake. Why are first impressions so important? When we first meet people, we judge them on a number of factors. These include

- their physical appearance
- how they are dressed
- their posture
- their apparent level of self-confidence
- their ability to communicate (speak articulately and listen actively)
- their social graces
- their smiles
- the nonverbal signals they send (positive or negative, harmonious or conflicting)
- their eye contact
- what they transmit

We then filter all of the above data through our own unique mental filter and draw one of the following conclusions:

- I like this person.
- I don't like this person.
- I respect this person.
- I don't respect this person.
- I trust this person.
- I don't trust this person.
- I accept this person at face value.
- I sense that this person has some hidden agendas.

Things such as a genuine smile; a firm handshake; confident, open body language; good, erect posture; appropriate eye contact; attentiveness; good verbal skills; appropriate attire; good hygiene; genuine interest; and a good attitude contribute to a favorable first impression.

Too much talking; not paying attention; an uncomfortable demeanor; bad posture; a lack of adequate eye contact; inattention; and an uninspiring handshake all contribute to an unfavorable impression.

In short, stand or sit up straight, smile, maintain eye contact, know of what you speak, listen, and look good. The rest will take care of itself.

DEVELOP A SLIGHT EDGE

More than thirty years ago, while I was a distributor for a major franchise organization, I was introduced to the "slight edge" concept. Being in my midtwenties and having had little exposure at that point to motivation and personal development, this concept was revolutionary to me. Today, many of you may be familiar with both, either formally or informally. But just what is the slight edge, and how do you obtain it?

> *Think About It*
>
> Make one extra call a day—that's five extra calls per week, fifty a year—and you will outearn and outshine your counterparts. Just think: What could fifty extra calls in a year do for your income?

In sports, in business, in education, and, indeed, in all walks of life, the people who win (however they choose to define winning: not necessarily beating someone else, but perhaps beating their own previous best) aren't necessarily one hundred or even ten times better. They simply tend to be a little better at the important things. They are generally not extraordinary: they just do the little things in an extraordinary way. Let me give you an example.

The hitter in baseball that hits over a .300 batting average will earn at least ten times as much as the player who only hits .250. The difference is one more hit every twenty times at bat. That's it! You don't have to be insanely productive to be a superstar. Simply exceed expectations and the competition—whoever or whatever your competition may be—on a consistent basis, and bingo, you are a super success! It doesn't take a major sacrifice. Just routinely do a little more each day and watch the balance sheet add up.

INTEGRITY AND ETHICS

The sales profession today needs people with integrity, honesty, and the ability to develop trusting relationships with customers, support staff, suppliers, and management. Read the following story and decide whether integrity rules in this scenario.

Be a Star

What little things can you do each day to outshine your competition? Try these tips to stay one step ahead:

- Make an extra telephone call.
- Obtain one more referral.
- Study your product or your job one more hour.
- Work in an additional appointment.
- Make one more closing attempt.

Randy, a new salesperson for the ABC Company, meets with a prospect. The prospect, Barbara, asks if Randy's product will satisfy her company's basic problem, which is high product costs. Randy affirms that his product will solve their problem. After discussing all of the features and benefits, Randy quotes a price for his product.

At this point Barbara resists, saying that she does not have enough money in her budget for this product even though she needs it to reduce costs. She understands that she needs it and that his product will solve her problem. She just doesn't have the money. Randy's response is to recommend a lesser version of the product that she can afford, saying it will work just as well. (It really won't satisfy all of her needs, but he wants the sale, and he justifies his action by thinking that Barbara's taking the lesser version is better than doing nothing.) She is concerned that by going to a lesser version, she will be sacrificing the ability to totally satisfy her needs and solve her problem. Randy assures her it will work, that this version lacks only a few of the bells and whistles of the original recommendation, and that she will lose nothing of real importance. He closes the sale.

What do you think? Is our sales friend lacking integrity? Is it OK, from time to time, to tell just a little white lie that doesn't do major harm to the relationship? If it is OK to tell little white ones, under what circumstances are they acceptable? Ethics is a major issue for many people, including customers, vendors, and prospects. What are your standards? Do you stick to the truth no matter how hard it might hurt you now or the outcome later?

Truth at all costs? Is it a matter of personal perspective? Many people, sooner or later, in an attempt to avoid conflict or protect themselves or another person from pain and disappointment, will lie. However, when you do, you set up the relationship for failure. Misrepresentation, shading the truth, little white fibs, or outright lies can never help you in your sales career or with a client relationship. In my opinion, truth, although it might cost you the sale, is always the best policy. It was Mark Twain who said, "When you tell the truth you never have to remember what you said." Amen.

In my opinion, truth, although it might cost you a sale, is always the best policy.

PEOPLE BUY FROM PEOPLE THEY TRUST

Over the years, of course, much has changed in the sales environment. Nevertheless, one thing is and always will be a certainty: People buy from people they trust. Your product is an extension of you. If a customer can trust you, then the customer can trust buying your product from you.

So has anything changed in selling over the past fifty years? Those of you who have been selling for less than five years most likely will answer that question with a no. Those of you with battle scars going back to the 1960s, 1970s, 1980s, and 1990s will probably answer with a resounding "a whole lot." Some of you are just not sure or can't articulate what the changes have been. As you begin your sales career, you might want to make a mental note of the following changes in and current realities of the sales profession:

- People have better, and often instant, access to information about your products and services *and* those of your competitors.
- People want you to help them make better-informed decisions, especially in this age of information overload.
- There are three major segments of prospects: millions of baby boomers, millions of retired folks, and millions of people under the age of thirty-five in positions of power.
- More women are in positions of influence with respect to purchases.
- There are increased opportunities to sell to people from different cultures.
- There are fewer layers of management to go through to get to your decision maker.
- Technology is changing buying patterns and attitudes.
- People will not tolerate poor quality or poor service. Instead, they will do business with your competitor.
- Your prospects have a countless number of options and plenty of vendors from whom to buy what they need.

Not everything has changed. Some things are tried and true and are here to stay:

- People buy what they want and desire.
- People want a fair value.
- People do not want to be lied to or misled.
- People do not want to pay too much to solve their problems or satisfy their wants and needs.
- People buy from people they trust.
- People do not buy just because they like you: You must fill a want or need of theirs.

The world is constantly changing, and the sales profession is no different. Keeping up with and even ahead of the times is often one of the elements that makes for an extraordinary salesperson. So study and stay up to date, and you will remain ahead of your competition.

LIFE IS PERCEPTUAL

No one looks at life or its events, conditions, or circumstances in the same way. We see life not as it is, but as we are. Each of us has a mental filter through which we interpret other people's behavior, events, and circumstances. Ten people can look at the same piece of art, the same auto accident, movie, or sunset, and see it differently. This gives life diversity and its relationships their challenges. Each of us has a mental filter with which we filter all of the experiences and observations in our life. For example: if I asked you to give me your opinion of this book so far, your comments would be completely your own and different from those of everyone else who has read the book. No one would describe its style, content, or objectives exactly the same.

One example I use in my seminar for couples is the idea of faults. Do you know someone who has faults? Be honest, now. Look closely at them for a moment. Aren't another person's faults simply the ways that person thinks, feels, or acts differently from how you think he or she should think, feel, or act? The assumption you are making when another person has a fault is that your way of feeling, acting, and so forth is superior.

As a salesperson, you should stop judging people and situations as "right" or "wrong"; you should think only of differences in perception. Passing judgment is one of the biggest issues in sales relationships that causes stress and conflict. You often feel like you need to change other people to your way of thinking because you think that their mentality is wrong and yours is right. Acceptance— learning to respect or at least recognize differences of opinion—is one of the biggest hurdles people face in relationships. It is also a major issue when it comes to motivating ourselves on a consistent basis. If we fail to perceive life and its events and people clearly, if we fall into the trap of judgment, we tend to fall into a number of demotivating traps, such as guilt, blame, resentment, anger, and any number of other negative emotions. These negative responses will color your use of your talent and how you treat others on a regular basis.

One of the best indicators of someone who is happy, successful, and living in a harmonious way is how clearly he or she is in touch with reality: not just his or her reality, but the realities of the surrounding world. Too many people believe that their truth should be everyone's truth.

HOW TO BE THE SALESPERSON YOU WANT TO BE

We have talked about some of the qualities you need—integrity, professionalism, willingness to work hard, and others—to be a successful salesperson. But you also need to know of some common mistakes salespeople make, some of the myths that may cloud the reality of sales, and how to handle the unfortunate, but inevitable, moments of rejection.

> *Think About It*
> Where are your perceptions about life, selling, people, events, circumstances, and your past, present, and future clouded? Where do you need a clearer vision and more accurate perceptual integrity?

Common Sales Mistakes

The marketplace is filled with poor and unprofessional salespeople. The sales profession is no different from any other when it comes to having its share of exceptional professionals as well as those people who could tarnish the reputation of the profession at large. Although many of the following traits are not perceived as unprofessional or unethical, they certainly go a long way toward painting salespeople—all of us—in a less than desirable light. And they are absolutely characteristics and actions to avoid, at least if you want to be able to afford a hot meal. Poor salespeople do the following:

- They talk too much.
- They give information before they get information.
- They fail to observe and integrate early prospect signals.
- They don't effectively manage rejection and failure.
- They sell when they should prospect and prospect when they should sell.
- They don't listen and instead take notes while the prospect is talking.
- They inject their own values, and perhaps buying prejudices, into the sales process.

- They don't effectively read buyers' signals and act accordingly.
- They sell features and price rather than value and customer benefits.
- They don't keep good records or evaluate their wins and losses.
- They fail to work as hard to keep the business as they did to get it.
- They don't ask for the business.
- They focus on making the sale rather than selling the relationship.
- They don't invest enough time and money in their self-development.
- They confuse the importance of knowing with that of caring.
- They misrepresent their products or services or both.
- They have poor knowledge of their products or services or both.
- They don't realize that they represent their organization and profession 24/7.
- They fail to honor their commitments.
- They are unprofessional in their behavior and demeanor.

When I was a new salesperson, one of the biggest mistakes I ever made occurred during an appointment with the president of one of my company's biggest clients. During the middle of my presentation I had to use the restroom. I excused myself right in the middle of the interview to go to the bathroom, which, of course, was extremely disruptive and reflected poorly on me. So always use the restroom before you begin an appointment, or, at the very least, limit your beverage intake before the appointment.

Common Sales Myths

Over the years, a great number of sales trainers, as well as sales managers, have perpetuated a number of sales myths. They may have been true at the time they were thought up, or at least people thought they were true. It is my belief, though, that in today's global economy, where change, technology, and value are driving consumers to new levels of satisfaction and understanding, these myths are not true no matter who is preaching them. I would like to share just a few of these with you, along with the reasons they are myths, not truths, and what the truth really is. Decide for yourself what makes the most sense, or what feels right to you.

MYTH: *Sales is a numbers game.*

TRUTH: *Sales is not a numbers game.* It is not a game at all. Selling is serious business. Some people say that if you see enough people, you will make enough sales. Bull. Selling is about *the right* numbers. If you see enough of the right people (qualified prospects), you will make lots of sales. The rationale here is that the number-one cause of failure in sales is the issue of rejection. If your strategy is to see lots of people, qualified or otherwise, sooner or later you are going to get more rejection than you can probably handle and will either quit or fail. If, on the other hand, you spend your time approaching *qualified* prospects, you are less likely to be burdened by needless rejection. Spend your valuable selling time with good prospects.

MYTH: *Salespeople can never give too much information.*

TRUTH: *Poor salespeople talk too much.* They give information before they get it. If this is your approach, you will tend to make one of two mistakes: giving unnecessary information or giving wrong information. Selling is not about giving a presentation filled with features and benefits that your organization has decided are important for the prospect to know. It is about giving only that information that each prospect (and they are all different) wants or needs to make an informed and intelligent buying decision. This is the difference between an organization- or product-driven focus and a customer-driven focus.

> **Think About It**
> Your prospect's enthusiasm for your product or service is in direct proportion to your own enthusiasm.

MYTH: *You can fake it until you make it.*

TRUTH: *Successful salespeople spend their time learning, growing, reading, observing, and developing habits, attitudes, approaches, and techniques that work.* They know what works because their purpose is to be good at what they do. If your approach is to fake it while you are learning, sooner or later you will get caught, and in my experience, it is sooner rather than later and more often versus less often.

The key is not to use the same approach with everyone, but to learn which approach is appropriate on each call.

MYTH: *In every sales appointment you need some small talk, or a warming-up period.*

TRUTH: *Each prospect deserves a unique and custom-designed sales approach based on his or her personality and style. Some people want and need warm-up time, but others don't. The key is not to use the same approach with everyone, but to learn which approach is appropriate on each call.*

MYTH: *I only need to hear six more noes from poor prospects, and the next one is sure to buy!*

TRUTH: *You can hear one hundred straight noes and still hear no from the next person, too. You can also get seven straight yeses if you are calling on good prospects.*

MYTH: *People buy from people they like.*

TRUTH: *People buy from people they trust.*

MYTH: *People buy because of your product's features.*

TRUTH: *People buy because your product or service solves a problem for them; answers a need, want, or desire; or offers an opportunity for gain.*

MYTH: *Everyone buys your products and services for the same reasons.*

TRUTH: *People buy from you for their reasons, not yours.*

MYTH: *You can sell anybody anything!*

TRUTH: *You can't close everyone. If you have been selling for at least a month, you have figured this out already.*

MYTH: *Everyone is a prospect for you.*

TRUTH: *You must seek and find viable prospects.*

MYTH: *The close is the most important part of the sales process.*

TRUTH: *Prospecting and qualifying are the most important.*

MYTH: *The best salespeople make the best sales managers.*

TRUTH: *It requires more than good sales skills to be a good manager.*

MYTH: *People always want the lowest price.*

TRUTH: *People do not want to spend more than they need to, but they really want the highest value (that is to say, the lowest cost to them over time).*

MYTH: *Salespeople are born, not made!*

TRUTH: *Successful salespeople develop their skills and attitudes. They are not born with these.*

MYTH: *Everyone buys a product or service for the same reason.*

TRUTH: *Not everyone has the same sense of pain, urgency, or desire.*

Psychological Debt

More than forty-five years ago, when I was failing in my first sales position and struggling every step of the way, I had an important mentor in my life who gave me the most valuable insight I have ever gained in my entire sales career. Here is a very condensed version of a conversation that took place in the early 1960s.

"Larry, I don't understand it. Everyone I give a presentation to tells me how good I am, how knowledgeable I am, and how successful he or she believes I will be in selling. But they still don't buy."

"Tim, you are experiencing what I call psychological debt."

"What's that?"

"During a presentation, you do a lot for your prospects. You give them your time, energy, and the benefits of your insight, wisdom, and experience. You are nice to them, and you educate them. In other words, you do a great deal for them in the span of an hour or so."

"What's your point, Larry?"

"A little impatient, aren't we? You see, Tim, you have done a lot for them, and they feel they owe you, psychologically, that is. And they don't want you leaving, owing you, and they don't want to buy for whatever reason, so they give you a compliment. Once you accept the compliment, the debt is paid, and you can leave without an order, supposedly feeling good about yourself because of the compliment. Problem is, sooner or later, with lots of compliments and no sales, you will starve. You'll feel good, but you will be broke."

"So what do I do?"

"It's simple. When you get an order and a compliment, say thank you. When you get a compliment instead of an order, refuse the compliment. Then the debt still exists. Here's how: 'Bob, if I were that good at what I do, we would be doing business together today, and since we are not, I'm afraid I don't deserve that compliment.'

"Tim, new salespeople tend to have a problem with this issue. Since they are new, they have a need for approval. When they get it, it strokes their ego, their need for acceptance, and makes them feel OK. Problem is, if they don't deal with it successfully, they will fail. You can't pay your mortgage with compliments."

I haven't seen Larry in more than forty years, but his advice has helped me avoid losing hundreds of sales during my career. Thanks, Larry, wherever you are.

Don't Shoot Yourself in the Foot

Many salespeople could be so much more successful than they are. All they need is a willingness to stop behavior that hurts their success and replace it with actions and attitudes that will ensure success. What are some of the factors that will limit your success? They include the following:

- believing that success in selling will be easy and fast
- the inability to keep motivated regardless of the circumstances
- living in the past or the future
- a lack of consistent effort
- letting yourself off the hook when you fail to reach your goals
- a lack of clear focus, direction, or goals
- inadequate planning time
- not investing enough time and cash in yourself, your skills, and your attitude development
- easily attainable goals
- an inability to manage rejection and failure with a positive attitude
- turning the responsibility for your success over to someone or something else: your company, the economy, your boss, or anyone
- an out-of-control ego

During my first year in sales, when I was selling advertising, I recall not following up with a client to see if he was satisfied with our services. Three months into his contract, he canceled the order. I called and asked him why he was canceling. He said, "The program isn't working." I said, "Why didn't you call me to tell me?" He said, "Why didn't you call me sooner to find out whether it was working?"

Another valuable lesson learned, folks.

Of course, the most important thing is learning what to do to prevent these self-sabotaging attitudes:

- Get up an hour earlier than usual every day and spend the time planning your day, year, career, or life.
- Start investing 10 percent of your income and time in self-development.
- Start a goal-setting journal and live it: every day.
- Develop a greater degree of patience, faith, and trust in yourself and the world.
- Give yourself away a little every day: your time, ideas, energy, or other assets.
- Count your blessings and live with gratitude for what you have.
- Take full responsibility for your life, yourself, your career, your future, your past. Take full responsibility for everything in your life.
- Kill your ego.
- Accept the reality that not everyone you meet, try to sell to, or whatever, is going to like you. It's just not that kind of world.
- Relax and enjoy the ride.
- Embrace change and let go of attachments to the past.
- Start a "good stuff" jar.
- Work as if you will live forever, and live as if you will die today.

> *Think About It*
> Keep your focus on what you want, can do, or have, not what you don't want, can't do, or don't have.

Managing Rejection

What is the number-one cause of failure in sales? It's the inability to overcome the fear of rejection. Why do people let this fear negatively influence their behavior?

Here are a few thoughts to consider that I hope will prepare you for the inevitable rejections and prevent them from becoming commonplace:

- Not everyone you try to sell to will want to buy from you.
- Expecting everyone you meet to like or accept you is to live in fantasyland.
- If you don't ask for something, it is unlikely you will ever get it.
- The fear of rejection prevents you from asking probing questions, asking for an appointment, or asking for the order.
- The fear of rejection is one of the major causes of failure in all areas of life, not only sales.
- The fear of rejection is not a skill issue and can't be overcome with the latest self-help technique or fad that forces you to behave in ways that are not comfortable for you.
- The fear of rejection is an attitude issue and can only be overcome by strengthening other attitudes, such as confidence, self-belief, patience, and trust, and by working on your self-image.
- The fear of rejection is a symptom of a need for validation.
- The fear of rejection sends a loud nonverbal message to your prospects that you lack confidence or belief in yourself, your product or service, your ability to help them or solve their problems, or all of these things.

Of course, rejection will happen. The key is how you react to it.

Of course, rejection will happen. The key is how you react to it. Do you think about what you could have done better, learn any lessons, and forge ahead? Or does the fear of rejection ever prevent you from doing any of the following?

- picking up the phone and making that next call
- asking for the business
- asking difficult, probing questions

- asking for referrals
- asking for a bigger order
- asking for a letter of testimony
- asking for anything you want
- asking for more responsibility in your position or for a raise
- following up with a customer who has had a problem
- asking for an appointment with an important person
- asking for a cash deposit
- asking for a long-term contract

If you answered yes to any of these, you need to address your fear of rejection immediately. You cannot succeed in the long term if common failures interfere with your ability to do your job and sell.

Failure Is Inevitable

Failure is not negative, nor is it positive. Failure is an event that does not need to be attached to some value of rightness or wrongness. Some people fail and quit, while others fail and get better, wiser, and stronger. There is an interesting difference between people who fail and then succeed and those who fail and then pack it in—and which type they are is based entirely on their attitudes.

I have never met anyone in my career who was successful who hadn't also experienced numerous failures. To succeed, you must stretch yourself and reach beyond your previous limits, boundaries, and skills. If you do this, sooner or later you will fail. Sometimes you will even crash and burn. I've been there several times, my friend, but I am still here—still selling, still writing, and still failing. I love to fail. When I am not experiencing temporary failure, it is a clear message that I may be stuck in my comfort zone.

> **Think About It**
> Learn to fail often so you can succeed sooner. If you are not failing, you have to ask yourself: Am I stretching, reaching, and going beyond my limits, or am I stuck in that which is comfortable?

Learn to use failure, adversity, problems, and risk as tools for self-improvement rather than reasons to whine and complain. Accept the fact that people who succeed must often first fail. Their failures give them the confidence, character, humility, and courage they will need to succeed. Success is not easy.

Frank Bettger, one of the great sales speakers of the last century, put it this way, "The price of failure is always higher than the price of success. It always costs more to fail than to succeed. So use your failures as learning opportunities."

Failures! Bring 'em on. Get ready to learn, grow, and stretch. Get out of your comfort zone and watch yourself accomplish great things.

The Cause and Cost of Discouragement—and the Cure

Ever lost a sale? I mean, a sale that you were really counting on? A really big sale, one that could make your entire year? If you haven't, then you might find it difficult to relate to the pain that other people who have had just such an experience feel. Then again, even if you haven't lost that sale of all sales, you might have been discouraged for other reasons and can recognize the tremendous doubt, fear, uncertainty, and hopelessness that can crush a salesperson's spirit.

Discouragement is right up there with fear as one of the biggest negative factors that affects your actions, decisions, attitudes, and life and career outcomes. I have been discouraged on a number of occasions, and I know the painful and exhausting feeling that you get when it seems like no matter what you do, your project is doomed from the start. I am not talking here about clinical depression, but temporary emotional despair.

Get the picture? I am talking about a temporary inability to lift yourself out of the mud and back into the sunshine.

What's the cause of this temporary malaise?

There are many potential causes, but here are the common ones:

- unrealistic life and/or career expectations
- living in the future rather than in the present
- assigning responsibility for your life to other people or outside circumstances
- a pessimistic attitude or negative mental focus
- not having clear goals and a clearly defined path toward them
- not spending adequate time in self-development activities like reading great books and listening to motivational CDs

- surrounding yourself with negative, pessimistic people who enjoy whining and complaining

What is the cost of staying in this gloom and doom mentality for too long?

- It can damage your business and personal relationships.
- It can make you physically ill.
- It will make you lose more sales.

What can you do to get out of this funk?

- Start reading and listening to personal development messages every morning after you wake and just before you go to bed at night.
- Keep a daily journal and refer to it when you feel discouraged or just need a little lift.
- Have a "Count My Blessings" page in your journal and read it every day.
- Surround yourself with positive, optimistic people.
- Start or join a Mastermind Group with other salespeople you know and respect, so that you all can share positive and creative ideas and methods for improving.
- Go to lunch every day for a week with a really successful salesperson in either your organization or a noncompeting business in your market for the purpose of sharing and learning. (No whining allowed!)

Follow any or all of these steps—whatever feels right for you—and I guarantee that you will be out of your funk sooner rather than later. The most important thing is that you challenge yourself. If reading and writing in a daily journal seems pointless to you now, then you are just encouraging the status quo and you'll never come out of your malaise. You have to at least try. You have a responsibility to yourself to act *now* to change your attitude and your circumstances. Trust me—if you follow my advice, you'll see a marked change, not only in your sales, but also in your life.

CHAPTER 2

PERSONAL TRAITS
FOR SUCCESS

As a new salesperson in your organization, you will have to meet a number of expectations for your attitudes, behavior, and habits. You now represent your organization in the marketplace. Whether you are working, traveling, or off duty, your behavior will be closely observed by your prospects, customers, fellow employees, support staff, and suppliers. It is critical that your behavior always be professional and above reproach. You never know who is watching.

RELATIONSHIP SKILLS AND ATTITUDES

During your first year, you will form many new relationships. In my second sales position, selling insurance, one of my fellow salespeople—he also happened to be our number-one salesperson—told me I would never make it in the business. At the time, I didn't know why he felt the need to share his pessimistic view about my future with me. In hindsight, it was pure insecurity and jealousy. I was on track to replace his number-one status in the office and in the company, and he knew it.

Great Expectations

You will be expected to

- learn quickly
- adapt to the personality of your organization
- work hard
- work smart
- communicate questions, concerns, and needs
- accept corporate policies and operate within their guidelines
- know the marketplace
- learn about your competitors, their products and services, and their strengths and weaknesses
- sell
- dress appropriately
- behave professionally

A lot to expect, yes, but you are representing their entire investment in public relations, reputation, and success up to this point. You now have a role as an ambassador for them, and it is vital that you take this role seriously.

Chances are, you won't run into anyone who is so blatantly negative to your face. But trust me: You will find that you have advocates as well as saboteurs. All you can do is be yourself, be friendly, and know that sooner or later, results talk. It's called leverage. When you are new and just beginning to find your way down the path of success, you will stumble in some of your relationships. Just learn from your mistakes. Before you know it, you too will be one of the superstars.

CONTINUE YOUR PERSONAL DEVELOPMENT

Continued self-development is an attitude, not an event. Don't think of taking a course, reading a book, listening to a tape, or attending a sales seminar as a onetime activity. Self-improvement is a lifestyle. Devoting yourself to lifelong learning is a philosophy that will pay you handsome dividends over time.

One approach I implemented early in my sales career was to invest 10 percent of my time and 10 percent of my income—on a weekly, monthly, and yearly basis—in my personal growth. Over time this investment will repay you thousands of times over.

If you want to improve your income, you must improve your value.

Think of yourself as an independent contractor. You are selling your time, skills, attitudes, and effort to your current employer. Your value is represented by your income. If you want to improve your income, you must improve your value. You do that by investing in yourself. I am not talking here about attending only mandatory company-sponsored learning programs. I am asking you: What are you doing on your own with your own available resources?

If your organization did not continuously improve its products or services, it would fail in the marketplace. If you do not invest in yourself, you may reach a point in your career where you are no longer able to increase your income, simply because your value has not increased. Develop the habit—in your first year—of investing regularly in yourself and, specifically, in your skills and attitudes.

THE IMPORTANCE OF MOTIVATION AND GOAL SETTING

Motivation is a very personal issue. Research has concluded that everyone has the potential for great motivation, but many people are not willing to pay the price to achieve their dreams, desires, or hopes. Many fail to really ask themselves one critical question: What motivates me?

For years, thousands of managers, hundreds of speakers and trainers, and dozens of authors have been preaching the benefits of self-motivation and goal setting as a way to achieve success, wealth, and happiness. And for good reason. Find what motivates you and pushes you to strive for the top, and keep that in mind when the going gets tough or you simply need or want to reach a higher level. A motivator is one of your tools for success.

What Motivates You?

These are some of the more traditional motivators:

- money
- security
- fame
- power
- prestige
- ego gratification
- winning
- being the best
- doing your best
- your family
- your future
- your past
- not losing
- personal satisfaction
- approval of others
- proving a point
- getting even
- feeling worthwhile
- impressing others

Do any of these drive you? Keep you going when you are on the verge of quitting, giving up, throwing in the towel?

But just as there are motivators, there are demotivators. A demotivator is anyone or anything—a person, circumstance, situation—causing you to be negative, passive, or self-destructive.

Fortunately, there are tangible ways to address self-motivation. Six basic steps will allow you to reach your peak-performance behavior and results:

1. Know what you want.
2. Know why you want it.
3. Know how you will get it.
4. Know what may stand in your way to achieve it (external obstacles: circumstances, people, and events; internal obstacles: attitudes, emotions, fears, and doubts).
5. Be aware of the external and internal demotivators, and develop a plan to deal with them, prevent them, or manage them.
6. Do something. Begin. Start.

A Bad Rub

I can think of hundreds of examples of demotivators. Here are some of the more common demotivators:

- negative people
- people who invalidate you
- people who don't listen, don't care, or are uninterested in you or your ideas
- an incorrect personal interpretation of failure, problems, or adversity
- goals that are consistently too high or too low
- managers who rely on fear and punishment as motivators

Demotivators come in all shapes and sizes. They can be your personal demons that no one but you is ever aware of, or they can be a corporate policy or family rule that contributes to an "I don't care anymore" attitude. Apathy is one of the most destructive emotions when it comes to performance, productivity, happiness, success, motivation, and overall behavior.

Audit Your Demotivators

Conduct an internal as well as external self-audit of your demotivators. Identify them, question their purpose and value in your life, and decide if it is time to rid yourself of their power over you, or learn to live with the consequences of keeping them in your life. One of the best ways to improve self-motivation and personal performance is to eliminate the demotivators from your life, whatever form they take.

Develop a Goal Philosophy

Even a goal to do nothing is a goal. Everyone has goals. People are constantly in the process of defining their goals, and then they either move toward or away from them with a variety of perspectives or rationales. There are two primary reasons for setting goals: First, they give you focus; second, they give you direction.

Focus

Without focus, it is difficult to hit a bull's-eye, take a good picture, or avoid getting killed on a busy highway. Focus is an essential characteristic of successful people. It keeps your eye on the ball. Yes, there are distractions, unexpected circumstances, and unknowns that will affect your ability to keep your focus, but your goal is to overcome and learn to ignore things that challenge your focus.

> *Think About It*
> Personal organization is defined differently by each of us. The key is, can you be productive with your current organizational style?

Direction

Ultimately achieving your goals is less important than your ability to continue working toward them. Many people achieve their goals and are disappointed once they reach them. A goal achieved is a milestone, yes, but you can't just sit back and rest on your previous success.

When winners don't reach a goal, they reexamine what needs to change and then change the time frame to achieve it. When losers don't reach goals, they reexamine and then change the goal itself.

Don't worry about the destination. Keep your eye on the ball in the present with what you can do now, not tomorrow. Do something every day to move a little closer to your objective. Remember that while you can't have everything in your life that you want, you can have anything. Keep this principle clear in your mind.

To set goals without any accountability is like whistling in the wind. You are living in fantasyland if you think you will achieve your goals without some checkpoints along the way to chart your progress.

At every checkpoint, you should consider these questions:

1. Are you satisfied with your progress toward your goals?
2. If not, which ones are you behind on? Why?
3. Are you ahead of schedule on any of your goals? Which ones? Why?
4. Is it time to let go of any of your goals?
5. Is it time to add some new goals to this year's list?
6. Who or what is affecting your lack of progress?
7. Who or what is helping the progress you have made?
8. If you could go back to last year and begin this goal-setting process all over again, would you have done anything differently?
9. What are you going to change in the next three months to ensure you are on target for your important goals?

How to Set and Reach Your Goals

Not only must you create goals, but you must decide ahead of time the best way to reach them. Of course, the best way to reach a goal may change over time, which is why progress evaluations are so important. First things first, though. As you go through the process of setting ambitious yet reasonable goals, you must consider the following:

- Set deadlines for your goals.
- Know the difference between tangible and intangible goals.
- Reward yourself when you reach a goal.
- Update your goals at least once a year.
- Share goals with other people who can help you, who influence you, or who will be affected by them.
- Set both short (hourly to six months) and long-term (six months to lifetime) goals.
- Record your accomplished goals in a journal.
- Be willing to abandon a goal when you have lost interest.

- Accept the fact that patience and faith are virtues.
- Know your reasons for wanting to reach a goal.
- Relax and enjoy the process.
- Life is not about the result, but the process of becoming.
- Accept the fact that you can't do it all, have it all, learn it all, see it all, become it all, or share it all in one lifetime.
- Goal setting is not a short-term fix, but a lifetime philosophy.
- Life can change in a heartbeat.
- Goals change as your interests, age, and circumstances change.
- Don't edit the goal-setting process as you proceed through the steps. ("I don't have the time now," "I can't afford it now," etc., are never valid excuses.) Don't worry about being realistic in the beginning. The purpose of the process is to discover what you can and cannot do, to learn to accomplish your goals in a realistic and practical way.
- Goals should be achievable, but they also require some stretch.
- Get in the habit of working on paper with your goal setting.
- Recognize that achieving goals takes effort, commitment, time, and skills.

THE IMPORTANCE OF BALANCING YOUR CAREER AND PERSONAL LIFE

Balance in life means many things to each of us. There are entire books written on the subject. Here are a few of the key ways to achieve a balanced life:

Common Contributors to a Lack of Goal Success

- a lack of commitment to the process
- impatience
- a lack of follow-through
- a lack of self-honesty

- consistently setting goals too high
- not anticipating roadblocks
- not allowing for enough time to reach your goal
- setting only long-term goals
- setting only tangible goals
- a lack of support, resources from people who can help you
- working toward a goal you don't believe in or really want
- not believing you will ever reach your goal
- quitting too soon
- not starting to work toward your goal

- Move consistently and purposefully toward meaningful goals in all seven areas of your life (page 53).
- Live in the present: one moment at a time. The present is where your plans are made, memories created, and relationships built.
- Live life from the inside out, not from the outside in; take full personal responsibility for the quality of your existence.
- Let go of your emotional baggage. It keeps you stuck in the past and prevents you from experiencing true joy in living.
- Accept the fact that life just is! It is not perfect. Everyone has his or her share of pain, problems, disappointments, mistakes, and struggles.
- Count your blessings daily.
- Live without regrets. Regret is a debt you can never pay. It will haunt you until your final day.
- Make thoughtful choices. Choices become our ultimate destiny. Wise choices create a life worth living.
- Live a simple and humble life. Keep your ego out of your actions, relationships, decisions, and plans: You will find inner peace.
- People, not things, are what really matter. In the end, it is not what you have accumulated that gives your life meaning, but rather your relationships with people.

PERSONAL MANAGEMENT

I'm sure you will agree we live in a very stressful world. Everywhere you turn there are people, events, and situations that cause stress and anxiety. There are two ways to respond to stressful situations: to learn from them and use them to help highlight where you might have some room for personal growth; or to whine about a situation you see as unfair. But obviously, life isn't always fair—in life we have an equal number of opportunities to either improve or stay stuck in the mud.

There are two ways to improve the effect of stressors on your life. One is to modify your life outlook and attitudes, and the other is to get better at personal management. I am not referring to better time management—better time management is just one factor included in better personal management. Here are a few ideas for you to consider:

1. Go to bed an hour later than you used to every day or wake up an hour earlier; you'll have extra time to arrange your daily affairs.
2. Evaluate repetitive time wasters and cut them out of your daily life.
3. Spend fifteen minutes planning out each day—it will save you hours.
4. Use your lunch hour to relax or learn.
5. Let go of emotional issues that sabotage your attitudes, success, and happiness.
6. Spend time on the essentials and let the unimportant items go.
7. Stay in control of the thoughts that fill your mind. Never allow yourself to dwell.
8. Develop a do-it-now philosophy.
9. Be careful who you let into your life. People have an influence on you.
10. Say no more often.
11. Have some fun every day.
12. Laugh more—at yourself and life.

By improving your personal management, you will undoubtedly create more free time for yourself each month. Why not use it in the following ways:

- Set some goals.
- Make some specific plans.

- Find creative ways to solve your problems.
- Reflect on last year, the last two years, or even your entire career.
- Write in your personal journal.
- Give something back to society.
- Devote yourself to personal relationships.
- Read a couple of self-help books.

KEEP GOOD RECORDS

To chart a more effective course for the future, you need to know where you have been. You need to know precisely where you must modify behavior, improve skills, or change approaches. Professional salespeople ask themselves regularly, "What is working, what isn't working, and what used to work that I have stopped doing?" They keep immaculate records on activity, results, mistakes, and anything else they need to improve. Whether they use a journal, a spreadsheet, or some type of call report doesn't matter. What matters is that they bring their personal history into their present, therefore changing their future.

Professional salespeople ask themselves regularly, "What is working, what isn't working, and what used to work that I have stopped doing?"

Many sales managers and sales organizations require call reports of your activity and results. See these as an opportunity to improve, not as a waste of your time. Take them seriously. In addition to these reports, I also suggest you keep additional records (whether daily, weekly, or monthly) of your successes, problems, challenges, needs, activities, questions, concerns—whatever will help you keep track of your history, progress, failures, and triumphs.

PERSONAL TRAITS FOR SUCCESS

CAUSES OF SALES SLUMPS

Sooner or later, every salesperson experiences a down period of sales results. These periods, where your continued activity seems to yield less-than-satisfactory results, are normal and to be expected. None of us can keep up a pace of two hundred miles per hour day after day, month after month, year after year. The key is to keep your attitude positive, your focus on what is working, and your activity levels high regardless of the results.

There are a variety of sales slumps. Let's just discuss four: the attitude slump, the prospecting slump, the presentation slump, and the closing slump.

The Attitude Slump

An attitude slump is where you find it difficult to maintain your confidence, poise, commitment, dedication, persistence, and motivation. This can be due to a number of causes, including losing belief in your organization's products or services; not reaching your objectives according to your schedule; being under a great deal of stress because of deadlines, expectations, or loss of control of the sales process; or having other issues in your life that are affecting your attitudes.

The Prospecting Slump

A prospecting slump is where you lack adequate qualified leads and are spending a great deal of time calling on poor prospects. As a result, your close ratio is a disaster. This could also be caused by your poor prospecting strategies—that is, you are still (after several months selling your products or services) spending a lot of time cold-calling.

The Presentation Slump

A presentation slump can be caused by your lack of up-to-date product knowledge, poor presentation skills, or poor communication skills, such as listening, speaking, or writing. It can also result from your lack of knowledge of the prospect's needs or use for your products or services. You therefore give an organization-driven rather than a customer-driven sales pitch.

You can't pull out of any of these slumps by just focusing on the one area that you feel might be your problem. You have to work on all of them.

The Closing Slump

A closing slump can be caused by your lack of control of the sales process, poor prospecting, poor sales presentations, or many of the items in the attitude area that we have already discussed.

BREAKING THE CYCLE

As you can see, there are a number of areas in your sales approach that can lead to a down cycle. The thing to consider is that all of them are related. In other words, if you are experiencing an attitude slump, it will have an impact on your prospecting, presentation, and closing. If you are in a closing slump, it will affect your attitude as well as other areas of the sales process.

You can't pull out of any of these slumps simply by focusing on the one area that you feel might be your problem. You have to work on all of them. The way out of a slump is to go back to what works, or what has worked for you in the past. It is also an excellent time for reflection and evaluation of your progress, success, weaknesses, and strengths.

BECOMING AN EFFECTIVE SALESPERSON

From day one, there are numerous things that you can and should do to start developing your skills and attitudes for success, from learning as much as you

can about your product or service to
streamlining your responsibilities and
managing your time wisely. The sooner
you have a plan and organize in your
mind the most efficient and thorough
methods for doing your job, the better off
you will be.

> ### Think About It
> Some prospects are worth more time, energy, and re-
> sources than others. The key is to know which are worthy
> and why.

The Importance of Product and Industry Knowledge

People need to know how much you care, but they also want and need to know
that you have the competence to guide them and recommend the best option
for them regarding your product or service. Product knowledge is a vital sales requirement if you are to compete successfully.

There are a variety of things you need to know from a product-knowledge
standpoint:

- what your product or service does
- what your product or service can't do and what it isn't
- how your product or service is unique
- how it is different from your competitors'

Key Success Factors in Your First Year

You will have a lot to learn during the next several months. Depending on the type
of sales position you're in, you will determine the key factors for your success. You
will need to consider whether or not

- it is purely an inside sales position
- you have leads provided
- you are taking over existing territory
- you will be selling a low-price service or product or a high-price one
- you will have inside sales support

- you will be selling an intangible service or a tangible product
- there will be weekend or evening appointments

How you spend your time, what obstacles you encounter, what you will have to learn, and what new habits or attitudes you need to develop will all depend on your particular circumstances. In this book, you will find keys to all of your challenges regardless of which ones you face.

This is just a start. The key is to know what you need to know and what your prospects need you to know to address their needs, questions, challenges, or problems. In this information-laden age, winging product knowledge is no longer an acceptable strategy.

This is especially true when you are dealing with a complex product or service and have knowledgeable and sophisticated buyers. Don't fake product knowledge. Learn what you need to know as quickly as you can. Product knowledge does not make up for poor people skills, selling skills, or poor attitudes, but if you have all four, you can achieve greatness in sales.

Learn to Compartmentalize

One of the ongoing challenges for many salespeople is the ability to compartmentalize areas of their lives. Let me explain.

As a writer, it is important for me to be able to set aside all life challenges, issues, and problems once I sit at my computer to create and write. Setting these aside is often easier said than done, whether we're talking about a salesperson or a writer. For example, suppose your spouse just announced, after twenty-five years of marriage, he or she is leaving. Your car has just been repossessed, and your teenager is in trouble. Not a pretty picture. Fortunately, not many of us have this much hit us simultaneously. However, we all have our battles, big and small, that we must face on an ongoing basis. The ability to keep these issues separate while you are trying to sell is vital.

Salespeople who cannot separate their personal challenges from their career responsibilities generally reveal in some nonverbal or emotional way that they have problems. We all have problems. We all will always have problems. If you don't, get some quickly. Problems build character. I can just hear someone reading this screaming, "I have had enough character building!" Maybe yes, maybe no. But consider this: If you still have problems anywhere in your life, you may not have built as much character as you need to fulfill your mission or destiny on this planet. When you cannot separate these personal issues from your work roles, you will tend to

- reduce your positive state of mind, which will compromise your success
- increase your stress, which will affect your health and ability to be creative
- send mixed messages to your prospect or customer
- lose your competitive edge

The following are a few steps to consider to help you compartmentalize your life so that one area will not have more control over another area than you choose to give it:

- Focus on something positive rather than negative in the area of your life that concerns you.
- Spend time before each call in relaxation and/or a short meditation period.
- Focus on your long-term life goals and your progress when life throws you a curve.
- Develop little routines or positive anchors to use when you are troubled.
- Carry with you some personal physical reminder of what is positive in your life or in that area that is causing you grief or worry.
- Call someone who will give you emotional support, feedback, or just warm fuzzies to help you refocus on what is positive.

Start Networking Your First Day

There has been a networking myth circulating for years that says, "It is not what you know, but whom you know, that will determine your success." Not so. It isn't whom you know, but who knows you. I am not splitting hairs here, trust me. I know a lot of people who don't have a clue who I am. So it really comes down to how you define the word "knows."

The key to effective networking is to start. Make it a routine part of your selling and nonselling time. Join organizations where you can meet prospects as well as people who can refer you to prospects. Develop a 24/7 prospecting awareness. Take business cards like they're candy, and be sure to file all your contacts electronically. Then start a mail campaign: E-mail, call, and even send paper notes to those special people who you feel might one day be able to help you. More on networking in chapter 3.

> *Think About It*
> Start an advocate list of the top twenty-five people you want to cultivate as your key support group. These people can give you ideas, feedback, help, and contacts. Select these people very carefully.

Mastering Time and Territory Management

As I've already mentioned, productive time use is essential. And part of using your time wisely is managing your territory efficiently.

Time management and effective time use are the result of many skills, attitudes, prejudices, habits, and personal philosophies. If a person has a time-management problem, it is most likely because of a weakness in some other area of his or her life, such as managing resources, people, decisions, problems, emotions, failure, activities, or success.

Need more time to sell?

Over the years I have done a great deal of research on how much time salespeople actually spend selling, and you would be amazed by the outcome of this research. I have polled the members of my audience for more than thirty years on how they spend their sales and nonsales time—asking them to include how long they spend on waiting time, developing proposals, windshield time, meetings, paperwork, and more. How much time do you think most salespeople actually spend selling? The truth is, the average salesperson spends less than 15 percent of each day selling—face-to-face or on the phone with a client, not trying to solve logistical problems or arranging appointments, but actually selling a product or service. Now, think about what you are earning using 15 percent of your time. Now imagine what your earnings would be if you increased this to 25 percent or 30 percent. I'm not saying you have to do anything differently—just spend more time doing what you are supposed to be doing, and you will double your sales and possibly your income.

And how can you up the percentage of time you spend actually selling? First, decide about what that figure is. For one week, why not carry a stopwatch (a silent one, of course), start it when you meet a prospect or customer *to sell*, and stop it when you leave. After the sales visit, don't reset the clock, but keep a running total of time spent selling in one week. I bet that if you do this faithfully for just five workdays, you will discover you are spending less time selling than you think. For the next five days, keep a running log, in fifteen-minute blocks, of how nonsales time was spent. At the end of each day, total your time in the following categories:

1. Paperwork
2. After-sales service
3. Other administrative duties
4. Market or client research
5. Prospecting for new business
6. Meals alone or with clients
7. Travel time
8. Time with coworkers
9. Time spent in meetings: formal or spur-of-the-moment
10. Planning
11. Thinking
12. Other

Between these two exercises, you will get a fairly accurate picture of where you need time management and/or territory improvement. You can't fix what you don't know is wrong. So before you launch into some sophisticated time management program, remember, you cannot manage time. It passes with or without you. What you do manage are activities, decisions, people, resources, success, problems, failure, materials, and actions. What these two exercises are designed to do is help you determine where you are out of balance.

THE BALANCING ACT

Each of us has numerous demands on our time, energy, and resources. One of the keys to sales success is the ability to balance multiple

- demands
- expectations of customers
- requirements of our position
- personal needs and desires
- tasks
- routine activities
- family roles
- expectations of supervisors
- personal growth possibilities

It is no wonder that many salespeople burn out early in their careers because of the inability to successfully handle all of these issues, challenges, and requirements. If success is one of your agendas, you will ultimately have to

- eliminate something from your plate
- better manage all of these issues and roles
- get better organized

Or else live with the continued stress of poor organization.

I am sure you know the feeling of being overwhelmed: the need to satisfy everyone and everything in your life. This combines with the desire to create a sense of peace in your life and ensure that, while working on other people's issues, expectations, and demands, you have not abandoned your own requirements for achievement and success. You also know how you have felt when you end a day, week, or month with a great deal of unfinished business. If you hope to do more, have more, become more, learn more, and contribute more, sooner or later you will have to confront your own needs and personal organization style. No one can tell you how to organize your life and career. What learning can do is help you identify where growth, change, or a new philosophy is needed so you can regain some sense of harmony while climbing the ladder of personal success, whatever that means to you.

Hints for Managing Your Time

To improve time use, a person must identify these impeding tendencies, attitudes, or weaknesses and then develop skills and abilities to address and overcome them. You can't improve time use: It is a nebulous concept. I challenge anyone to manage the next minute or hour. It can't be done. However, there are a couple of points of self-knowledge that can help you maximize your time and results.

The Keys to Improving Time Use and Territory Management

- Know yourself.
- Know your tendencies.
- Know your strengths.
- Know your weaknesses.
- Know your goals.
- Identify your common time wasters.
- Have a prospecting strategy.
- Establish regular planning times.

Know Your Prime Time

What is Prime Time? It is that time of the day or week when you are at your best. Are you a morning person? Late-night person? Other? Does your energy fade during a certain time of the day or week?

Know Your Prime Time *Plus*

That is, know the combination of time when you are at your best *and* your customers and prospects can see you. For example, if you are a morning person and a client or prospect wants a conference call in the morning, this is your Prime Time

Plus. However, if you are an afternoon person—your energy, creativity, and imagination peak in midafternoon, and you are not at your best in the early morning—it is best to schedule your meetings in the afternoon, during your Prime Time or Prime Time Plus. The key is to schedule critical sales activities during Prime Time Plus and nonsales activities during your non–Prime Time Plus.

Schedule critical sales activities during Prime Time Plus and nonsales activities during your non–Prime Time Plus.

Time Block Approach

This strategy helps you blend the goals and objectives in your life with the available time at your disposal. It ensures that you don't neglect any area of your life while moving toward your goals and life purpose.

The Value of Lists

Working from lists is one way to ensure that you

- don't forget to do something important
- work on the important stuff first
- feel good about your day
- end the day, week, and month without neglecting an important task, activity, or role
- enjoy the time you have
- get more satisfaction from your responsibilities
- get more done
- sell more

Work from lists of things to do. Here's how:

1. Make a list.
2. Prioritize the items on the list according to your goals, needs, desires, activities, and demands.
3. Start with the important ones (must-dos).
4. Finish these before you move to the less important ones (should-dos).
5. Finish these before you move to the unimportant ones (will do if I get time).

Work from lists, and you will get more done in less time. As a result, you'll have more time for planning, contemplation, relaxation, and fun. All valuable activities that, while often overlooked, can give you an additional edge.

Develop the habit of spending a certain amount of time each day or week in solitude, or on minibreaks for recharging your battery. It doesn't matter if it is a walk in the park; a slow, relaxing meal; meditation time; or just sitting down and doing nothing.

You start with a month or week. You list your top five or ten goals in all or some of the important segments of your life:

- family
- career
- finances
- socializing
- education
- physical needs
- spiritual needs

Start with a clean month or week. Nothing included. Now take your number-one priority, whether it be time with your spouse, exercise, reading, sales appointments, or something else. Block out the time for this area in the week or month. Now go to your second priority.

Continue to fill in blocks of time in your schedule according to your top priorities. As the week or month fills, you now become acutely aware of how precious your time is and how you want and need to spend it.

If you begin with a month, all you have to do is transfer this information to your weekly or daily list of things to do. Another way to approach it is to take a year. Using the same philosophy, block out time for critical tasks, responsibilities, and activities. Become more detailed as you move from the year to the month, week, and day.

This process ensures that you don't neglect any important area of your life as you live it. Your career, personal life, financial concerns, social interests, and family get the attention they deserve.

The Joys of Journaling

Start a journal. There are a number of outstanding reasons to keep a journal. Here are a few of them.

A journal can

- increase your effectiveness
- help you learn from your failures
- improve your relationships
- help you achieve your goals
- keep you headed in the right direction
- help you learn from others
- save you time
- reduce your stress

Keeping a record of your insights, thoughts, ideas, successes, mistakes, errors, achievements, and failures and their causes will do more for your career than any other single activity.

Realities

Paperwork is not going away, not in this lifetime, anyway. No matter how technically oriented your organization becomes, there will always be paper: information to share, something to write, forms to complete, reports to evaluate, or some piece of paper that finds its way to your desk. The key is to determine honestly and effectively whether you want or need to spend time on this stuff, or whether you can discard it without negative consequences. Let's take a brief look at a few of the paperwork demands on your time:

- expense reports
- call reports
- territory reports
- customer reports
- customer history reports
- forecasting reports
- goal or quota reports
- competitor evaluations

Here are a few ideas to consider while managing paper:

- It is a myth to believe that you can handle each piece of paper once.
- Technology will never replace someone's need or desire to have a hard copy of something.
- Who wants the information—a customer, your boss, a fellow employee, or another department—will determine your attention span and response time.
- Most people are not good communicators on paper. They either go on and on with endless drivel, or they give us far too little information to help us make a decision.
- You need a priority system for handling your administrative tasks.
- File any notes you take during telephone conversations or appointments.
- Establish a reading file.
- Use expandable file pockets instead of hanging folders.
- Keep your briefcase organized.
- Have an effective follow-up system.
- Have an effective suspense-action system.
- Do difficult tasks first thing in the day.
- Use a pencil for scheduling appointments.

- Confirm all appointments.
- Send yourself e-mails as reminders.

Territory Management

Territory management is the ability to maximize your results, reach your goals, and effectively build your business in your territory while satisfying the demands and expectations of your management team and customers. There are several keys to this.

Let's take a brief look at a few of the issues that will require your attention as you attempt to better organize your time, territory, career, and life.

Streamlining Paperwork

Here are some tips that will make your life significantly easier and free up your time for the good stuff:

- Allocate a specific amount of nonselling time to administrative requirements.
- Don't let paperwork and reports get in the way of your Prime Time selling activities.
- Make a daily or weekly appointment with yourself for reports and paperwork.
- Categorize your administrative tasks into "must do immediately," "do as soon as possible," and "do after completing the previous."
- Form the habit of keeping daily records so that at the end of the week it isn't as big a chore to complete a report or an administrative task.
- Organize your routine tasks, such as reports and your various roles, in such a way that they can be completed easily.
- Delegate what you can to a subordinate, staff person, or another department.
- Have your mail screened by a support person.
- Create files for your paperwork: routine, urgent, archive, action today, action this week, action this month, suspense, action this year, pending, to review, to read, when I get time, from my boss, customer requests. Get creative here: The more you have, the easier it is to keep track of everything.

- Subscribe to a book review program.
- Spend a half day each week or month in the library catching up on industry information and trends.
- Write responses on memos/faxes/e-mails rather than creating a new document.
- Keep things brief, short, and to the point. Avoid editorializing.
- Keep your memos, reports, and correspondence accurate, not perfect.
- Develop a template for all of your routine reports.
- Have a self-rating system for how well you think you are doing managing your paperwork.
- Develop the habit of asking yourself, Do I need to do this? Do I need to do it now? Can someone else do this?

Improving Your Territory Management

One of the fundamental aspects of effective territory management is the ability to qualify prospects before giving them your time, energy, or corporate resources.

Let's look at a few ways to better manage your time and territory management:

1. Ask more effective questions earlier in the sales process.
2. Pay attention to the answers to determine whether it is a good time to try to sell to this prospect.
3. Develop a customer profile to use as a template for your prospecting.
4. Audit your sales call activity by dividing the number of calls you make in a week by the number of miles you drive in that week. This number will give you your call-route effectiveness.
5. Spend more prospecting time getting referrals.
6. Develop strategic alliances to help you improve your prospecting activity.
7. Plan your call activities early in the week, month, or day.
8. Don't give poor prospects more time than they deserve.
9. Develop a daily checklist of what you will need to do to be effective.
10. Try to get more of your prospects to visit your location, plant, or office.

11. Don't spend time giving presentations to people who aren't the ones who make the decisions. Territory management, like time management, is a function of many attitudes, habits, values, skills, and beliefs. It is also a function of the

    - geographic size of the territory
    - number of clients and prospects in the territory
    - method of travel through the territory—that is, plane, car, or whatever
    - nonsales responsibilities within the territory
    - degree of administrative sales support

Efficient Versus Effective

It is important to know the difference between two words: "effective" and "efficient."

"Efficient" means to do things well or right.

"Effective" means to do the right things well or right.

Note the difference? It is one thing to end your day tired after completing your list of activities. It is another thing to end your day having completed the important things: those things that needed to get done, and not just those things you wanted to do because they were easy, fun, or new.

To effectively manage a sales territory, it is critical that a salesperson have a prospecting strategy—a rationale for how much time, energy, and resources to give to each type of prospect or customer. Many salespeople travel hundreds of unnecessary miles each week or month and still do not effectively cover their territory. Without a prospecting strategy, it is impossible to get the maximum use out of one's time and have effective territory coverage.

In this chapter we have begun to evaluate your attitudes, expectations, and reasons for beginning your sales career. We have looked at your motivation, goals, and personal organization. Now the real work begins. It is time to put much of what you have learned in chapter 1 and chapter 2 into practice. So let's get to it. Don't stop now: You're on a roll.

CHAPTER 3

THE POLITICS OF SALES

Every profession, every position in any organization, will have a certain amount of politics that you will have to learn to manage if you are going to make your first year successful without an unnecessary amount of stress. Many people dislike playing political games; however, learning to play these games effectively is an important skill that you must master during your first year in this profession.

WHAT TO EXPECT

During my sales career, I encountered a wide variety of political challenges that often came very close to permanently derailing me professionally. But I made it because I learned the skills and developed the attitudes that guaranteed my survival. Each of us must confront our own personal issues. Each of us will face unique circumstances as we learn the ropes in this profession.

Each organization and sales culture is unique. Some management philosophies embrace and honor the salespeople who represent their products and services in the marketplace. Others, unfortunately, regard salespeople as a necessary evil. In these organizations, management is always playing with sales territories, compensation plans, rules, procedures, policies, and strategies, often with the objective of keeping their salespeople's incomes within certain acceptable parameters.

I have always held that one of the opportunities this profession offers is the ability to determine your own income and destiny. Any organization that limits your financial growth has an agenda to keep you within historical income guidelines. If you find yourself in such a company, I am not suggesting that you become a crusader your first year and attempt to change your organization's philosophy. But you need to become aware of this manipulative political tactic.

SPECIFIC POLITICS AND ISSUES

There are other political issues you will have to learn to handle. As mentioned previously, what you specifically encounter will depend a lot on the organization you work for. Nevertheless, there are certain issues that are quite common, and no doubt you will come across several of the following situations.

Department Rivalries

One of the common rivalries is the conflict between the finance and sales departments. The finance department is driven by lower sales costs and higher margins. Often in sales you will have to sacrifice profit margins to close a deal. Often you will have to "spend money to make money." Unfortunately, this rubs the controller, accountants, and other finance personnel the wrong way, and sometimes you will need your sales supervisor or officer to intercede for you.

Conflict and Competition with Fellow Salespeople

Sometimes there may be a salesperson who is threatened by your presence or your success. Although it is unlikely that one of these people will let the air out of your tires late some Monday night after work, it is possible that individuals may go out of their way secretly to sabotage your success at work. They may steal your accounts, bad-mouth you to management, give you wrong information, lead you astray, or adopt any number of subversive tactics. Keep your eyes and ears open; learn as much as you can as quickly as you can; don't get caught playing political games. By all means, when someone proves to be an adversary,

be careful about what information you
share with him or her. Be the bigger person, and avoid taking sides in any political squabble. Just keep your eye on the
ball, and do what you are paid to do
without getting immersed in all of the
nonsense on the side.

> *Think About It*
> Favorable first impressions can improve your ability to sell more. You don't get a second chance to make a good first impression.

SPIT-SHINING YOUR IMAGE

How you carry yourself and how people see you can go a long way in affecting how they treat you and whether or not they drag you into the rumors and hair pulling mentioned above. We've all heard the saying "You never get a second chance to make a first impression." And think about it: Every day in sales you are making a first impression on someone. Image may or may not be every-thing—but it certainly counts for a lot. So what is image? Many things.

How You Dress

Many organizations today are becoming more casual in their dress code. I sug-gest that regardless of what your company's dress code is, always err on the con-servative side. If you can't afford $1,000 suits and $400 shoes, that's OK. Just make sure what you do buy always looks professional, neat, clean, and appropri-ate for the prospect you are calling on.

Talk Isn't Cheap

What comes out of your mouth plays a big part in how you are perceived. We've all heard someone who curses like a sailor without hesitation. What is your per-ception of such a person? Avoid profanity, off-color jokes, snide remarks, sexist comments, political arguments, religious discussions, bad-mouthing, racist re-marks, invalidating anyone, dealing in rumors, culturally insensitive comments, and lies (even little ones).

Your Work Ethic and Style

Have fun in your new job, but be serious, too. Get to work early and leave late. And keep busy in your downtime with productive activities, such as learning your product or service, studying up on your industry and your competitors, reviewing your organization's policies and procedures, understanding the marketplace, and establishing who the key players are in your industry. I also highly recommend that you spend at least one day a month in the library researching your prospects' and clients' industries.

Your Performance

You will be judged in your first year not only on your results but on the habits you develop, the routines you follow, the activities you engage in, and the lessons you learn. No one likes a complainer, a whiner, or someone who always plays the role of victim. None of these traits are attractive, and none further your career—they usually have the opposite effect. You are under constant surveillance, especially when you have to deal with difficult emotional circumstances. The best policy is to understand that as you are learning, you will make mistakes, lots of them, so relax and learn everything you can from them. Napoleon Hill, in *Think and Grow Rich,* wrote: "You will experience failure, rejection, and disappointment: guaranteed. Embrace it, accept it, and learn from it."

Great advice from one of the great minds of the twentieth century.

Every adversity, every setback, every failure, every problem carries within it the seed of an equivalent or greater benefit. So look for it, uncover it, and then learn from it.

Who You Hang Out With

Be careful who you hang around: Other people influence how you feel, how you talk, what you believe, and how you perform. If you want to become an eagle, fly with the eagles, not the ducks. If you want to be successful, spend your time with the people in your organization who are successful and soak in everything you can. You don't have to mimic them; just learn to pick and choose what they do that fits with your personality, philosophy, goals, and lifestyle. Travel with losers, and you will learn how to lose. Travel with winners, and you will learn how to win. This isn't rocket science, folks.

HOW TO BECOME A PRO

Now you know what it takes, but how do you get there, step by step? There are many ways to jump-start a career that are unique to the particular job and company. At the same time, though, there is a definite foundation that you need to become a bona fide sales professional. Read on and learn.

Network

Once again I will return to the cliché "It isn't what you know, but whom you know." To further counter this argument, I would like you to consider the following ideas:

- Success isn't about whom you know, but who knows about you.
- Success is about who knows you and what you do.

You can know a lot of people, but if they don't know a great deal about you, the value of the contact is limited. One of the keys to effective networking is the ability to both accumulate a variety of

> **Think About It**
> I have met tens of thousands of people in my career, but I would venture a guess that fewer than five hundred can contribute to my success by being able to introduce me to potential clients.

contacts in your database and make sure these people are aware of your skills, abilities, interests, and needs.

Networking Basics

Networking is finding people who can be centers of influence for you, taking the opportunity to get to know them, and giving them the opportunity to get to know you.

Most salespeople are very poor networkers. They fail to join organizations where people who could benefit them congregate, or if they do belong, they fail to get involved or even participate in various meetings and networking opportunities.

How are your networking skills? Do you promote yourself with regularity in areas where influential people mingle? Do you belong to industry associations? Do you attend some of their meetings? Do you keep a database of contacts, where you met them, and how they might be of value to you? Do you have some system to keep in touch with them, like a newsletter or periodic notes, telephone calls, or e-mails? Whom have you met in the past five years, and lost touch with, who could be of some value in your new sales career?

Be Professional

Selling is not what you sell, but how you sell what you sell. How are you doing when it comes to being a pro? How do your clients or customers think you are doing? How do you think your competitors think you are doing? How does the marketplace think you are doing? Don't wait for the results to come in from these sources. If something needs fixing, fix it now.

Don't Get Stuck in Your Comfort Zone

Over time it can become easy to get stuck in one of a number of comfort zones when it comes to behavior, performance, techniques, or attitudes. Let's look at a few of the common ones that many salespeople fall prey to:

- calling only on clients or customers whom you like or who like you
- selling only the products or services you make the most money on, know the most about, or have the easiest time selling

- slowing down your sales activities at certain times of the month or year (sandbagging)
- once you have exceeded your quota or manager's expectations, adjusting your performance accordingly
- selling only to certain types of buyers
- avoiding certain buyer personality types
- avoiding learning new applications of your products or services
- spending too much time with customers with whom you have a lot in common regardless of their purchasing potential
- having nonproductive routines that keep you away from the real role of a salesperson
- spending too much time on after-sales service issues that keep you from selling more to new prospects

Now it is your turn. List some of the areas where you feel you are locked in a comfort zone of some type. After you have completed your personal list, answer the following:

- How long have you had this behavior or attitude?
- How is this attitude or behavior sabotaging your sales success?
- If continued, how will it affect your career (long-term, short-term)?
- Why haven't you done something about it?
- Have other people noticed or mentioned the pattern?
- What can you do to change this attitude or behavior?

Sales is not an easy profession. It isn't something you do because you can't do anything else or because you want to make some fast, easy money. The real success stories in sales over the years come from people who have forced themselves out of their comfort zones and refused to settle for the easy route. If you want to make an impact in this profession, help your clients, and make an exceptional income in the process, you must leave the comfort of what you know from time to time and venture out into the unknown. You must take, as the poet Robert Frost wrote, the road "less traveled."

Get Out of the Box

Getting a fast start out of the box in your new career is one of the best ways to ensure a successful sales year. Many salespeople get lulled into a relaxed state as they begin their new career. Why not get an edge on your competitors before it is too late?

Pour it on. Make the first days as productive as possible. The quick-start concept discussed in chapter 1 is a valid way to ensure a great month as well as a great beginning of your new career. It is called momentum. Don't wait. Do it now.

To accomplish this great year, you have to be prepared. You have to plan. You have to be ready. And when is the best time to get ready? Now. If you wait, you may lose. Go for it. Today. You will be glad you did. You have nothing to lose and everything to gain by using the quick-start approach to your new sales career. You may even surprise yourself in addition to surprising your boss. Wouldn't that be a kicker?

Formula for Success

Here is a simple formula for success:

Self-Evaluation + Planning + Preparation + Extra Effort + a Winning Attitude = Success

Now, go out and do it!

Avoid Naysayers

Sooner or later someone is going to cross your sales path and attempt to discourage you, dissuade you, or even sabotage you. People like this can take many roles in your life. They can be spouses, parents, friends, in-laws, supervisors, children, neighbors, or associates.

Tune them out and keep your eyes on the road. Don't give them any room in your consciousness. Forget the notions *I'll try another day; if I am lucky; if I meet the right people; when I have enough money; if I belong to the right groups or clubs; if I had gone to the right schools or had the right parents; if I were the right age, color, or sex; if I weren't too short or too tall, too beautiful or too ugly.*

Get Real

People often say, "I just want you to be realistic." Being realistic is often an excuse for being negative. Or, "I don't want you to be hurt, disappointed, or to fail." Tune them out. Don't give them any room. Avoid them. Don't let them influence your dreams, desires, or destiny. Let them worry about their own lives.

I have met a few of these people in my sales career, and I am sorry that I did not recognize them earlier for what they were. If I had, I would have saved myself a great deal of grief and accomplished my goals sooner rather than later.

Who are the naysayers in your life? They are easily recognizable—they're the ones who seldom encourage you, pat you on the back, support you, or believe in you.

Get them out of your life—if not physically, then mentally and emotionally.

Learn How to Bounce Back from Adversity

Everyone, at least once in his or her life, experiences some form of adversity, failure, or loss in at least one area of life. Adversity can strike with or without notice. It can hit a relationship, a loved one, your career, your business, your health, or your financial status.

Stages of life end. For example, youth ends and is followed by adulthood. All careers end, either with retirement or the choice to start something new. Relationships end.

Setbacks are often signals that some aspect of life has come to an end or needs to come to an end. They are wake-up calls, or what I call choice points, in life. Many people, including me on a number of occasions, have resisted endings for various reasons. Sometimes, however, we embrace or encourage them. We want to continue life, business, or a way of being forever. Most people die with unfinished business. There is always something more that could have been said, done, seen, learned, or shared by someone who has passed on.

Bouncing back from an event—such as a lost sale or lost client—is vital to your success, regardless of whether the challenge was out of your control or a function of your own attitudes, decisions, behavior, or actions. What gives adversity its power over feelings and responses? Why is adversity a tool used by some to improve or change, while others use it as an excuse to give up or to whine and bemoan their circumstances? Where is the potential lesson in a setback?

Fair Versus Unfair

Life isn't fair, and it isn't unfair. It just is. It brings each person unique opportunities to learn and grow as a result of each person's particular circumstances. Everyone, I repeat, everyone, regardless of age, sex, nationality, religion, career status, or financial position, is a student of life. Some people may seem to have it made, at least superficially. But do not judge by appearances only. Everyone is fighting inner battles of one kind or another.

No one is immune to the teachings of life—class is always in session, and we never graduate. We don't get to select the curriculum, but we do get to do all the assignments and take all the quizzes. If we pass, we get to move on to other, sometimes bigger or higher, lessons. If we fail, we get to repeat the same lesson again and again until we finally learn whatever it is we need to learn as we travel through life.

> *Think About It*
> Adversity and problems are normal. Successful salespeople use them as learning tools.

The repeated lesson might present itself in a different client, career situation, or any number of new or different circumstances, but the lesson will be the same.

Many of us, by choosing to see ourselves as victims, bring repeated adversity of one kind or another into our lives. To see yourself as a victim and fail to take responsibility for your circumstances is to live in an inner world dominated by blame, guilt, and resentment. I once heard a friend ask, "Why is this happening to me again?" There *was* a common denominator in all of the repeated events: him.

No one is immune to the teachings of life. Class is always in session.

Adversity Is Opportunity

Adversity gives us the opportunity to do a number of things as we move through our lives. Some of them are reevaluating old patterns that are not working; seeing ourselves more clearly as contributors; developing new attitudes about life, relationships, money, people, work, and the like; and observing how we handle the lessons we are given.

There is a law in the universe called the law of cause and effect. There is also the saying "Be careful what you wish for because you will probably get it." Still another says, "What you are seeking is seeking you." There is a great quotation from baseball legend Yogi Berra, who observed, "Expecting different results from repeated behavior is a mild form of insanity."

As you can see from these various perspectives, a great deal of the adversity and loss in our lives is self-inflicted through our conscious actions, expectations, perceptions, and thoughts or our subconscious values, beliefs, judgments, and paradigms.

All behavior is the result of a person's consciousness. To attempt to change behavior without first changing consciousness is to invite failure, whether the problem is with eating habits, communication patterns, work ethic, or everything in between. The reason so many people fail at altering their behavior is that they try to change from the outside in rather than from the inside out.

What does this have to do with adversity and bouncing back in sales? Everything. Our state of mind is often fertile ground that attracts adversity into our lives. Our state of mind will determine how we will respond to or overcome the events that come to us. Our perceptions, or filters (how we see life), will determine our interpretation of whether something is adverse or not. Give twenty different people the same adverse event, and I guarantee that some will see it as negative,

> **Think About It**
> Failure and adversity are teachers on the highway of life.
> They test your resolve, commitment, and attitudes.

some will see it as positive, and some will see it as devastating. The event is the same; the interpretations are unique and personal.

When we are confronted with a situation, regardless of its nature, that we perceive as a threat to our comfort, security, sense of well-being, or the status quo, we tend to imagine the worst. Fear takes over: *How will I survive alone? Will I make this sale? Will I ever find a new job or career that I will be successful in? Will I ever find another lasting, nurturing relationship? What will my life be like with only memories of the past? Am I destined to struggle my entire life? How can I ever get over this tremendous loss?* There are others, but I am confident you see my point.

When we operate out of a consciousness of fear, we tend to lose our perspective. We don't think right, see clearly, or feel safe. We therefore see ourselves as victims and so are not in control of our lives.

Adversity can be an emotional tool for positive change, just like any other. If we hear the wake-up call, we can listen carefully to what we believe it is trying to teach us. This takes awareness, courage, self-love, and patience. If we are too hard on ourselves and beat ourselves up, thinking, "I am such an idiot," "I'll never get this right," or "I deserve all this bad stuff," we will find it difficult to create the proper mind-set to change direction. Adversity needs to be looked at with precision, careful observation, and honest introspection. It needs to be seen as one of life's teachers, and not some villain that is out to get us or beat us down.

Having said all this, I want to emphasize that we should not let ourselves off the hook with justification or acceptance. It is vital to learn to become more comfortable with where we want to be or who we want to become, rather than where we are or who we are.

So a question you should ask yourself is, What kind of student am I as I pass through the classes in life? Am I a willing learner, or am I resisting the teaching, and thus the opportunity for personal growth?

BOUNDARIES AND LIMITS OF THE PROFESSION

Every profession has limits and boundaries. Sales is no different. Sales, however, has fewer limits than do most other professions. This is the one profession where you can truly determine your future in terms of your income, lifestyle, relationships, and freedom. The key to this freedom is your effort, willingness to learn, and your resilience. This is one of the few professions where you will be judged not by the number of hours you work, but what you put into those hours; not by what you know, but by how you use what you know; and not by whom you know, but by how you cultivate those relationships to further your success.

Conquering Adversity

Here are a few things you can do if you find yourself smack in the middle of a situation that is uncomfortable, challenging, or trying to teach you something—in other words, adversity:

- Try to keep the situation in perspective. Will this be as big an issue in one hundred years as it is today?
- Evaluate the situation in light of your entire life.
- Focus on what you have, not what you lost. This isn't an easy step when you are neck-deep in pain, sorrow, or grief, but continuing to focus on what no longer exists tends to keep you locked in the past and in a state of "no positive action."
- Do something, anything, to refocus your thoughts, energy, and activities in a positive or more healthful direction. Remember that you can't change what has happened, but you can change the future. And you change your future in your present moments. You also create all of your memories, positive or negative, in your present moments.
- Keep in mind the concept that you don't always get to determine what comes into your life, but you always get the choice of how to respond to it.
- Dealing with loss or adversity of any kind is painful and difficult as long as you continue to focus on the problem. To wallow indefinitely in the negative circumstance, failure, disappointment, or loss is to remain stuck and out of control. Life is neutral. It doesn't care how you react to its teachings.

All professions require intense study, mastery of certain skill sets, and the development of productive attitudes. Many professions require years of formal education and years of climbing the corporate ladder; many also require licenses. In sales, though, you can outearn your peers and exceed your wildest dreams for financial success in your first year. All it takes is a willingness to work—not through clocking an eight-hour day and five-day week, but through applying extraordinary effort and persistence. Your boundaries are set only by your own thoughts and self-limitations. You are the only element that can prevent your ultimate success.

There are a few limitations that you will want to become aware of as you begin your first year:

- your geographic territory or assignment
- your organization's compensation philosophy
- your organization's attitudes about developing its employees
- your management's willingness to give you latitude in your approach to your sales activities

Even though some of these may be out of your control, you can still control your success by remaining flexible, adaptable, and open to the changes that will naturally occur during your career.

One of the reasons many salespeople fail is their negative response to circumstances, policies, and procedures that they can't control. Sooner or later your philosophy, prejudices, expectations, and attitudes will be challenged by your coworkers, your manager, or your customers. It is vital that you learn from these situations while at the same time keeping a close guard on your emotions, reactions, and attitudes. Refuse to fall prey to negative rumors and people. Be rigid in your development as you learn, grow, and master the skills necessary for success. Refuse to let other people or circumstances bring you down and discourage you. In the end, all you have is your attitudes. And your attitudes will determine your destiny.

You are reading a book on sales written by someone who failed in his first sales position forty-five years ago. Success is the best revenge. I succeeded because I refused to give in to limitations in thinking, creativity, imagination, and actions. I have broken a lot of rules in the process, but playing it too safe is for people who do not want to reach the top of the mountain.

The Importance of Leverage

As you read the story below, "Starting with Zero," you should know that it has a happy ending. I went back into the same business with a different company, and twelve months later, I was one of the top salespeople in the state in that industry. Several companies came to me and tried to recruit me. You can't possibly imagine the offers I received. Thinking back, it was all because of leverage.

When you are your organization's number-one salesperson, there won't be much you can ask for that you won't get. Why? Leverage. If you are at the bottom of the list of salespeople in terms of your performance, I challenge you to walk into your boss's office and tell him or her you are taking the afternoon off! Never going to happen. However, if you are producing more than anyone else on the sales team, you can simply walk in and say, "I am taking the rest of the week off," and I guarantee you won't get much resistance.

Starting with Zero

Let me tell you about my first year in sales, more than forty-five years ago.

I was excited about the opportunity to become successful in a new career. I was willing to learn, work hard, and put the necessary time in to achieve the freedom that I desired. My employer, a major insurance company, hired hundreds of salespeople each year. Some survived, and many did not. I was one of the ones who didn't. The cause: I expected my company to train me, to give me the necessary skills to achieve success. In the first six months I didn't sell anything. Nothing. After that, I was determined never again to put my destiny in the hands of my employer. Their limited resources had a negative impact on my ability to learn and succeed. I turned over my success to their training budget and the ability of my manager to teach me. His abilities were limited, so his limitation became mine, or so I thought at the time.

What did I know? I was only twenty-four, and this was my first sales position. I had nothing to use as a benchmark for their approach to training and developing their salespeople. Unfortunately, my lack of sales experience, insight, maturity, business acumen, and awareness of what to expect, both from my employer and from my prospects and the marketplace, contributed to my demise. The point is, your success is up to you, not your organization's financial position, philosophical attitudes, and management abilities.

So how do you get this leverage? It's really quite simple: Succeed, do well, be number one, and you will be amazed at how much freedom you will have, how much support you will get from other departments, and how little resistance you will get for most of your reasonable requests. Work on getting leverage during your first year and continue with a high performance, and you will get to call the shots for years.

YOU ARE YOUR FUTURE

Each of us creates our future, one decision, moment, action, and thought at a time. Some people are creating futures filled with pain, loneliness, heartache, insecurity, resentment, guilt, and fear, while others are carving out futures filled with joy, happiness, peace, love, and security. Why will some salespeople spend their years coping with negative circumstances while others spend them in comfort, growing, sharing, and learning? Here are a few thoughts to consider today as you move through the decisions and actions that will determine the quality of your life tomorrow:

- All decisions have consequences: some positive, some negative, some immediate, and some long-term.
- To see yourself as a victim is to secretly wish that your present circumstances will continue.
- We become a lot like the people we are around; be careful whom you surround yourself with or let into your life on a regular basis.
- Habits, both mental and physical, are created by us, and then they re-create the new us in the future.
- You cannot escape the truth that each of us is responsible for our life and its outcomes. To cast blame, anger, and resentment on anyone or anything other than ourselves is to live in a fantasyland of denial and immaturity.
- If you do not spend adequate time planning for and moving toward the future you desire, you will spend your future days in frustration and anxiety.
- To live without balance in the critical areas of your life—physical, mental, familial, spiritual, financial, social, and professional—is to set yourself up for disappointment, frustration, failure, stress, and any number of negative conditions in some area of your life.

REDISCOVER YOURSELF

This is the age of rediscovery.

Bookstores are filled with hundreds of books on how to rediscover your childhood, relationships, sense of balance, your mission or purpose in life, and meaning in your career. Everywhere I look, I see people who are working harder at trying to have fun and find a sense of meaning in their jobs and in their lives in general.

> *Think About It*
> You create your future, one moment at a time, day by day.

People by the tens of thousands are leaving corporate America in search of freedom, fulfillment, and a sense of control over their lives. People are leaving relationships by the millions in search of something more or better, whatever more or better may mean to them.

There is increasing evidence that many of these people, in spite of their renewed search for more, are still leading lives of "quiet desperation," as Henry David Thoreau put it. This was true when Thoreau wrote it, and it is still true today. Despite an increasing number of choices of careers, playthings, people, activities, travel destinations, and interests, many people are still frustrated, dissatisfied, or confounded by all the choices before them.

What Is Rediscovering Yourself?

Admittedly, I am not an expert in linguistics, but I have my own definition of "rediscovery": rediscovery means already having found what you seek once before and, for whatever reason, needing to find it again. I believe herein lies a part of the problem. Most people have never truly discovered themselves the first time, so they are really embarking on an initial discovery.

Cruising Through Life, or Not

I have a client in the cruise business. I recently spent three weeks cruising the Caribbean and working with the crews. I know it was tough duty, but someone had to do it. I had a lot of free time to observe a wide variety of passengers and their behavior.

People would push and shove to board the ship before it left port, and they would shove and push just as much to get off the ship when the cruise was over. They all brought on board more than bathing suits and healthy appetites; they brought their relationship frustrations and agendas, their fears and prejudices, their anger and their hopes, their unmet needs and their attitudes.

One would have thought that these people, because they were on vacation, would have been able to relax and enjoy life at least for a week. Not so. If they were unhappy onshore, they were just as unhappy on board. If they were angry onshore, they were just as angry on board. Of course, if they were happy onshore, they were just as happy on board.

To me, rediscovering means experiencing an awakening of your true self; to feel those real feelings, fears, hopes, longings, and values that have shaped your life. Often because of our expectations of ourselves, other people's agendas for us, the rules of society, the rules of business, and our personal needs, we build protective walls around ourselves. But these walls shield us from more than just the outside world; they shield us from ourselves and our own expectations. Few people really know themselves. Most people go through life on autopilot.

Instinct and experience have taught us how to react. We play our parts with precision. And many of us have lost the childlike spontaneity and curiosity that are the hallmarks of peace and happiness. I know because I, too, have spent years building protective walls around myself. It has only been in the last few years that I have been willing to find the courage to be real. I must admit that I have a long way to go, but at least I have begun.

There are risks in being real. There are times when rejection cannot be avoided. There are times when others' judgments will, if we let them, creep into our behavior. John Powell's book *Why Am I Afraid to Tell You Who I Am?* is one of my favorites. In it John talks about the value of vulnerability and the pitfalls of hiding. I wish I had read it years before I did. I am confident I would have had fewer years of guilt, disappointment, struggle, and pain as I worked on becoming a human being rather than a human doing. Note the subtle difference.

FIND A MENTOR

Do you have a mentor? Someone who believes in you, helps you in your new career, and is willing to take time to contribute to your personal and career growth? Mentors offer their

- experience
- knowledge and wisdom
- contacts
- time and energy
- insight and counsel, as well as compassion, understanding, and feedback

A mentor can save you time, mistakes, money, energy, years, and effort. A mentor will not do it for you or make excuses for you. A mentor can accelerate your career, save you the trial-and-error approach, and generally add a wealth of experience to your cause, no matter what it might be.

A mentor can accelerate your career, save you the trial-and-error approach, and generally add a wealth of experience to your cause.

Over the years, I have had a number of mentors. Each, in his or her own way, contributed something to my life, growth, and success. Some stayed with me for years, while others served as my mentor for only a short time. Each of us, as we grow, may become more, learn more, or accomplish more than our mentors. We may outgrow their ability to contribute to our lives. By the same token, some mentors may be with us for life. We might have less contact with them over the years, but when we do spend time with them, it will be invaluable.

Several years ago I started a Mastermind mentor group called Master Speakers International. Our group is made up of eleven speaking and training veterans.

We meet once a quarter to share ideas, get feedback, and generally brainstorm creative ways we can each build our business and career. We have been meeting only every three months, but I can tell you that the ideas that have surfaced and the camaraderie I receive are priceless. I wouldn't miss one of our meetings.

Is there a group somewhere that you can get involved with that could be a mentor group? Is there someone out there who could help you by sharing time and wisdom with you? If not, why not start a group? That's the best way to surround yourself with like-minded people. It doesn't have to be a big group. A group is three. If you don't want to start a group, find someone you know who can contribute to your career in some way. Ask if he or she will be a mentor for you. I am currently a mentor for fifteen authors and speakers. It is a lot of fun, and they give to me as much, or more, than I give to them. Find a mentor and begin learning and growing from another's experience.

CREATE A PERSONAL MISSION STATEMENT

The trend for the past several years has been for organization leaders to run off to a secluded resort, hover around a conference table for hours, and labor over a mission statement. Why? What is the value? I must admit that I have spent hundreds of hours during the past few years working with clients to develop mission statements, vision statements, core belief statements, and the like.

The purpose of creating a mission statement, as I see it, is to develop a focused purpose and direction for an organization. Wouldn't this also be beneficial for a salesperson?

I have had a personal mission statement for years, and I'm happy to share it with you: to learn as much as I can and share as much as I learn. This purpose has driven my career and life since 1973, the first year I worked as a full-time speaker. A personal mission statement can

- help you through the rough times in your life
- keep you focused on what is really important
- determine who and what gets into your life and stays there
- give your life and career a sense of meaning
- help you wisely make critical decisions

- save you time and effort
- help you have a more fulfilling and satisfying career and life
- help you live longer (I'm not sure about this one yet, but I hope so. Glad to see you're still with me.)
- reduce the stress in your life
- help you avoid career and life mistakes that drain your energy and creativity

If you don't yet have a personal mission statement, why not get started developing one today in your new sales career?

CHAPTER 4

CREATING POSITIVE RELATIONSHIPS

Make a sale, and you will make a living. Sell your client a positive relationship with you and your company, and you can make a fortune in sales.

Today, sales relationships are tested and strained in all senses: redefined with entirely new rules, expectations, and limits. As a result, the model of what makes a good sales professional is being radically modified.

These constant and increasing changes notwithstanding, managers are asking salespeople to increase sales volume and margins as well as improve customer loyalty and retention. This is no small order when you consider that, at the same time, budgets are decreasing, the number of support staff is dwindling, contact with management is declining, and expenditures for sales training are shrinking.

Whether you, as you set out in your first year of sales, are selling a service or a product, a high-ticket onetime item or a low-cost consumable, I think I can safely assume that you are experiencing unprecedented shifts in consumer attitudes and purchasing habits. Let's consider these issues:

1. Why and where sales relationships go sour
2. Sources of conflict in sales relationships
3. How to anticipate and satisfy customer or client expectations
4. How to manage conflict in relationships
5. Twelve steps to maintaining positive relationships

WHY AND WHERE SALES RELATIONSHIPS GO SOUR

Sales relationships that deteriorate generally share at least one of the following characteristics—in one or both people:

1. Hidden personal agendas
2. Out-of-control, inflated egos
3. Unrealistic and uncommunicated expectations
4. A lack of trust, respect, or both
5. An unwillingness to agree to disagree
6. Greed, selfishness, or both
7. Ineffective patterns of communication or behavior
8. Unethical behavior or lack of integrity
9. Arrogance or ignorance
10. Inconsistent standards or rules
11. Unmanaged old baggage
12. Inflexibility or an uncompromising stance
13. Clouded perceptions
14. Critical or judgmental behavior

Quite a list. Nevertheless, I've seen some sales relationships that have been affected by one—or many—of these factors that survived. At the same time, I have witnessed situations in which only one of these factors put an abrupt end to the relationship.

The characteristics or history of a relationship can help it survive and even prosper, but equally important is the willingness of both parties to continue working together. People will always have high expectations, jaded perceptions, issues of trust and respect, and other beliefs that can sink a sales relationship. Those will challenge the security of any relationship. If either you or your client has a less-than-honorable intent, even the smallest miscommunication or error in judgment can alter the relationship. Everything that is a part of this relationship, regardless of its source or direction, will pass through what is essentially a new filter. Events that by themselves might not be relationship busters somehow become the final straw. And that final straw, like the one that breaks the camel's back, ends the relationship.

If the filter is not clogged with detritus, whatever passes through it maintains its integrity. This means that as long as you and your client want the relationship to work, you can manage any relationship issues, whatever they are. For example, shattered trust can be repaired, but you can't do it alone: It won't work if the other party brings other issues, such as old baggage, mistakes, and repeated misperceptions of trustworthiness. Your client must be willing to stay in the present. If his or her motive is to blame or manipulate rather than establish a mutually profitable relationship, then that agenda will sabotage any success at rebuilding trust.

SOURCES OF CONFLICT IN SALES RELATIONSHIPS

All relationships experience conflict from time to time. This is normal. Whether the relationship is three months or twenty years old, conflicts will arise. A relationship that never has any conflict is most likely lacking in growth, passion, integrity, and awareness. But in sales—as in life—your goal should not be to eliminate conflict, but to manage it.

Let's take a look at some of the common sources of conflict in sales relationships. As indicated by the length of the aforementioned list, there are lots, but these are some of the most important ones:

1. *Different personality styles.* Everyone is different. Each of us has distinct likes, opinions, needs, feelings, attitudes, expectations, communication styles, and ideas. If everyone were alike, the world would be a very dull place. The benefit of different personalities is that some people can push our buttons, while others are able to motivate us to peak performance—to do our absolute best. Learn to accept that no personality is good or bad. We are all just different.

Each of us has distinct likes, opinions, needs, feelings, attitudes, expectations, communication styles, and ideas.

2. *Unrealized expectations.* Each of us comes to every relationship with expectations that are based on our previous experiences and desires. If we don't manage these expectations properly, they can lead to a great deal of disappointment and frustration. Learn to communicate your expectations effectively while ensuring at the same time that you clearly understand the expectations that others have of you.

3. *Poor follow-up.* One of the biggest sources of conflict in sales is when you make a commitment to a prospect or customer and don't follow up. Here is my general rule for follow-up: Anytime you do anything for a prospect or customer, follow up. Anytime your prospect or customer does anything for you, follow up. Effective follow-up can take many forms. You can send an e-mail, make a telephone call, write a letter by hand, or even drop by for a visit. The idea is to make it clear to your customers and prospects that you don't think of them only during your sales calls.

4. *Inconsistent messages.* Congruence is when what you say and what you do are consistent. Get in the habit of never committing to something if you are not sure you or your organization can do it. In other words, make sure that if you talk the talk you can also walk the walk.

Whenever you have two people involved in a relationship where egos are in control, you are guaranteed to have conflict.

5. *Assumptions.* Assumptions happen when you are not communicating clearly with your client or prospect. Assumptions can range from a simple misunderstanding about a commitment to which you alluded, to a significant miscommunication about some aspect of the sales process, such as delivery arrangements, financial terms, quality expectations, or anything else that can be misunderstood.

Remember: anything that can be misunderstood probably already
has been by someone, at some time.

6. *Out-of-control or inflated egos.* The ego wants to control, manipulate,
seem successful, and be right. Whenever you have two people involved
in a relationship where egos are in control, you are guaranteed to have
conflict. The key to avoiding this type of conflict is to realize and accept that the world does not revolve around your opinions, experience, desires, needs, or expectations.

7. *Increased stress levels.* One of the major reasons that conflicts occur in
relationships is that one or both parties are under a great deal of stress.
People under stress tend to have short fuses, communicate poorly,
jump to conclusions, be physically and mentally fatigued, lack patience, and have unreasonable expectations.

8. *Hidden agendas.* A hidden agenda is when you want to say something
to someone but don't because you want to avoid a conflict, or you
don't want to hurt the person's feelings. Hidden agendas are part of
every relationship to some degree. In a sales relationship, however, if
your customer has a hidden agenda, you can lose a sale or even your
best customer. How? The customer stops doing business with you for
whatever reason but won't tell you why. You just don't hear from that
person anymore, and then you discover—probably by chance—the
customer is doing business with your competitor.

Let's look at the two major causes of conflict in relationships: personal issues
and organizational issues.

Personal Issues

Why and how do personal issues contribute to conflict in sales relationships?
Each person believes that he or she is right, whether the person admits it or
not. The issue may be how a product should be designed, priced, or distrib-
uted. People see the world as they think it is or should be, not as it is. People's
views of a situation will always vary, even if only slightly. Expectations, assumptions, and perceptions are emotional issues that arise from thousands of
sources, both internal and external. That people interpret things in various

ways is what gives life its color, but also its conflicts. Everything in life comes in pairs: up/down, in/out, night/day, good/bad, and so on. If everyone saw all of life in exactly the same way, imagine how dull the human experience would be. So if we are to experience the joy of these differences, we must also learn to accept the challenge of the differences themselves.

> **Think About It**
> Conflict is normal in every relationship. The key is to maintain a high level of trust and respect to ensure the conflict contributes to the success of the relationship and not to its failure.

Personal issues give us the opportunity to grow, learn, and modify our beliefs or behavior as we get in touch with the source of these issues. Many people are attached to their own views and seldom are willing to see another perspective. When this happens, conflict is inevitable.

Organizational Issues

Organizational issues are a little less personal and more a function of the organization, its culture, and its communication style. Let's take deadlines as an example. Whether a deadline is short or long is a function of several factors. First, who wants something done (the president or a file clerk, a minor customer or your biggest customer)? Second, what are the consequences if you miss the deadline (will your biggest customer have to shut down an entire division while waiting for your parts)? Third, how are you empowering your own people with the responsibility to get the job done? Fourth, what is the history you have established with regard to meeting this customer's deadlines? And finally, how realistic are the deadlines under which you operate? Do you typically pad a deadline—that is, build in a little extra time—and does the customer, through experience, know it? Or are your deadlines realistic and well thought out?

HOW TO ANTICIPATE AND SATISFY CLIENT EXPECTATIONS

Most customers are looking for the same things from their vendors or suppliers. They want a fair price; responsiveness to requests and problems; a friendly, comfortable sales climate; empathy for their needs and wants; people who are interested; and people who listen. They may want many other things as well, but most fall within these general areas.

The secret to anticipating customer needs or problems is really quite simple. All you need to do is pay attention and integrate previous customer experience into your current actions, decisions, or behavior.

> *Think About It*
> Professional and effective after-sales service separates winners from losers.

The buying public can, at times, be quite demanding, rude, and insensitive. It is important for you to realize that the behavior that people exhibit is often a cover for some other hidden emotional issue or need. For example, much anger is rooted in fear, and arrogance is the product of insecurity. When a customer is angry, you can choose to react to their anger, or you can look past it to try to determine what it is they are afraid of. (Some anger, of course, may be fully justified, as when a salesperson fails to deliver what he or she promised.)

You can't make every customer 100 percent happy all the time.

Successfully anticipating customer needs and expectations requires you to do various things. One is to listen; another is to be interested; a third is to see the situation from the customer's point of view; a fourth is to show empathy and understanding. The fifth and final task is for you to effectively communicate your awareness, empathy, and understanding.

You can't make every customer 100 percent happy all the time. This is an unrealistic expectation on your part. What you can do is ensure that what you have suggested, solved, or anticipated is reasonable and acceptable to each client. Let me reiterate: You will never be able to resolve every customer issue to that customer's complete satisfaction. The best you can hope for is to be reasonably successful with most people. Keep in mind that it is not always the solution that is of primary importance to many people, but rather the manner in which you handle the situation.

HOW TO MANAGE CONFLICT IN RELATIONSHIPS

Again, conflict in relationships is normal. It is impossible to successfully antici-pate ever person's opinions, judgments, prejudices, and expectations. Everyone sees life through the filter of his or her own experience and beliefs. Some people's filters allow them to have a more realistic view than others. Other people's filters are clouded with erroneous perceptions in the form of old baggage, unrealistic ex-pectations and values, and beliefs that in no way resemble reality. You will dis-cover that it is very difficult to manage conflict with these types of people.

Conflict results when two people have different points of view. You can use the conflict as a tool that will help you grow, or you can use it as a defense against modifying actions, beliefs, or behavior. Conflict is, in itself, really neu-tral. What makes it positive or negative is how you and the other party manage the source of the conflict. If you manage it in a positive way, you may each end up with a better understanding of the other's views. By exacerbating instead of resolving the conflict, you cause greater stress, tension, mistrust, and, ultimately, the breakdown of the relationship.

You cannot change or manage other people's behavior. All you can do is modify your own.

To manage conflict, you must first look at your own expectations and agen-das and think about where you tend to find fault in a given situation. This will allow you to determine under what circumstances you are likely to become de-fensive, critical, or judgmental. Once you are in touch with these triggers, your next step is to monitor your emotions and reactions to other people's stuff (atti-tudes, perceptions, opinions, and the like).

If you find that certain behavior from another person tends to push your buttons, what you must do first is look back at yourself and ask why you are re-acting this way. Why is what this person is saying or doing affecting you the way it is? You cannot change or manage other people's behavior. All you can do is modify your own. You can't do that until you have a clearer picture of why you tend to react the way you do.

The answer to the question of how you can better manage conflict, then, is not to try to eliminate it. This will never happen. Sooner or later, something else will trigger a negative response from you. Learn to see conflict as a teacher, one that can instruct you about yourself and your tendencies. It takes two people or more to have conflict. If one of the two sees the source of conflict as an opportunity to learn, the negative dynamics of the situation can be quickly neutralized. As long as both people stay locked in an ego battle for power, there will be no hope of a positive outcome.

TWELVE STEPS TO MAINTAINING POSITIVE RELATIONSHIPS

There are twelve steps you need to remember in your effort to cultivate and maintain positive relationships with your clients. These are the most important—the essentials, the foundation of any positive relationship.

1. **Be someone your client trusts. People buy from people they trust, not people they like.** The first step in building positive sales relationships is to ensure that all your words and actions contribute to building and maintaining trust. Honor your commitments. Don't make promises you can't keep. Follow through. Follow up.
2. **Anticipate client problems and defuse them in advance.** This can and must be done by planning, learning, communicating in a timely fashion, and understanding why the client views the situation as a problem.
3. **Listen and read between the lines.** Read the feelings and emotions behind the words. Have a sense of how your clients feel about you, your product, and your overall relationship.
4. **Be a resource for your clients.** Get past your selfish need to make a sale or earn a commission. Be ready and willing to offer your assistance, counsel, ideas, and support.

5. **Build bridges, not barriers.** Tell your clients what you can and will do, and do not tell them what you can't or are unwilling to do. Facilitate the relationship instead of complicating it.

6. **Be your clients' ambassador within your organization.** If you don't represent and relay your clients' needs and wants within your organization, who will?

7. **Be a creative problem solver.** Break the rules, push the envelope, and don't accept the status quo or outdated paradigms. Be solution oriented. Keep your clients' ever-changing needs and wishes in mind and work for ways to satisfy them.

> ### Think About It
> Avoid practicing your techniques and strategies on your best prospects. Practice with your peers, a manager, or friends.

8. **Be available both when things are going well and when they aren't.** Everybody loves sunshine and beautiful days, but how you handle yourself when the storms hit is what truly defines you. Be there through the worst of times as well as the best.

9. **Know your clients' businesses, goals, culture, objectives, frustrations, needs, and desires.** Study their industries and competitors, as well as the trends that have an impact on their businesses.

10. **Create team spirit, a spirit of cooperation.** Achieve this between your organization and your clients' organizations.

11. **Be willing to learn from failure, mistakes, and adversity.** You will learn much more from these than from your successes. Use them to refine your philosophy, strategies, attitudes, and approaches.

12. **Understand that relationships are either getting better or worse.** They are dynamic, not stagnant. Monitor the progress and dynamics of the relationship to be sure that you are in touch with its issues and its potential.

Sales relationships, when managed in a positive and mutually beneficial way, can be rewarding for everyone involved. Your future success in sales will hinge on your ability to develop, maintain, and manage all of the relationships that affect your career.

The Benefits of Positive Relationships

It is impossible to sell successfully today, and in the long term, without developing and maintaining positive relationships with your clients. There are many benefits to successful sales relationships and success in sales. Here are just a few:

Repeat business. It is easier, less stressful, less time consuming, and less costly to sell more to a present customer than it is to focus on selling only to new customers. The average cost of a sales call today is more than $500. Add to that the cost of acquiring a new customer, and you can easily reach a figure ten times that size. When you have a solid relationship with a client, the client will tend to want to give you more business.

Making mistakes. Positive relationships allow you to make mistakes. Sooner or later, every organization makes a mistake, in shipping, manufacturing, finance, operations, or customer service. These mistakes are inevitable. If you miss a shipment date with a new customer, this can send the message that you or your organization can't be trusted. When you miss a shipment date with a customer with whom you have been doing business for several years, or even just a few months, you have already shown that the customer's interests and ultimate satisfaction are your primary concern. When mistakes occur, they don't become deal busters.

> *Think About It*
> Remember: you don't do business in a vacuum. Your competitors are after your customers every day.

Price hikes. A good relationship with a client makes it easier for you to raise prices. Every organization has to raise prices. I have raised my fees every year for the past five years. My clients do not resist this rise for one reason: I have, over time, credibly established my high value to my clients. Unless your clients perceive your high value, they will see no solid reason for continuing to do business with you when you have to increase prices, eliminate a product line, or do anything that they might view as negative.

Referrals. Positive client relationships mean that you will get more and better referrals. One of the best sources of new business is referrals from your current customers. The longer a relationship, the better chance you have of getting a consistent flow of well-qualified referrals.

Learning. You will have the opportunity to learn more about your client's business. Your customer's business is changing every day. There are new demands from customers, profit challenges, competitors, and constant changes in the marketplace and economy. The better your relationship with your clients, the more you can learn about their business needs, challenges, concerns, and opportunities.

Reduced stress. A good relationship is less stressful than a problematic one. Life is stressful. Business is stressful. Selling is stressful. Doing more business with current customers is one of the best ways to reduce the stress of uncertainty. Starting a new sales relationship can take a lot of time, effort, and creative thinking. Better to give all of this to a present client from whom the rewards are greater and more certain than with a new client.

There is only one way to own the business: through trusting, successful, and mutually beneficial relationships.

Business growth. Strong relationships contribute to solid business growth. To increase your income, you have to sell more, improve margins, and reduce sales costs, all in a fixed territory. There is only one way! Maximize your sales results with your current customers while keeping your competitors at bay.

Less competition. You will competitor-proof the business. Your competitors want your customers' business, and they will do almost anything to get it. They will lie, misrepresent themselves, make outrageous promises, give stuff away, even buy the business. The only way you can keep the business in this kind of climate is to own the business. There is only one way to own the business: through trusting, successful, and mutually beneficial relationships.

Lower costs. You will have lower sales costs. Your turn: why?

Higher income. You will make more money. This should be self-explanatory by now.

DEVELOPING POSITIVE RELATIONSHIPS WITH YOUR COWORKERS

Your coworkers, regardless of their experience, tenure, or achievements, can contribute to your success. They represent the same products or services that you do, and all are experiencing similar outcomes based on their activities and attitudes. Cultivate these relationships. Be interested in your colleagues, both their personal lives and careers. You don't necessarily have to socialize with them, but develop the habit of sharing success stories, frustrations, lessons learned, experiences, and needs. Use them as a resource for your development, but don't be selfish about it. Try to contribute to their success as well.

Everyone can contribute to your personal growth and success, even people who are not like you or don't agree with you.

You may have coworkers whom, for whatever reason, you don't like, don't agree with, or don't relate to well. Fine. But remember, everyone can contribute to your personal growth and success, even people who are not like you or don't agree with you.

SELLING POSITIVE RELATIONSHIPS

Poor salespeople focus only on closing the sale. Successful salespeople focus on closing the sale and establishing the relationship. Which is your approach?

For many salespeople, the close of the sale typically comes at the end of the sales presentation. It is unfortunate that these poorly informed salespeople lack adequate understanding of the role of selling in today's competitive world.

Sales is not only about closing the current prospect on a particular product or service that solves one pressing problem, need, or desire. It is about building a trusting partnership by becoming a resource, helping solve ongoing problems, and satisfying the prospect's continuing needs and desires.

Salespeople, for years, have been taught that to close a sale, they need to use devices, or "closing techniques." Some examples are the "which would you prefer?" or "get it before the price goes up" closes. These techniques, while occasionally successful, tend to focus only on how the current product or service satisfies a current need or want. The sales relationship must begin somewhere. The question is, How can you become a resource for a prospect, therefore beginning the partnership, if you haven't even closed this sale?

First, you must evaluate your selling intent, or the philosophy that underlies your approach to the sales process, and how it affects both this sale and the future of the relationship.

If your focus is on the short term rather than the long term, your intent is most likely only to move products or services now. If your intent is to develop a long-term, mutually beneficial relationship with this new prospect, you may not close this deal, but that does not prevent you from beginning to build a positive relationship that can one day end in success.

It also depends on how you choose to define a successful sales relationship. All relationships, sales or otherwise, are dynamic. If a sales relationship is to improve, you need to pay constant attention to several areas. They are trust, respect, acceptance, integrity, communication, intent, the relationship's direction, personal agendas, and a willingness to make the relationship work.

It is possible to begin to develop all of these with a prospect that you have not sold or "closed" yet. You can provide information, guidance, recommendations, solutions, feedback, and a variety of other services that would turn your nonrelationship into a relationship that is improving and moving forward.

I am not suggesting that you give away that which you sell. If you sell information or guidance, for example, don't give it away. That only weakens your ability to build a successful relationship. But if you sell, say, widgets, ask yourself, is there some other area in which you can help that strengthens your position in your prospect's eyes?

Giving to Receive

During the past twenty-plus years as a speaker and trainer, I have given away to clients and prospects hundreds of books and audiobooks by other speakers and authors. You might wonder why I would introduce a competitor to a client. Do I have brain damage?

No. This philosophy has served me well for years for multiple reasons. One, it shows prospects and clients that I am just as interested in their success as I am in my own success. Two, it communicates that I am secure enough in my own business and that I am not threatened by other potential resources that are available to them. Three, it shows them I am on the lookout for information or ideas in my field that can contribute to their long-term success.

In many instances, I have sent these materials to prospects before I have done any business with them. But in many more instances, this approach has helped me distance myself from my competitors. Customers want value today. By showing an interest in them before closing the sale, I am encouraging them to think, "If Tim does this much before he has sold us, we can assume he will do as much or more after we buy from him." Granted, once I sell them, I have set up a high expectation for service and results, so I'd better work as hard to keep and develop the business as I did to get it. Otherwise, not only will I lose this business, but I'll also lose the potential of getting referral business and references.

It takes more time, resources, and energy to cultivate a new customer than it does to keep an existing one. It is also easier to do more business with a present customer than it is to find more new ones. What is your approach? Are you investing a greater proportion of your time and resources in finding new business or in satisfying, developing, and keeping existing business? I agree that a continual flow of new business is the lifeblood of growth and success in sales; don't, however, make the mistake of underestimating your ability to use your present customers to help you with that mission.

Few customers will simply give you their business with no effort on your part. You must ask for it, but you also have to earn the right to get it. In my opinion, closing is more of a philosophy than a skill. It is more an attitude than a strategy. It is more about giving than getting, and it is more about service than your sales compensation.

WHAT IS A CLOSING PHILOSOPHY?

A closing philosophy says, "I am here to help you. I am here to do business with you. I am not on an educational crusade, nor am I a professional visitor." We all make the same income, regardless of what we sell, on the sales we don't close—that is to say, nothing. But successful salespeople leverage their time, energy, and resources by earning their customers' willingness to either directly sell new business for them or indirectly support their overall sales efforts with other potential customers.

"Closing the relationship" is not something that begins at some magical point during the sales process. It is an attitude you bring to every good selling situation.

COSTS OF POOR RELATIONSHIPS

Poor relationships will cost you directly, indirectly, and every way in between. If you have a poor relationship with one customer, odds are he or she will spread the word to another customer. Here are a few examples of the problems caused by poor relationships:

- **Increased sales costs.** Every new customer has an acquisition cost. This is what the company invests to make a sale, e.g., travel expenses, sales commissions, and the cost of promotional materials. A new sale to an existing customer will have a lower sales-acquisition cost than one to a new customer.

- **Lost sales.** When a customer has a poor relationship with the supplier, the customer becomes more vulnerable to the promises and commitments of the competition. As a result, customer loyalty can be difficult to maintain when there is a strain of any kind on the relationship.
- **Poor communication with your customer.** Communication is the result of many factors in relationships. It is also an excellent benchmark for how well a relationship is doing. Poor communication between the customer and the supplier will lead to trouble.
- **Wasted time and effort.** Spending time trying to salvage a lost relationship can be very frustrating as well as costly. Many salespeople attempt to save a relationship that is well beyond the saving point. As a result, they are not spending time with better prospects and customers.
- **Lack of customer loyalty.** Most customers would rather do more business with their current vendor than start a new relationship. When trust or respect leaves the existing relationship, customers may feel violated and will, without guilt, take their business elsewhere.
- **Increased customer pressure for lower prices and more benefits.** When a relationship lacks mutual respect, integrity, trust, and understanding, a customer will tend to feel the need to be more aggressive in attempting to get lower prices. One reason for this is that nobody wants to feel that he or she is being taken advantage of.
- **Increased stress for you, your boss, and the organization.** Whenever you lose a customer your organization has invested in maintaining, there is naturally going to be a lot of frustration on the part of many people. This customer now has to be replaced, and the cost of acquiring a new customer is always going to be higher than that of keeping one happy.
- **Uncertain business growth.** Growing a business in any economy is difficult, costly, and often frustrating. One of the best ways to build a solid, growing organization is with repeat customers and referrals from them. Without a strong, positive working relationship with your customers, you can't count on anything from day to day or customer to customer.

- **Your failure.** Sooner or later, if you are not cultivating strong working relationships with your customers, you will find that you are always on the lookout for new business. Since often there is limited new business, you may find that you have no one else to sell to, so you will be looking for work elsewhere. New business is always necessary, but maintaining your current business is even more important.

COMMUNICATION IS CRITICAL

Communication in relationships is one of the biggest challenges today. Whenever you put two people together in a sales relationship, each brings different values, beliefs, expectations, history, education, agendas, goals, personality style, communication style, feelings, life outlook, and old baggage. It is difficult, at best, to communicate effectively with another person even without all of these differences. The key to better communication in a relationship is recognizing these differences and being willing to

> *Think About It*
> Nonverbal messages are always more accurate than the verbal messages people send you.

be flexible, accepting, understanding, and nonjudgmental of the other person's views, opinions, or communication style. Granted, this is not always an easy task.

Creating and Sustaining Positive Communication

The first step in improving communication with another person is to look inward rather than outward for the cause of your communication difficulties. Since we all tend to "fall in love" with our own stuff, this is usually not easy. Most of us are doing the best we can with what we have at our disposal at the present time. Remember, when you judge other people, you are saying more about who you are than about who they are. You are defining your own prejudices and opinions when you choose to see the problem as solely the other person's fault.

Effective Communication Techniques

Meet people where they are emotionally before you try to take them where you want to take them.

Let me explain. Let's say a husband walks into the kitchen and says to his wife, "I am so upset. I thought Bill would have called me back by now. He is so irresponsible." She responds with, "Don't worry, honey, I am sure he will call soon." Seems like a simple and innocent enough remark, right? Wrong. The wife met her husband where she wanted to take him, which was that it would be OK, that Bill would call, regardless of her husband's feelings at the moment. But the husband was angry, frustrated, disappointed, whatever. She should have met him where he was emotionally and not where she wanted to take him.

What could the wife have said to meet her husband where he was? "Honey, I know you feel frustrated and disappointed." Or she might have responded, "Honey, I can feel your frustration and disappointment; you have every right to feel that way"—meeting him where he is—"but it will be OK. I'm sure Bill will call soon" (taking him where she wants to take him).

Let me give you one more short example.

Your teenage son walks into the house after school and says, "Well, I didn't make the baseball team." You respond with, "Don't worry, Tommy, there is always next year. It all works out for the best." Again, an innocent enough remark. Encouraging? Yes. Hopeful? Yes. Positive? Yes. But does it satisfy and soothe Tommy's current feelings? No, you simply are telling him that it will be OK in the future. He is disappointed *now*—that is his principal emotion at the moment, and that's the emotion you have to acknowledge.

Let's take another look at this example. In response to Tommy's remark, you say, "Tommy, I know how angry and frustrated you are" (meeting him where he is). "You worked very hard to make the team, but all your hard work will pay off when you try out again next year. Don't lose faith; it will all work out" (taking him where you want to take him).

This same principle applies just as strongly whether you are dealing with employees, customers, friends, siblings, strangers, or vendors. This simple technique can dramatically improve the quality of your communication and your relationships.

Don't Invalidate Others

What is an invalidator? It is a person who puts other people down, insults them in public, disregards their opinions, does not listen, lets his or her own ego try to control other people, is emotionally manipulative, or negates others' feelings. Not a pretty picture, is it? Invalidators are everywhere: in homes, the classroom, the boardroom, on the golf course, and everywhere else. I have had the fortune (and misfortune) to have had several invalidators in my life. It isn't fun, but you have a choice of how to deal with them. You can hide under a rock, lock yourself in the closet, fight back, give up, or run. I have done all of the above. How do you know if you work with (or for), live with, or just hang out with an invalidator?

Invalidators are everywhere: in homes, the classroom, the boardroom, on the golf course, and everywhere else.

1. Invalidators interrupt you a lot.
2. They ignore you or don't really care about your feelings.
3. They say things like, "you should," "you never," "you always," "you don't," "you owe me."
4. They say "don't you" rather than "do you."
5. They don't listen to you.
6. They are only concerned about their own needs and don't give a rip about yours.
7. They communicate things like, "What will people think?" and "You make me angry."
8. They also can be heard saying, "How could you do that to me?"; "See what you made me do!"; "It is your fault"; "If you really loved me you would!"; "Why can't you be more like . . . !"; "I expect you to!"

I could list many more characteristics, but I am sure that you can now identify whether you are an invalidator or if you have one in your life.

Avoid Misunderstandings

Misunderstanding is a major cause of relationship stress—and it can range anywhere from verbal confusion to improper interpretation of another person's motives, agendas, verbal content, and emotional meaning.

These are some of the causes of misunderstandings:

1. Uncommunicated expectations
2. Poor verbal skills
3. Insecurity
4. Poor self-esteem
5. Emotional immaturity
8. Wrongful intent
9. Unrealistic expectations
10. A conscious or unconscious desire to invalidate the other person
11. A lack of desire to communicate effectively

How do you deal with people who have these characteristics, and how do you avoid misunderstandings in the first place? Some of the following approaches might help:

1. When you are unsure of the other person's meaning, ask for clarification.
2. When you feel misunderstood, ask the other person to explain what he or she thinks you meant.
3. Keep an open mind while listening to the other person.
4. Hold off on your judgments, personal opinions, and expectations while listening to the other person.
5. Try to make increased eye contact while the other person is speaking.
6. If you don't understand a concept or idea, ask the other person to define it.
7. Observe the nonverbal messages behind the content.

8. Listen for feelings as well as words.
9. Stay in the present moment.
10. Control distractions that may interfere with the message.

Misunderstandings do not need to take as great a toll on sales relationships as they do. If both of you share the responsibility for the message—its accurate delivery and receipt—you can dramatically reduce the stress, anxiety, and frustration that you experience from communication problems.

When You Make a Point, Follow It with an Example, Story, or Illustration

We have lost storytelling as a tool in selling today. Years ago the most effective salespeople were good (honest) storytellers—they understood the value of narrative. People need an anchor to understand your sales points. One of the best ways to accomplish this is by giving examples (choose ones that they can relate to) to help them understand your points. Let me give you an example.

I recently spoke to an audience of more than five hundred salespeople. Half the audience was older than forty-five, and the other half was under thirty. Whenever I used an example that the over-forty-five crowd (baby boomers) could relate to, I watched as the other half (the Generation X and Y folks) looked at one another blankly. They were saying to themselves, "What does he mean by that? I don't get it." At the same time, the boomers were nodding their heads in agreement and smiling. They got it. When I made a point that related to the under-thirty group, they smiled and said, "Right on" while I got the same blank stares from the boomers. Obviously, this anecdote proves that stories can both alienate and engage your listeners. The key is to find a good story that profoundly resonates with your client—because if you do, your client will be hooked thereafter.

Years ago the most effective salespeople were good (honest) storytellers.

People Always Think That They Are Right

Keep in mind that people are least responsive to your ideas, opinions, or information right after they have given you their opinions, ideas, or information. They tend to fall in love with their own opinions. When someone offers an opinion and says, "I think this is the best way to handle this problem," and you immediately respond by saying something like, "I think this would be a better solution," you send the message that you are not listening, don't care, or are not interested. Whenever anyone offers an idea or opinion, always ask him or her a probing question before you offer your response. We are not talking about agreement here, just sending the message "I am not invalidating your idea or opinion."

Polish Your Vocabulary

The tools of the professional salesperson are words. We paint word pictures, we tell stories, we describe product or service features and benefits, we influence, we inspire, and we hope to convince people of the benefits of doing business with us. All of this requires a command of language.

> **Think About It**
> If you don't improve your vocabulary, you can't expect to express yourself accurately in any situation.

It amazes me how many salespeople have poor vocabularies. These people fail to realize that they are limiting their success, negatively affecting their destiny and lifestyle because they lack the ability to use the right word at the right time.

The key is having a good enough vocabulary to be able to effectively communicate with people of all demographics. In all cases, you need to be able to use words that your prospect or customer can understand. The ability to articulate your feelings, attitudes, needs, skills, desires, and knowledge is one of the most important ingredients for success in sales and in life.

How is your vocabulary? Do you often find you overuse certain words because you don't know any words that mean the same thing? Do you ever find yourself searching for just the right word for a particular situation? Is your poor vocabulary getting in the way of your future success? Do you tend to overuse profanity?

I have listed some ways for you to improve your vocabulary in the sidebar below. Take a few minutes and list as many ways you can think of to improve your ability to use words and thus increase your chances for success in life. If you really try, I'll bet that you can come up with at least a dozen that you could put into practice immediately.

Talk Smart

Your ability to effectively persuade your prospects and customers depends entirely on your ability to communicate effectively. Yes, sometimes having a product to demonstrate, the ability to use third-party references, and carrying proof sources (articles, case studies, letters of reference, brochures, news stories, and the like) can help you achieve sales success. I believe, however, that your single strongest tool is your ability to use language effectively and correctly when selling to your prospects and customers.

From A to Z

You can improve your vocabulary in many ways. One of the best: read more.

Here are a few others: Do crossword puzzles, play Scrabble, read magazines, and learn one new word a day—that's 365 new words every year. In five years, imagine what kind of vocabulary you could have. When someone uses a word you are unfamiliar with, ask that person what it means. Get a word-a-day calendar. Find a CD on vocabulary improvement and listen to it as you drive.

Improve your vocabulary—improve your life. Pretty simple.

Over the years I have seen hundreds of salespeople—who represented a variety of organizations and sold both services and tangible products—lose sales and customers because of their inability to articulate concepts, ideas, and benefits professionally.

All of us have one thing in common: Regardless of what we sell, how long we have been selling, and whether we are succeeding or failing, we all use words to communicate. I do not mean to play down the importance of nonverbal communication (actually, it makes up a very large percentage of the meaning of the messages we send and receive), but I can't overemphasize the importance of our words. I can think of various areas to cover, but I would like to focus on just one: how to prevent misunderstanding by using words that prevent the possibility of confusion.

As you read the following examples, see if you can determine my meaning:

1. Our product is better than our competitors'. (What is better, how much better?)
2. Our service will exceed your expectations. (How much, when, how?)
3. Our prices are lower than everyone else's. (How much, everyone? All the time?)
4. We guarantee your satisfaction. (How, for how long?)
5. We have the fastest delivery in the industry. (How fast?)
6. We are the best in the world. (Best what? Best at what?)
7. We are the only company that can . . . (Your turn.)

In all of the above examples, you are setting yourself and your prospect up for disappointment, misunderstanding, confusion, and uncertainty. The way to avoid this possibility is to deal in specifics, not generalities; to use words that create clear mental pictures rather than clouded ones; and to clarify how the other person is interpreting your message by asking probing questions.

Effective Listening

Hearing and listening are two different skills. Hearing is a physical capacity. Listening is a mental one. The ears collect sound waves and send them to the brain for interpretation. Only when the brain analyzes and interprets sound waves does "listening" actually take place.

One of the biggest complaints many customers have is that people don't listen. Salespeople don't listen. Many kids don't listen. In some cases, their attention span is less than thirty seconds. Employees often don't listen; they have their own agendas, and they are thinking about them instead of listening to their supervisors or coworkers. Some parents don't listen to their children because they are too busy, distracted, or simply not interested.

Why don't people listen?

1. They don't care about the other person.
2. They are more concerned with their own ideas or thoughts.
3. It takes too much work to listen, so they just fake it.
4. They don't know how to listen.
5. They think they are listening.
6. They have no interest in the subject.
7. Their egos (the need to manipulate, control, or look good) get in the way of their listening.
8. They don't like the other person.
9. The other person's nonverbal communication style gets in the way.
10. They don't trust the other person.
11. They think that they know more about the subject than the person talking does.
12. They don't respect the other person.
13. They don't believe the other person.

When your prospects and customers share their feelings, fears, wants, needs, dreams, or frustrations with you, they are looking for one of the following:

> **Think About It**
> In sales you will spend more than 50 percent of your communication time listening. Do it well.

1. They want your honest feedback, opinions, or feelings.
2. They want you to agree with them.
3. They want you to disagree with them.
4. They want you to share your feelings, experiences, or beliefs with them.
5. They just want you to listen.

Guess which one most people want most often and get the least? If you guessed anything other than listening, you may find you are having some communication problems in a sales relationship.

Here are a few things to consider the next time your prospects and customers share their feelings with you:

1. You don't have to like the message to be willing to listen.
2. Listen for the central theme of the message, not only for the specific points.
3. Stay in the present moment. Don't rush ahead or get mentally stuck in old baggage.
4. Offer feedback to demonstrate that you are listening.
5. Ask questions when you don't understand something they say.
6. Don't offer your opinions unless they are solicited.
7. Make lots of eye contact.
8. Stay focused on the other person rather than on yourself.
9. Don't become impatient when others digress while they are talking.

Listen to This

Listening takes place on two levels: the conscious and subconscious. When you listen to a person consciously, you are paying active attention to their words, intent, feelings, attitudes, and meaning. When you listen subconsciously, you catch their words, but you may miss the subtleties of their intent and meaning.

10. Don't rush them.
11. Recognize that some people are only looking for support or understanding, not your opinions.
12. Resist the tendency to consider your response before they have finished speaking.

Remember, one of the greatest compliments you can pay other people is being willing to listen to them whether or not you are interested in the subject. Learn to listen well, and you will be amazed at how your sales relationships improve.

Are you a good listener? One way to find out is to observe how often you interrupt others.

Nonverbal Communication Techniques

Everyone communicates on two levels, verbally and nonverbally. Verbal communication, or our spoken or written words, represents a very small portion of our overall message. People can lie or mislead you with their words. Nonverbal language carries more than 50 percent of our total message. Effectively reading nonverbal cues can dramatically improve your sales relationships as well as your sales results.

> ### Think About It
> To communicate effectively you must always mean what you say and say what you mean.

If you detect an inconsistency between the verbal message and the nonverbal message that you are getting from a prospect, I would advise you to pay more attention to the nonverbal message. The nonverbal message will always be a more accurate representation of the person's feelings, attitudes, or beliefs.

We communicate nonverbally in multiple ways. We use gestures, facial expressions, eye movements and eye contact, posture, tone, inflection, pauses, pace, and volume. The way people dress also sends nonverbal signals.

An easy way to determine what people are thinking or feeling is to observe whether their signals are open or closed. Open signals represent acceptance, willingness, enthusiasm, and approval. Closed signals represent the opposite of all of these. Closed signals are crossed legs, arms, and hands. A lack of eye contact, rigid posture, leaning away from you, and placing the hands on top of the head are also examples of closed signals. Open signals are exactly what they imply: open hands, uncrossed legs, eye contact, leaning forward, and so on.

I suggest you spend the next few days observing and trying to interpret people's nonverbal messages.

Getting Below the Truth Line

What do I mean when I say "getting below the truth line"?

Let's say your prospect says, "The price is too high." Is that really what he or she means? How about, "I need to think this decision over." Is that the truth, or is there something more going on? How about, "I want to talk with some additional suppliers before I make my decision." All of these comments can have one thing in common. They are statements that the prospect makes that may not be the truth, or they may not be a reflection of what is really going on in the prospect's mind. How do you know?

You must learn to get beneath the truth line in every conversation or sales presentation. You must learn how to bring the real issues to the surface so that you can address them. If you don't, then you will not be dealing with the real objections or resistance. Traditional sales training asks you to use a variety of clever techniques to "overcome" these objections. I would rather you change your paradigm and see these kinds of statements not as sales objections but unanswered questions or concerns.

Let's go back to the previous three examples. What is the prospect really asking when he or she says the price is too high? *Why should I pay so much? I can't afford it. I don't have good enough credit to buy it. Can I get it cheaper somewhere else? If I pay this much, will the product satisfy my needs? You haven't convinced me it is worth what you are asking.* How about the second one, "I need to think this decision over." What could the prospect be asking or saying? *I don't have the authority to make the decision myself. Should I get someone else involved in this decision? What if I buy it and it doesn't work; how will I look to my boss, customers, etc?* And the last one, basically "I need to shop around." What could this really mean? It's your turn. See if you can come up with your own answers.

There's a technique that I have used for more than thirty-five years, whenever I have gotten information that I am not sure is genuine. I ask, "In addition to that [whatever I have been told], is there anything else that will get in the way of our doing business together?" I ask this for three reasons. First, in doing so, I am not challenging the prospect's opinion, view, or statement. Second, I am accepting whatever the prospect is saying (not necessarily agreeing but accepting the explanation for the time being). Third, I am positioning myself to determine what else might be going on (below the truth line) that might stand in our way. Did you notice I put a trial close at the end of the question rather than simply asking the question?

The purpose of this is to send the message "Tell me everything you have, now, that will prevent us from doing business together." I still have to successfully deal with all of these issues to close the sale, but at least I know whether this will be possible. If I can, I have a sale and won't get a whole new list of issues after I deal with these.

CHAPTER 5

THE IMPORTANCE OF MENTORS

One of the biggest mistakes I made in my early sales career was not immediately establishing mentor relationships. My assumption was that my employer would give me all of the tools, knowledge, and sales and career information I would need to be successful. I couldn't have been more naive. Yes, they did train me, and yes, they did give a certain amount of coaching, but I was soon to learn that every organization has its failings and shortcomings. There was so much more I needed to know that I could never get from my company, managers, and fellow salespeople. Success requires more than knowledge; it also requires wisdom.

The difference between the two is significant. Knowledge is what you know, and wisdom is knowing how and when to apply what you know. Every organization has its limitations. What's more, the world is changing faster with every passing day, and what your organization taught you yesterday could well be out of date, inappropriate, or even wrong today. You need a variety of resources and experiences to succeed and compete in this ever-changing world. In part, a mentor can teach you how to stay on top of your area.

MENTOR RELATIONSHIPS

There are many professional as well as personal advantages to having mentor relationships. But let me ask you a simple question before we get started: If you had the opportunity to cultivate relationships with people who could save you time, mistakes, and money, as well as accelerate your career progress, would you? Why?

Start Now

In the Mastermind Group I belong to, Master Speakers International, we meet four days a year to share and to evaluate, critique, and support one another's progress, ensuring that even the most experienced of us continues to grow personally and professionally. I have learned more in the seventeen years I was in this group than I have in the decades I worked as a full-time speaker. Why does it work? I have finally put all of the pieces together successfully. Don't wait more than forty years, as I did, to find people who want to help you and who want your help. It can be just what your sales career needs to set new sales records year after year after year.

What Are Mentors?

Mentors are people who have an interest in contributing to your success, can add to your knowledge and understanding, are willing to help you, and put you in charge of what you do with the knowledge they share with you. They can also improve your results by sharing their experiences with you. Often they are more successful than you are in some area of life, have already done what you are beginning to do, and are older (but not always).

If you had the opportunity to cultivate relationships with people who could save you time, mistakes, and money, as well as accelerate your career progress, would you? Why?

I am currently a mentor to a number of aspiring speakers and authors. Each of my mentees has different goals, agendas, experience levels, challenges, and needs. They also have other mentors besides me. The more people you can get in your corner helping you, the better off you will be and the sooner you will succeed.

Types of Mentors

Mentors come in a variety of packages. They can be friends, relatives, business associates, or even a combination of these. They can be in different career positions, have similar or dissimilar backgrounds to yours, and live near you or across the country. They can be less successful than you (depending on how you choose to define success). They can be retired, a former teacher, a previous supervisor, a distant uncle. Get the picture? Mentors can take many forms and come from varied backgrounds. What they have in common is their willingness to share their ideas, honest feedback, positive and negative experiences, encouragement, criticism, out-of-the-box thinking, knowledge, and time.

Some can be in your life for a few months, while others may fill the role of mentor for years. This may sound a bit strange to some of you, but some of my mentors are people I have never met—authors who died years ago, yet who share their insight and wisdom through words that were written before I was even born. Wait a minute, Tim, you just said that one of the requirements for mentors is that they give you their time. What gives? How can someone who is dead share his time? There are different types of mentor relationships. Don't limit your thinking. Anyone who can help you grow with his or her insight and knowledge can fill the role of mentor. Some might call these people heroes. Call them what you want. I have a great many heroes who have departed this earth who help me succeed every day. People like Mark Twain, Will Rogers, Norman Vincent Peale, George Burns, and many others. They help me daily because of their willingness while they were alive to put their thoughts, ideas, frustrations, encouragement, experiences, dreams, and fears on paper.

Good Mentorship Gone Bad

Years ago I was in a business relationship with one of my mentors, whom I'll call Harry. He was a few years older than I was and more successful in business than I had been to date. We used to meet once a week to share ideas and goals. As our relationship grew, it became apparent that we had a great deal in common, but that we also complemented each other's weaknesses. We began discussing the idea of going into business together. We spent hours discussing business opportunities and our strengths and weaknesses and eventually decided to start a business together. For the first year, our relationship and mentoring grew successfully. But the mentor-mentee relationship was now cluttered with the details of our shared business.

Over time we began to communicate less openly with each other. I stopped trusting him and he stopped respecting me. Well, you don't have to be a genius to figure out the outcome. The relationship ended badly, both personally and professionally. I have not seen Harry for years, but I have spent time reflecting on where we went wrong. It was simple: a clash of egos. In the beginning we were both willing to give up control, but over time we became less so. I lost a good mentor, but more than that, I lost a good friend.

So as you read this chapter, think about people in your life—past, present, or future—from whom you could benefit. How can you benefit from people you haven't met yet or don't know? Create a list of skills, attitudes, and ideas you want to learn, and then find people who have those qualities. Whether you know them or not is of no significance. Don't let the fact that you travel in different circles from the people you eventually want help from prevent you from the possibility of one day benefiting from their knowledge and life experience.

> **Think About It**
> Don't limit your thinking. Anyone who can help you grow with his or her insight and knowledge can fill the role of mentor.

The Roles of Mentors and Mentees

Mentors play many roles while they are on your career team. Let's take a look at a few of their roles and responsibilities:

- They are your best critics.
- They are your biggest fans.
- They play devil's advocate.
- They share ideas with you that you might not be in a position to learn otherwise.
- They are your best cheerleaders.
- They hold you accountable for your actions.
- They keep you in touch with reality.
- They help you avoid mistakes.
- They help you stretch your professional and personal limits.
- They help you learn new concepts.
- They keep you thinking straight.
- They give you new ideas or paradigms.
- They tell you the truth, even though you might not like it.
- They save you time.
- They expect a lot from you.
- They meet with you or talk with you regularly (or, if they are teaching you through their writings, you read them regularly).
- They introduce you to people who or resources that can benefit you (perhaps in the form of other books, if they themselves are not around).

Quite a lot, wouldn't you say? This relationship is not a one-way street. To deserve all of this from them, you too have some responsibilities:

- Listen.
- Grow.
- Try new things.
- Be willing to let go of old habits, routines, or attitudes.
- Ask questions.
- Be prepared each time you meet with or talk with them.
- Give them updates on your activities or results.
- Give something to them: Don't just be the taker here.
- Learn new skills, attitudes, or behavior.
- Do something with what they give you.

- Be honest.
- Do not withhold information that would help them help you.
- Be appreciative for the gifts they give you, and show it.

Seldom will you have a relationship where both the mentor and the mentee fulfill every above-listed responsibility. What I have described is an ideal set of circumstances and traits. This doesn't mean that you shouldn't try to fill all of these roles—you should be sure to try your best to meet every qualification.

How to Select Mentors

The first thing I recommend is to understand how you want to benefit from a mentor relationship. This may not be an easy task. How can you create a list of what you want to know or learn when you don't know what you need as you are beginning in this new career?

What Mentors Expect from Mentees

Here are a few of the requirements I have with my mentees:

1. They must initiate the call or meeting.
2. They must send me, in advance, the question, need, challenge, or issue with which they want help.
3. They pay for the call.
4. As we end the call or meeting, they must put together a written action plan of things they will do with what I gave them or what we shared.
5. When they call or request another meeting in the future, we first discuss their actions from the previous meeting. If they haven't done anything with that information, I won't talk with them or meet with them until they have. They don't have to have been successful, only to have tried something.

Those are only a few. Every mentor relationship is unique. The purpose is for both of you to gain—the mentor by sharing and you by learning.

Following are a few things to consider as you begin to create your list of expectations, needs, and wants for the relationship.

Your reasons. Why do you want a mentor relationship? What are your expectations, agendas, needs, and desires? Decide what you hope to get out of a mentor relationship before you get into it. Explain to your potential mentors what your expectations are and discover whether or not your choices for mentors will be able to fulfill your needs.

Your weaknesses. What are your weaknesses? Before you can find mentors who can help you overcome your weaknesses, you must be honest with yourself about what they are. Each of us has blind spots when it comes to our own weaknesses. To grow, you must get in touch with them.

Your expectations. What are the expectations of your new career that you lack the experience or knowledge to fulfill? Any new career requires specific skills, attitudes, and knowledge. Your company or your manager may share these with you, but you may have to learn many of them on your own over time.

> *Think About It*
> A mentor relationship is a two-way street.

Your personality. Are you willing to let go of your ego and change your opinions and attitudes? If you are stuck, for whatever reason, in a set of values that can sabotage your success, you must be willing to change them. Many people surround themselves only with people who mirror their beliefs. The problem is, you all may be wrong. The ego wants to maintain control, look good, be right, and look successful. To change requires a willingness to be vulnerable, and to admit that you don't know everything—or even anything—about this new career and its requirements.

Over the years I have had many people in my sales seminars who had no intention of changing their behavior. All they did was try to convince me or themselves that their ways were better or right, and that there was no need to change. I have often wondered why these people even bother to attend such programs. Why waste the time if you are in love with your own viewpoints? Have you ever read a book or listened to a speech and thought, "They don't know what they are talking about. My way is better." I know I have, and I also have learned over time that I missed numerous opportunities to grow. Looking back, if I had had a more open mind or a more open disposition, I could have saved myself a lot of grief, time, and money.

Your goals. What do you want to learn or change? As you grow in this career you will need the benefit of knowing others who have been there. Make a list of skills, contacts, ideas, solutions, needs, whatever, that you feel you need now. This list will change within the next year. Develop the habit of continuing to ask yourself, "Where am I now in this career, and what do I need to believe, feel, or do differently to succeed in the future?"

Stick to Business

A few years into my sales career, I had a proven track record. I was doing well, but there was still a great deal I needed to learn. In the organization, the best salesperson was a woman. We were both single. She was bright, successful, and willing to share her experience and knowledge with me. Initially our relationship was strictly business, and I couldn't put a price on her advice and encouragement. Then it happened. We became involved personally, and the relationship changed. She was no longer a mentor. When the relationship ended, we both remained at the organization, but I had lost a valuable resource and mentor.

What went wrong? I should have known that sooner or later a romantic relationship at work, if it failed, would have an impact on the professional elements of the relationship. In hindsight, if I had to do it over again, I would have resisted the impulse to get involved personally, knowing that her friendship and mentorship were too valuable to lose.

Your aims. What type of relationship would you like? Do you want to meet with someone regularly? Will you be satisfied to just talk once a week or month? Do you want a mentor who is older or younger? The same or the opposite sex?

Your contribution. What can you bring to the relationship? What have you learned or done? How can you help? Understand and relay to your mentor what you bring to the table and how your relationship can be mutually beneficial.

Once you have answered the above questions, you will be ready to take the next step. Don't rush through the questions, though. If you answer them honestly, it can save you a lot of time.

Good Mentorship Stayed Good

When I owned a franchise in the mid-1960s, I had a wonderful relationship with a fellow franchise owner named Dave.

Owning my first business was, to say the least, a scary concept. I had invested thousands of dollars to buy a franchise in a business I knew nothing about. Looking back, I see that it was a good decision made for the wrong reasons and at the wrong time. Needless to say, I needed help—lots of help. I found the help I needed in Dave, who had been in the business for several years and whose franchise was consistently one of the top performers. Dave and I became good friends. I trusted his advice, and he respected my willingness to learn. We were only a few years apart in age but had similar lifestyle desires. He was there; I wanted to get there. We would spend endless time on the phone. He would challenge my ideas, views, opinions, perceptions—you name it, he challenged it. He was also my biggest advocate and cheerleader. When I was successful, he was there with a big congratulations. I miss Dave, who died several years ago. But I will always be grateful for his insight, toughness, his holding me accountable, and his friendship.

Why do you think this relationship worked?

The next step is to make a list of people who may fit the profile and who can give you what you need or want. Don't try to figure out whether they'd be willing to help you. Just make the list. Put as many people as you can on it. Don't limit it to people you know or those who are alive or live close; be open-minded.

Craft this list carefully. We are not looking for volume, but quality. Don't worry now about how you will meet or get to know the president of the nation's largest conglomerate; if that person fits your profile, put him or her on the list. I have many people I would like to be my mentors whom I haven't met yet. I may never meet them, and they may never become my mentors, but I have at least identified them and created a strategy to learn about them, get to know them, and get them to know who I am.

Start the Dialogue with Your Prospective Mentors

Next determine which ones on your list would be the most beneficial to contact to begin the inquiry process. It makes no sense to spend months unsuccessfully trying to start a relationship with a potential mentor when there may be someone next door who could help you today. Choose ten potential mentors from your list with whom you can begin a dialogue now. Tell them that you would like to meet to discuss the possibility of a mentor relationship. If they are receptive, start. If they are not, move down the list.

When you meet with someone, you will want to discuss your list of expectations and try to determine whether this person is willing and able to help you. We are not talking about a lifetime commitment here (although you may get lucky and establish a lifetime relationship); try to find only a short-term situation from which you both hope to benefit. Some words of caution: don't complete these steps until you have finished reading this chapter. You might even want to wait until you have finished your first run through the entire book.

How to Develop and Maintain Positive Mentor Relationships

Each person in the relationship has expectations. The mentee seeks information, contacts, and knowledge. Mentors want mentees to be accountable and willing to grow and to use what they learn. To have a mutually beneficial relationship, both people must have their needs or expectations satisfied. From personal experience, I can tell you that I have had no desire to continue to give my time and expertise to someone who is lazy, is looking for the easy way, wants me to do all of the work, or fails to adhere to the rules we have established for the relationship. There are some things you can do to ensure that this relationship remains positive.

Politics and Mentorships

In my second sales position, I had an informal mentor relationship with one of the officers of the company I worked for.

I was working for a manufacturer in a sales-development position. I had a lot to learn about the products, services, and markets of my employer, as well as about selling a high-ticket product. My first position was selling an intangible that was easy to understand and describe to customers. I just lost my passion for the business over time and decided to leave. When I began my new sales position, I was filled with optimism and hope. But at every turn, I was discouraged by how much I had to learn and how few people were available to help me. I befriended the senior vice president of manufacturing. He was twenty-five years my senior but took an interest in me. We would meet informally once or twice a month to discuss how I was doing and what I needed to do to succeed. This was a wonderful relationship that lasted more than two years, and then something happened. He began to have difficulty with my direct manager.

I was between a rock and a hard place. I had to make a decision about where my allegiance was. I chose my manager. That was perceived as a bad decision by the VP, and our relationship ended quite abruptly. My career at that company ended shortly after that. I am not implying that you can't have a mentor relationship with someone else in your organization. I am only cautioning you that these relationships have to be managed delicately. What went wrong? I was unable to successfully manage the politics in these relationships. I lacked the skill and finesse to be able to keep both my supervisor and my mentor happy. As a result, I lost my job.

Ground rules. Establish the rules and expectations early in the relationship and keep the lines of communication open regarding these rules. If for any reason, personal or otherwise, you have to change them, break them, or ignore them, be sure to let your mentors know what you are doing and why. Give them the benefit of the doubt. Keep in mind that they have entered into this relationship to help you. They are giving you their time and knowledge for free. Don't abuse these mentor relationships, or you may find you will lose valuable resources that could contribute tremendously to your career growth and future success.

Time limits. Recognize that no relationship will last forever. Your mentors' agendas, needs, expectations, resources, and availability may change, and they may not be able to continue to give as freely as they have in the past.

Honest communication. Don't play games with your mentors. They deserve better. Keep in mind that they have lives and possibly careers also. If you can't or won't do something, say so. If you don't have an answer or don't know something, admit it. If you want to end the relationship for whatever reason, do it. Return phone calls, answer e-mails, and make these relationships a priority in your career.

Mutual benefits. Find ways to contribute to their success. Whether it is information you run across, books or websites that might be of interest, customers you can bring to them, or problems you can help them solve, share these freely and openly with them on a timely basis.

Trust counts. Maintain a high level of trust and respect. Every relationship, sooner or later, has conflict. This one will, too. If you have a high level of trust and respect, any conflict involving different viewpoints, attitudes, or opinions will be resolved quickly and easily.

Reap the Benefits of Another's Experience

My father has always been a powerful mentor in my life.

My father is now in his mideighties. He has been retired for more than twenty years, but I can tell you that every time I have a significant challenge or desire, a big plan, or a serious problem, he has been there with an unbiased attitude. I didn't always like what he had to say, but somehow, I knew I should pay attention—that someday his words of wisdom, counsel, or chastisement would come in handy. Not all of us are blessed with parents who have both the love and the knowledge to help us in our later years as life and business challenge us. I was one of the lucky ones. He gave me both, and still does. Keep in mind he knows nothing about the business of speaking and writing. Mentors don't have to know intimately what you do. They only have to be willing to give you their honest feedback and appraisal from their years of experience.

Show respect. Respect their time and knowledge. Your mentors may at times share valuable personal insights, beliefs, and philosophies with you. You don't have to agree with them, but you can learn from them.

Listen and learn. Recognize the challenges to maintaining successful relationships. You are in a new career; you will be changing, learning, and growing every day. Your mentors may have already been where you are. When they offer counsel, advice, or feedback, it is most likely given with a positive and respectful agenda. Recognize that they are sharing what they believe you want or need. They may recognize this before you do. There is a great old saying: "When the student is ready, the teacher appears." They may at times have insights that you are not ready for. Accept them and store them away for future review and consideration.

> *Think About It*
> To be successful, a mentor relationship must have rules and clearly expressed expectations.

Keep records. Start a mentor journal and record all of the ideas, information, insights, and questions you have received or asked, or those that you want to ask in the future. Write everything down for future review. You can create sections for the following topics:

- expectations you have of your mentors
- expectations they have of you
- questions to ask
- things to share with them
- lessons you have learned
- changes you have made
- actions you will take
- results you have achieved
- thoughts you have had
- experiences you want to share
- realizations you have come to
- views or opinions that you have changed
- a history of your meetings and telephone conversations

This is just a partial list. Keep only those items that you think are appropriate for you in this relationship. If you have more than one mentor relationship at a time, you can keep all of this in one journal; you don't have to have fourteen binders on your desk.

Don't Force It

Early in my speaking career, I started a Mastermind Group with a dozen other speakers.

Over the years, I reaped the benefits of sharing ideas with like-minded people. Another purpose of the Mastermind Group was to help facilitate mentor relationships that were wins for the mentor and mentee both. In the early part of my speaking and writing career, operating as a sole business owner, I knew I needed input, feedback, and ideas from other successful speakers and authors. So I invited a group of people in my business to form a Mastermind Group in which we would share ideas and critique one another's materials, marketing plans, and products. From the beginning, it was clear that this group would not succeed. There were too many individual agendas and competing philosophies. We lasted for less than six months as a formal group. Each meeting was a struggle to accomplish anything worthwhile. I ended up wasting a great deal of time and money in this effort.

What went wrong? I was trying too hard to make the relationships work. A collaborative relationship, if it is to be successful, must flow. It should have very little stress.

How Do You Know When the Relationship Is Working?

Well, folks, we are in the home stretch. I hope that I have convinced you of the importance of establishing, maintaining, and learning from mentor relationships. There are just a few other things I would like you to think about. How do you know when a relationship is working, and how do you know when it isn't—when it's time to end it and move on?

There are warning signs when a relationship is not working, just as there are signals when it is a mutually beneficial and worth continuing. Mentor relationships are like any others—they take effort, commitment, energy, and time to develop and maintain. No relationship, if it is to be worthwhile, will come easy.

You and your mentor are bound to disagree and have misunderstandings. These, however, do not have to cause the relationship to end. If a relationship is working, it will generally be free of mistrust, stress, hidden agendas, unspoken expectations, unresolved conflicts, and old baggage. It will be respectful, helpful, encouraging, honest, and safe. If and when you lose any of these characteristics, it may be a sign that the relationship is coming to an end. If so, how do you know when it is time to move on?

There are several ways to tell if the relationship is no longer working. Here are a few of the common signals:

1. One of you has stopped communicating on a regular basis with the other.
2. You are now performing out of obligation or guilt rather than desire.
3. Trust, respect, or both are no longer part of the relationship.
4. Your mentor can no longer help you. Your needs and desires have outgrown this relationship. Keep in mind that even if the mentor relationship ends, you can still maintain the friendship, if you had one.
5. Your mentor is too busy for you.
6. You have lost interest.
7. The relationship is becoming destructive and critical rather than supportive and positive.

I'll leave you with a question before we go on to chapter 6. What are you going to do with the information in this chapter?

CHAPTER 6

THE GREATEST
CHALLENGES IN SALES

Every profession has problems, challenges, and risks. No one is immune to these hazards, but everyone can benefit from the opportunities they present. If you pay close attention during your first year, you will notice that some of your peers will do exceedingly well with the tools, training, and opportunities that they are given. Others, in contrast, will misuse or not use these benefits at all. You will also become acutely aware of how some of your fellow salespeople do poorly while others chart a very successful financial course into the future. Why, if two people are given the same opportunities and products or services to sell, plus the same challenges, economy, management team, and risks, would one do well while the other does poorly or even fails?

I have asked myself this question over and over again during my forty-plus years as a trainer. Of course, there is no simple and conclusive answer; however, there are a few warning signs that I have observed that may help you avoid the catastrophe of failure. Remember, it always costs more to fail than to succeed in any area of life, and sales is no different.

The requirement of success is a willingness to learn, work, grow, and persist. The cost of failure is enormous emotionally, financially, and physically. Consider what you are up against if you fail:

- You have to look for a new position.
- Your track record will make it harder to secure a favorable new position.
- You may have to move to a smaller residence, perhaps unloading some of your possessions. In the process, your personal relationships could be dramatically affected.
- Your self-esteem will take a beating.
- You will have to learn a new career or job.
- You may have to cultivate an entirely new group of friends and associates.

Although you might not experience all of these, you would certainly encounter some, as well as face other unforeseen consequences. So it is best to avoid such catastrophic failure. Now we need to learn how to do that.

Remember, it always costs more to fail than to succeed in any area of life, and sales is no different.

PATHWAY TO SUCCESS

Your career, like most everyone else's, will probably be riddled with potholes, missed opportunities, and mistakes. At the same time, you will experience your share of opportunities to succeed. But to open life to the good, you need to learn how to deal with the bad. So let's look at some of the challenges you will inevitably face as your career develops.

LIFE VERSUS WORK CHALLENGES

As we discussed previously, you will need to learn to balance your new career and your personal life successfully. How best to handle that?

Maintaining balance is not easy in any career. It is especially difficult in the sales profession. Many people will want, need, or even demand your time. There are customers, suppliers, fellow salespeople, managers, and executives. Each of these groups has specific needs or desires for which you will be responsible. You will be required to be at your customers' beck and call and to travel to trade shows at the last minute. You will be required to attend seminars, company meetings, and briefings that can last well past normal working hours. There is no such thing as "normal" in sales. I have worked twenty-four-hour days and many seven-day weeks. You will have to plan your vacation time and your other time off around client and management expectations.

> **Think About It**
> Passion is the great equalizer. Your ability to maintain a high level of passion regardless of what is going on around you will greatly determine your success.

How to Prepare for the Balancing Act

The key to effective balance, to preventing these demands from overwhelming your personal relationships and interests, is to keep everything in perspective. Remind yourself regularly that this field provides the income that allows you to live the way you choose, but it, in my opinion, should never totally dominate your life. Life is meant to be fun, rewarding, and challenging, but you do not need to derive all your satisfaction from your career. It is important to love what you are doing so that you work the twenty-four-hour days out of love rather than out of obligation or guilt. The day that I am no longer willing to spend several hours each week on planes so I can have the privilege of speaking to an audience is the day both I and my audience will no longer benefit from my message.

> **Think About It**
> Selling and life can be hard, and sooner or later everyone wants to quit. But the key is to understand the difference between wanting to quit and actually quitting.

And the day I stop enjoying spending long, quiet hours at my computer—sometimes into the early hours of the next morning—is the day I will begin to wonder whether what I write has any redeeming value for my readers or gives me any real sense of satisfaction.

How to Manage the Balancing Act

The first thing you can do to manage this challenge is to accept its inevitability. At the same time, you'll need to recognize that if you don't, your success in sales could ultimately suffer. Depending on your age, relationship status, and emotional maturity, you will encounter different challenges.

The Balancing Act

Balance is about love: loving what you do, whether it is work or play, being alone or with friends or family. Sooner or later you will have to make some hard choices. Should you have a family weekend or spend two days boning up on a new presentation? Should you leave work early to attend your six-year-old's birthday celebration or put the finishing touches on an important proposal? These choices will never be easy, but you'll have to make them anyway. Balance is about goals. We have spent a great deal of time discussing the importance of goals. Again, without clear, carefully thought-out goals, you will never enjoy real balance, harmony, and inner peace in your life. You will always feel as though, in some area of your life, you're being cheated or things have spun out of control. You will add unnecessary stress to your life. When you come to that point—and you will—you will have to make some difficult choices. Better to have a road map that shows you why you decided what you did so that you can devote your full energy and total passion to what you are doing at the time.

If you are in your twenties and single, your new career will most likely affect only your social life (although don't discount this—losing your social life may jeopardize future family happiness). However, if you are in your thirties or forties and married or divorced, you will confront an entirely different set of problems: children, a spouse or ex-spouse, and numerous social and family obligations. The key to managing these challenges successfully is keeping the lines of communication open and being honest with those people with whom you are close. As your responsibilities in your personal relationships change, you will need to grow into those obligations with clarity, flexibility, and patience.

How to Prevent Falling Off the Tightrope

In all honesty, I must say that you can't prevent your work obligations from affecting the rest of your life. This is true not only of sales but of virtually all professions. Success means making trade-offs. Life changes—get used to it. People change. Your desires, goals, and needs change. The best strategy is to remain aware that you will need to face these challenges eventually—if not today, then tomorrow.

HANDLING REJECTION

You must be able to emotionally handle the rejection that is inherent in sales. We all want to be approved of, validated, and accepted. No one likes rejection, whether it comes from a friend, relative, total stranger, or fellow employee. The rejection that you will experience in your sales career is a normal element of the profession. Sooner or later, you will encounter prospects or customers who don't like you, don't want to see you, or are even offended by your attempts to see them or sell to them. And even if they like you, they simply may not need the product or service that you're selling at that particular time. It is impossible to expect that everyone you attempt to see or sell to is going to want to see you or even be curious about what you have to offer.

> **Think About It**
> Anything worthwhile comes after you have overcome a challenge. If something comes to you without challenge, you won't give it much value or feel much satisfaction.

How to Prepare for the Inevitable Rejection

One of the biggest challenges you will face in your new career is finding the strength to effectively manage rejection, which, if you are not careful, can make you feel discouraged, frustrated, and even like a failure. I have been studying sales success and failure for more than forty years, and I strongly believe that the inability to successfully deal with this challenge is the number-one cause of failure in sales. Why?

Each of us has a fundamental psychological need to be liked. Each of us likes to be around people who agree with us and enjoy our company. We dislike spending time with people who are constantly pushing our emotional buttons or whose demeanor we find unpleasant. We have organized our lives to ensure that most of our time is spent in the presence of positive, like-minded people, rather than those who are our emotional opposites. The best way to prepare for rejection is to accept that life is not a popularity contest; understand that not everyone you meet will like you—nor will you like them; and recognize that once you overcome this fear of rejection, you will be well on your way to exceptional success in your new sales career.

How to Manage Rejection

You can take various approaches to dealing with this issue. Each will require some stretching, consideration, and willingness to set aside some of your current fears, expectations, and attitudes.

Talk with strangers. First you can start talking more to strangers, people you meet on street corners, in elevators, or in coffee shops. The key is to start a conversation with someone you don't know by bringing up a general topic that fits the situation: "Have you ever been here before?"; "Is the coffee good?"; "Have you ever tried the restaurant next door?"; "Good morning"; "Hi." (These you might want to consider saying first.)

Try *anything* that is nonthreatening. I have even used this tactic in New York City, a place where it is "against the law" to talk to strangers. Of course, some will see your attempt at idle conversation as an intrusion—but others will welcome the opportunity to talk with someone. The point is to develop the habit of talking to strangers and getting used to the rejection you get from some people. Recently I tried to start a conversation with a woman on an elevator in Washington, D.C., with a simple, unobtrusive "Good morning." She responded, "Are you addressing me?" I said, "Well, it's just you and me on this elevator, and I usually don't say good morning to myself out loud." She said, "Do I know you?" I replied, "No." Just use your imagination a little and you can quickly guess where this conversation went: nowhere. But I was no worse off for having tried to start a conversation—even though I was unsuccessful, the experience helped me remember that rejection and even rudeness aren't always that bad.

Cold-call. Spend fifteen minutes a day calling prospects who don't know you and who may have never heard of your organization. You will tend to get blown off a lot if you don't have a good opening approach. Again, the point is to develop some emotional stamina in dealing with rejection.

Here's one more: Make three cold calls a day. While I am not advocating cold-calling as an effective prospecting method, I am suggesting it as a way of learning to cultivate the ability to not take rejection personally.

Prevent rejection in the first place. You can't prevent every potential rejection that you will face in your career. Well, there is one way, I suppose—and that's to never attempt to see people, sell to people, or ask for the business. You will never experience rejection by staying in your office, in your car, or at your desk. But then you'll never sell anything, either.

FORGE AHEAD

Essential for success is the ability to stick with it—whatever it may be—during long periods of poor results. You must be able to face your failures, put them aside, and keep battling for the results you desire.

How to Develop Persistence

One of the critical skills for success in sales is persistence, or what might be called "the stick-to-it-iveness." That may not be proper English, but it gets the point across. Many people expect life and sales to be easy and to get immediate, positive results. One of the requirements for success in sales is the ability to fill up your prospect pipeline and then keep it full with regular prospecting. Nothing that is worthwhile ever comes easily or quickly—trust me, I know. If you expect immediate results, you will live with a great deal of frustration.

How to Sustain Persistence and Stick-to-it-iveness

Persistence is a habit that is formed over time. I won't go so far as to say that the ability to hang in there is in your genes, but if you have it as a trait, you most likely exhibited it during your early childhood, education, or any past activity. You can develop this habit of persistence now if it is not part of your mental makeup, but you will need patience and, yes, persistence, to develop the habit of persistence. Seems like a paradox, doesn't it, learning to stick with things by sticking with things?

I am by nature a persistent, do-it-now type in most areas of my life. I just refuse to quit. In fact, I have a sign over my desk that has been there for years that says, YOU NEVER FAIL—UNTIL YOU STOP TRYING. Any success I have had thus far in my life and career has had little to do with my education, luck, or contacts. I have achieved it purely with the attitude that no matter what, I will never give in to failure, discouragement, or challenges that appear insurmountable. How have I been able to do this in the face of relentless problems, adversity, setbacks, and failures? It is simple for me; my mind contains no room for giving up. I just refuse to accept failure as final. It is only a detour.

Success Can Lead to Failure

I recall, over twenty years ago, working with a new client in the real estate business in Washington, D.C. One of the newer hires, she had sold a new home in the half-million-dollar price range in only her second week as a part-time agent. She was feeling excited, confident, and almost arrogant. When I said that I thought this quick success was one of the worst things that could have happened to her in her new career, she was astonished. "Why?" she asked, with a little edge in her voice. I responded with the following.

"Sarah, long-term success in sales requires attitude management skills; effective prospecting; long, hard hours; learning to deal with rejection and disappointment; and knowing how to sell in different situations. Succeeding early, although I certainly congratulate you, was not the result of any of the previous factors. You were lucky. Now, luck is a good thing to have in life, but it won't guarantee your success if you develop the belief that this business is easy. What will your attitude be if you sell nothing for the next six months?"

"That won't happen to me," she responded. I could see I wasn't getting my point across, so I asked her one more question.

"Sarah, do you think all of your sales will be this easy, or come this quickly?" She responded with a confident "Yes." Well, to make a very long story short, she failed to make any sales several weeks later. In fact, she never sold another home. She quit. She did not develop the skills and attitudes necessary for long-term success.

I suggest that you learn persistence in the little things first. Get in the habit of having small successes. Then build on these as you strengthen your resolve, confidence, and commitment. Why not keep a persistence log? Track all of those activities, projects, and tasks. How did you do? Did you quit early? If so, why? Did you stick with them to their conclusion? If so, why?

How to Prevent Negative Perseverance

I have learned that sooner or later each of us will be brought to our knees in some area of our lives. The key to avoiding being undone by this is to not give any mental energy to anything other than your goals and how, why, and when you want to achieve them. If it takes your entire life, so be it. I have also learned that surrender—not giving up but letting life be—is an excellent way to live without the added stress that comes with yielding to discouragement and failure.

As we have discussed, failure, risk, problems, and the like are a part of life, just as are success, achievement, and overcoming challenges. The thing to remember is that one day you are going to want to give up. This is fine. Just don't do it.

BE WILLING TO WORK LONG HOURS

As I have suggested throughout this book, sales, especially in the early years, requires long hours and lots of effort if you want to succeed. Shortcuts to success in this field don't exist. If you can't manage the long, demanding hours, then you're going to have trouble finding success. If, on the other hand, you can out-work your competitors and peers, there is no limit to what you will be able to accomplish over time.

How to Prepare for Long Hours

Long hours and endless days require a lot of energy without any immediate positive return. But you can do some things to make sure you have the time, energy, and attitude to put in long hours on the job. Figure out what works for you.

Recipes for Success

You know that you have to study, put in your time, and have a positive attitude to succeed. But how do you do all that without burning out? Each person is different, but the following is a list of some essentials for optimal performance in your life:

- Eat a balanced diet.
- Manage the stressors in your life.
- Eliminate destructive mental and physical habits that will sabotage your energy.
- Play hard.
- Get regular exercise.
- Take minivacations.
- If you need to lose weight, do it.
- Nap on weekends when you can.
- Get to bed an hour earlier than usual.
- Take vitamin supplements.

There are other actions that will help, but these will get you started, and if you can do many of them, you will be amazed at how much energy you will have for the demanding tasks ahead.

How to Manage Working Long Hours

Many of the methods I suggested in the previous section take time, commitment, discipline, and persistence. There is no easy way to accomplish what you want. To do so you will need to manage your time better, and arrange your priorities and resources in your life and career with care.

SACRIFICE

Unquestionably, to be successful you must be willing to sacrifice many of your personal needs and agendas. It is important to have personal goals as well as career and sales goals—we have already discussed this topic. In this section I would like to offer an amendment to this perspective: Sometimes you have to accept that your personal and career goals may conflict with each other. Welcome to the real world. The most important thing is that you establish *clear* goals in all areas of your life. If you don't, you'll be ill-equipped to decide which should take precedence—your career or your personal life—and you might make sacrifices in either area for the wrong reasons. The secret to ensuring the least amount of disruption in any part of your life is to know why you are doing what you are doing. Many people who set goals fail to ask themselves the critical question: Why do I want this? When you have answered this question, you will have a clearer understanding of your real motives and how you can minimize their impact on your personal life.

Often your personal and career goals will come into conflict with each other. Welcome to the real world.

Preparing to Sacrifice

When you're choosing between private and business objectives in your life, there are many factors to consider, not the least of which are your personal opinions, expectations, and philosophy. Often some of these might conflict with those of your management team or organization. For example, let's say that your religion prohibits you from working on Sunday. What if you have a sales meeting or have to travel to a trade show on a Sunday? How will you handle this conflict? Some organizations and managers will be relatively sensitive to your personal beliefs, while others won't give a rip about your family, personal interests, or religious beliefs. I am not saying this is right or wrong: It's just the way it is in the world in which you have chosen to work.

The point is, sooner or later you may have to decide how you are going to handle the conflict between your professional expectations and your personal needs. Recognize that there may be little that you can do other than attempt to persuade your manager that your personal desires or obligations are important to you and that you respectfully request that he or she honor them. Sometimes this will work; often it will not. If you choose to remain with a company in which work always comes first, you must accept the consequences. Alternatively, you may look for a sales job that will be satisfying professionally but will also have managers who are more aware of and sensitive to employees' personal lives.

Sleeping on the Job

I recall that early in my career, I was tired a lot. I can remember instances in which I lost business because my competitors got to my prospects before I did. One in particular comes to mind.

I was in my first year of sales, and I had a tremendous opportunity to close one of the biggest sales in the history of the company. It required lots of planning, preparation, and research, which I had to do in the evenings and on a few consecutive weekends. At the time I had my priorities wrong and had put off some of the work because I was just too tired and needed a break from the pressure and sheer size of the workload. Needless to say, I lost the sale to a competitor who was better pre-pared and able to stick with the workload until he was done. I will never forget that early lesson. And, trust me, it will never happen again. I may lose the business be-cause I don't have the wisdom, experience, knowledge, support, or tools, but I will never lose another sale because I am not energetic enough to be up to the task.

MANAGING CONFLICT AND ACHIEVING BALANCE

What, then, can you do if a conflict arises between your career and some aspect of your personal life?

First, evaluate how important this priority really is to you. Second, if it is a family issue, discuss it with the appropriate family member to see if he or she is willing to be flexible. Third, discuss it with your manager to see if you can find an alternative that will work for everyone. Fourth, be open to developing a new paradigm. Fifth, if necessary, be willing to stand your ground, recognizing that you may win the battle but lose the war. In other words, think about whether the short-term gain outweighs any long-term loss.

Life is often about the ability to manage change and uncertainty in a positive way.

Life is often about the ability to manage change and uncertainty in a posi-tive way; to see new situations and challenges from a different perspective; and to be willing to let go of expectations, habits, rules, and opinions that may have served you well in the past but are no longer in your best interests.

Prevention

One way to reduce the stress and negative outcomes of these issues is to discuss many of them with your supervisor early in your career.

Years ago, when I was a salesperson, my wife gave birth to our first child. Try as I might to help, my wife never slept more than three or four hours a day. She was exhausted and needed me to help a lot more with our daughter's care. My boss's attitude was that you can't be representing our company and selling successfully if you are also babysitting. My response was that if I had to deal with the added stress of an exhausted mother of a daughter of whom I was equally a parent, I wouldn't be very effective as a salesperson, either. We reached a compromise. I adjusted my schedule so that I could satisfy his needs as well as my own needs, and those of my wife and daughter. It wasn't easy, but it did allow me to keep my job and succeed. I would make prospecting calls and do all of the studying I needed to at home. My boss made an exception in my case because I was working to do my part as well. I didn't expect a one-way solution.

THE JUGGLING ACT

Essential as well is the ability to handle multiple tasks simultaneously. At any given time, you may be required to solve after-sales problems with several customers at once; negotiate with in-house support staff over schedules, resources, or the allocation of funds; prospect for new business; attend meetings; conduct research for a new customer or prospect; learn about a new product for your customers; attend classes or seminars on sales skills or product applications; or create a variety of reports on territory status, customer potential, market conditions, or competitor strengths and weaknesses. This is just the beginning, and you will

> **Think About It**
> The type of obstacles you overcome will have a direct relationship to your success and personal satisfaction.

have to do all of this simultaneously. It may seem like a great deal to have on your plate, but remember, the more successful you become, the more you will have to juggle at once.

You might reasonably ask, then why become more successful if the result will be more work? This is the attitude that many salespeople take, and it leads to their ultimate failure. The longer you are in your position, the easier it will be to handle all of the additional responsibilities. With time, you will, I hope, develop strategies that enable you to pour it on without having to work that much harder.

The key is to learn to work more effectively—smarter, not harder. This is a skill that you can gain only with time. You have to learn the ropes: what you can do and what you can't, who is reliable and who isn't, what resources you have at your disposal and which ones you lack. The key is to learn the lessons as you go along. Resist the tendency to put off learning anything you can in this regard. A little extra effort in the beginning will pay handsome dividends later in your career.

The longer you are in your position, the easier it will be to handle all of the additional responsibilities.

How to Multitask

In the section on time and territory management in chapter 2, I shared a number of strategies to help you in this area. If you feel you are weak in this regard, you might want to go back and reread that section. You will find many ideas on how to manage your time and responsibilities effectively. Here are a few others to think about:

- Always spend the time necessary to do a task right the first time.
- Be careful that you don't get into a rut thinking that your daily responsibilities are unimportant. They are the reason you are working, and if you do them correctly, they will be the source of your success.
- Even when you have several tasks going at once, be sure to focus on only one thing at a time.
- Learn to concentrate and avoid distractions.
- Recognize that some things will always be more important than others; keep things in perspective.
- Avoid doing the easy things first, or the things you can get done quickly. You may get more done, but are you getting the right things done?

- Keep asking yourself, Is this the best use of my time now?
- Once a day/week/month, reevaluate your priorities.
- Spend adequate time planning your day/week/month/year.

The absolute key to multitasking? That's simple: Plan, plan, and plan some more.

STAYING MOTIVATED

Motivation is an inside-out proposition. Yes, some people are motivated by money, rewards, and threats, but in the long run, these are temporary. The key to maintaining your motivation in good times as well as bad is to understand the essence of motivation and how it affects you personally.

What Motivates You?

Everyone is motivated. Not everyone, though, is motivated by the same things. Some people get a rush when they are given a plaque in front of a hundred people, while others need only the quiet satisfaction of knowing they have overcome an obstacle and accomplished a goal. Some people measure their success and ability to stay motivated by how much money they make. I am not saying that any of these are better or worse than any others or that some are right and others wrong. The key to effective motivation is to know what motivates you and why. If you have never taken stock of this issue, now is the time to do it. It is also important to know what makes you unmotivated. Often eliminating something that strips your motivation is just as valuable as having a positive motivator.

The key to effective motivation is to keep in the forefront of your consciousness the reasons you are doing what you are doing.

The key to effective motivation is to keep in the forefront of your consciousness the reasons you are doing what you are doing. It is also important to recognize that the more control you have over your motivators, the more likely you are to remain motivated regardless of the circumstances. For example, if you are motivated by money and your company changes the sales compensation plan in midstream (yes, it happens all the time), you may find yourself losing your motivation, and there is nothing you can do to change the circumstances.

If, in contrast, you are motivated by completing a task, and you can control the circumstances surrounding its completion, guess what: You can better control your motivation itself. Don't get me wrong—there is nothing inherently bad in any form of positive motivation. Sales contests can be good for you and your motivation, but they can also reduce motivation for others.

Be sure to have some control over what motivates you.

The point is to be sure that you have some control over what motivates you. Even a redesigned sales compensation program can give you the opportunity to reevaluate how you are selling and to whom, to see if you can't improve your performance and income in spite of the new program.

In this chapter I have tried to illuminate the realities in the sales profession. If you feel I am being negative, or are wondering what you got yourself into, you may want to read more about the profession—or change careers. Turning a blind eye to the realities of this industry doesn't make them disappear. It is better to be prepared than be broadsided by circumstances, events, or people you could have avoided if you had had ample warning.

Let me repeat, I have made my living for over forty years selling. I love it. I love the independence, the success, the ability to help others, and, yes, the money. But I also love the challenges, the risks, and even the failures. It is all part of the game. Remember, you will win some, and you will lose some. You won't win them all, nor will you lose them all. I can tell you, though, that the smell and taste of victory far outweigh the negative experiences of defeat and failure.

CHAPTER 7

GOOD STUFF

During your first year, you will have many successes as you learn new skills and contribute to the lives of your customers. Your primary responsibility in sales is to help your customers improve their businesses and/or personal success, eliminate challenges and problems, and generally help them improve the quality of their lives, no matter what you sell. Many salespeople believe their major role is to improve the success of the organization that they themselves work for while also earning an income. Yes, these activities are important to your overall long-term success, but you can accomplish them in many ways. It is unfortunate that some of these salespeople shade the truth, mislead customers, and often even lie to make a sale. Your personal satisfaction and self-esteem can only come from an ethical approach to your position and its responsibilities.

ON SUCCESS (AND FRUSTRATION)

In the course of your career, if you choose to take the high moral ground, you will undoubtedly experience many situations in which you can be proud of your accomplishments. When you create win-win relationships with your customers or clients, you will set yourself up for a large amount of positive feedback, genuine appreciation, and, often, thanks that will compensate for all of the negatives you may also experience. Selling is a worthy career. It gives you the opportunity to make a difference in your customers' and clients' lives, and when you do, you can go to sleep at night knowing that you have made a wise choice in selecting this career.

> *Your personal satisfaction and self-esteem can only come from an ethical approach to your position and its responsibilities.*

Real *Success*

During my sales career I have received over three thousand letters of thanks for a job well done. I have included a couple of them in this chapter. Let me tell you, when I have seriously felt that the difficulties of this profession were so overwhelming that I wanted to quit and get a "regular" job, these were the letters that kept me going.

Now, when you are in a slump, down in the dumps, and the world has turned its back on you, your manager is breathing down your neck, you haven't made a sale in three months, and you just can't take another day, you will feel a renewed sense of purpose after receiving a genuine and heartfelt thanks from one of your customers. The key is to perform in such a way that people offer accolades truthfully and frequently.

Thank Me Now and Thank Me Later

What are some things that you can do to deserve letters and appreciation like this from clients, fellow salespeople, support staff, or even your suppliers?

Real Success—Part One

Years ago, I gave each employee of one of my clients a copy of a book I wrote. Several years later I received a letter from one of the employees:

"Tim, the words in your book came at a time when I was facing a serious crossroads in my career. I was discouraged, frustrated, unhappy, and ready to throw in the towel. After reading your words, I felt a renewed sense of dedication and commitment. I decided to give it all I could and never consider failure as an option. At the time the future was as bleak as it could be for anyone, anywhere. I was failing because of a loss of belief, passion, confidence, and dedication. I was looking more for how I would benefit than how my customers would from my relationship with them. Your words gave me a new perspective. Today, years later, I am one of my company's most successful and respected executives. I can only imagine what my life would have been like today had I not developed a new attitude. Thank you for saving my life and career."

That is why you do your job every day.

Go the extra mile. Do more for your customers than they ask, deserve, or even pay for. It means you are more concerned with what they get than how you benefit from a sale to them. Promise a lot and deliver more. Most salespeople promise a little and deliver less.

Give rather than receive. Develop the philosophy of giving rather than getting. This means that in the normal routines of your day you take the time to think about others more than yourself. It requires a loss of selfishness on your part. This will take some adjusting of your own self-expectations, and for some this is not an easy task.

Real Success—Part Two

After conducting a three-day in-house custom management seminar, I received the following e-mail.

"Tim, our business was on the brink of failure. Our customers were bailing out faster than they were coming in, our employees were leaving in droves, and my personal life was in shambles as a result. Your program couldn't have come at a better time. As a result of the information you shared, we are back on track headed for a record-breaking year. New customers are lining up to do business with us, we are turning away potential new employees because we just don't have the physical space for them, and my relationship with my spouse and children couldn't be better. I can't thank you enough for your insight, wisdom, ability to challenge us in a positive way, and your concern for our success."

Deliver more value. Develop the habit of spending some time every day doing a little extra for some of your customers without expecting a thank-you or a response. Do it because it is who you are, not because of what you will receive in return. You can send them an article you think they might enjoy that doesn't have anything to do with improving their business or your products or services. You do it because you want to send the message "I care about you, not just your business."

Focus and learn. Learn to focus on what you are learning and how it will help others, not only you or your organization. Spend time learning about your customers' industries, concerns, needs, and expectations, even when they have nothing to do with your product or service. Get inside their business. I remember years ago having dinner with several employees of one of my clients. One of the sales managers said over coffee, "You have been doing business with our company for over five years, and we no longer think of you as an outsider, but one of us. As a result, we know that your only interest is our success and not your own." That statement made my month!

Appreciate. Show appreciation for the things that people do for you. People in general tend to want to do more for those who show appreciation for what is done for them. Whether it is a thank-you call, letter, or e-mail doesn't matter. The mere fact that you have taken the time to acknowledge their thoughtfulness will go a long way in building favorable long-term relationships. I'll prove it.

Whom do you tend to want to do more for? People who say thank you or people who act like they deserve it or you owe it to them?

Show that you care. Show people you care and are interested in them by sending them birthday cards, flowers, or special recognition of some kind. I give away over two thousand books a year to people just to say thanks. I send out over fifty greeting cards a month acknowledging special events like business anniversaries, new product introductions, and promotions. You would be amazed at how

> *Think About It*
> Remember that money comes and goes, but your self-esteem is with you forever.

few salespeople go to the trouble to take these kinds of actions. Trust me, sooner or later it will pay off, not necessarily financially (but it can there as well), but in many other ways that will give you far more lasting satisfaction and meaning than your last paycheck or award.

Acknowledge your staff. Get in the habit of thanking and praising support staff for their effort on your behalf. Yes, they are paid to do the work, but a little praise and appreciation can go a long way. I remember in my first sales position, there was one secretary for the entire sales staff. Now, I ask you, if you need a proposal done on the computer or are out of town and need some samples sent to a prospect and there are ten other sales-

> *Think About It*
> Don't wait for others to give you what you can give yourself: Pat yourself on the back when you feel you deserve it.

people vying for this person's time, which salesperson's request is going to get handled first if the secretary can't get to everything today? You guessed it: the one who is the most thankful. I learned this lesson the hard way. I lost a sale because my proposal wasn't at the top of the pile one day. The tasks that got the secretary's attention were the ones not necessarily requested by the most successful or longest-term salespeople on the staff, but by those who were the most respectful, kind, appreciative, and courteous.

Say thank you. Don't underestimate the power of thanking your manager for his or her help and support. Your manager has a great deal to handle. You are not the only one who needs guidance and praise. Your manager has responsibilities up the chain of command as well as down. He or she also has a manager who has to be kept informed and met with. Managers have reports, business obligations, and most likely family obligations as well. Your manager is going to do his or her best to spread time, talent, and resources around as well as possible. Accept that you are not his or her only responsibility. Showing routinely that you appreciate your manager's time and effort on your behalf will go a long way in ensuring that you get support when you need it most.

Remember other departments. If it is appropriate in your position—and this can depend on what you sell—every once in a while show gratitude to the people in finance, distribution, manufacturing, design, customer service, human resources, and administration. These people are all on your team, and you need to have people willing to go to bat for you in a crunch.

Remember everyone. Show appreciation for the efforts of your vendors or suppliers on your behalf. Your suppliers have other responsibilities than to help you succeed. They have other customers as well. Whether it is joining you on a sales call, tracking down an order, or just following up with a customer, you will want them to be available for you when you need them. The only way to ensure this support is to let them know how much you appreciate their concern and help.

Acknowledge experience. Be thankful to the veteran salespeople on your staff for their guidance. Sooner or later you will need to ask for the help of one of the more senior members of your sales team. Like you, they have their own customers' demands and their career issues. In fact, because they have been employed there longer, I'll bet they have a lot more on their plate than you do. Appreciate their guidance and support. It could prove invaluable in saving you time, mistakes, and even failure over time.

Thank your spouse or partner. Finally, show gratitude to your spouse, if you have one, for his or her patience while you devote a great deal of your energy and time to your career. It is critical that you maintain a healthy personal life while you are in your new career. At times you may need to miss a meal, weekend, special event, or simply a night at home with your family. But keep this to a minimum, for ultimately it will affect your career. A personal life that is in shambles will eventually wreak havoc on your career and jeopardize your success. Regularly show your appreciation to those in your life who really matter. Tell them you understand the sacrifices they are making on your behalf in order to advance your career.

A personal life that is in shambles will eventually wreak havoc on your career and jeopardize your success.

The previous list might leave you thinking that all you will have time for is going around thanking people every day and that you won't have any time left to sell. This attitude of thankfulness is more a function of who you are than how you spend your time. Really, how long or how much effort does it take to give a support person a few words of praise once or twice a week?

Handling Recognition (Or Lack Thereof)

As wonderful and necessary as recognition is, if you don't handle it properly or you don't get enough, you will have to deal with this in a professional manner. Following are a few problems with recognition that you may experience, particularly early in your career.

No thank-yous. What if you feel like you are not getting enough recognition? As a new salesperson, you will want to know how you are doing as you progress. If your expectation is to have every deed recognized, you will set yourself up for a great deal of frustration. Your manager, depending on his or her competence, available time, and the size of the sales team, may not give you the feedback you want during your first months. Learn to accept the reality that your value is not directly related to who notices what you do or how well you do it.

Unequal recognition. Someone else on the sales team gets more recognition than you do for the same results. In your early career, your major concern should be how well you are doing, not keeping track of others. This is not a competition with the other members of the sales staff. This is about your success and your personal pace. As long as you are learning and doing your best, forget everyone else and what they get and how often. Believe me, if you focus on your own growth and not on the psychological need for a pat on the back every morning, you will survive and prosper. However, if your major concern is recognition, I guarantee that you will be disappointed and frustrated. Both of these emotions can take your eye off the ball.

Punch Your Own Ticket

Years ago I heard a speaker give the following example. I think it bears repeating here. She said, "Many people go through life holding out a ticket to be punched if they do something well." Many organizations use a similar approach. When you go into a coffee shop and buy a latte, they punch your ticket. Get ten punches and you receive a free latte. She went on to say, "The secret to happiness and emotional well-being is to learn to punch your own ticket when you do something good. Don't wait or expect others to notice, care, or bother to punch your ticket." I thought this was great advice and have used it ever since. Later in this chapter I'll show you how I have adapted it to suit my personal needs.

A swelled head. You receive recognition and it goes to your head. I have seen this happen more often than you can imagine. I have seen people fail in their sales positions after making salesperson of the month or year. Strange? Yes. True? Yes. Why? I could give you numerous examples from business, sports, entertainment, and education. Let's use sports as an illustration. How many teams have back-to-back championships in football, baseball, or basketball? How many people have won consecutive tournaments in tennis? Golf? Oh yes, there are some examples, but fewer rather than more. Why? Is it arrogance? Overconfidence? They stop learning or growing? They lose their passion, drive, focus, or commitment? You tell me! To avoid this trap, it's important to remember that

recognition, while nice and often well deserved, is not why you will succeed. You
will succeed because of your effort, commitment, willingness to learn, and many
of the topics we have discussed in this
book up to this point.

> **Think About It**
> Rewards are not always financial. The feeling that you
> completed a "job well done" or that you helped someone
> can be worth a great deal.

No praise. You get only negative feedback, and you never get any praise.
Some managers are uncomfortable giving positive feedback. Many are only capable of negative reinforcement. If you are unfortunate enough to be working
for someone like that, there are some steps you can take:

- Keep a journal of your successes and positive deeds.
- Start a "good stuff" jar.
- Spend time with your mentor.
- Meet with your manager and discuss why the only feedback you re-
  ceive is negative (make sure you are on solid ground here, and find out
  if you actually deserve the negative stuff).
- Ask your manager what you have to do to earn his or her praise.
- Ask your fellow team members for positive feedback.
- Rely on the positive feedback from your customers as enough.

There are numerous other recognition issues, but most that you will face
will tend to fall into the above four categories. The key thing to remember is
that the only recognition that really matters is that which you receive from your
customers. Remember, that's why your company is in business, and it is the
major responsibility of your career to always ensure that the customer comes
first. Some companies do not have this philosophy. Just remember, no matter
what your organization's philosophy is, without customers, none of you has a
job. So the only recognition that matters comes from your satisfied customers.
Work for it, achieve it, and you will never have to worry about your success or
whether you will have a job tomorrow.

SETTING AND REACHING HIGHER GOALS

In chapter 2 we discussed in detail the importance of setting goals and how to move toward them. My intent here is not to repeat the earlier discussion, but to take it to a higher level. Once you understand the goal-setting process and its importance, you will realize that your continued success is directly related to your ability to set bigger and more challenging goals. Your early goals might have been to

- improve your product knowledge
- master the fundamental sales skills
- learn new attitudes that would guarantee your survival
- reach your quota
- fill your prospect pipeline
- satisfy the expectations of your manager
- make a living
- increase your income

> **Think About It**
> Ask for testimonial letters from your clients and keep them in a binder. Whenever you feel discouraged, read them.

Now it is time to move beyond the basics and begin to think longer term and more broadly. It is time to accept the fact that you have survived, you are doing well, you like the role of selling and what it gives you, and you need bigger and more challenging goals in order to continue to grow in your career. This is what I have learned from personal experience:

- Increased recognition doesn't do it.
- More money doesn't do it.
- More freedom doesn't do it.
- Greater leverage doesn't do it.
- More knowledge doesn't do it.
- Being number one doesn't do it.

Then what does? That, my friend, is what you have to determine for your-self. I can only give you a few guidelines. Here is what you will have to consider as you begin to reach for more:

1. What keeps the passion growing for you in your career and life?
2. If you didn't have to work, how would you spend your time?
3. When do you feel really good about yourself?
4. Why do you want to earn more money?
5. If your manager said, "You will no longer be paid for your effort and results," would you continue in this career? Would you work for free? I know, I know, seems like a foolish question. But pretend you no longer need the money. You are secure thanks to your wise manage-ment and investment of your income over the years.
6. Do you like the intangible benefits of this career, such as the ability to help others, enough to stick with it for different motives?
7. Do you love the problems and challenges as much as the results and success?
8. Do you enjoy helping others, or are you in it for yourself?
9. Do you want to move into management and beyond?
10. Would you like to start your own business someday?
11. Is retirement an option for you? Or do you love what you do so much you never want to stop or do something else?

That's enough to get you started. Why not spend some time on these ques-tions and then come up with some additional ones of your own? Make them challenging and thought provoking. The value of the answers in life is related to the quality of the questions.

TAKING THE GOOD STUFF AND LEAVING THE BAD STUFF BEHIND

One of the skills necessary for success in sales is the ability to compartmentalize, to keep the good stuff in your consciousness and the negative stuff quarantined like a computer infected with a virus. What is bad stuff? I am confident everyone will define this differently. To me, the bad things are those circumstances that (a) negatively affect your attitude, (b) take your eyes off what is really important, (c) prevent your personal or career growth, or (d) cause you to fail. Bad is not a problem, but rather the inability to learn from it; a failure, but the inability to overcome it; a setback, but the unwillingness to find another way. Bad stuff can be good stuff. And good stuff can potentially be bad stuff. Good, bad, bad, good; so what? As you can see, it really only matters what you do with it.

Bad is not a problem, but rather the inability to learn from it; a failure, but rather the inability to overcome it; a setback, but rather the unwillingness to find another way.

Everyone does something worthy of praise. One of the things I learned early in my career was that if I didn't blow my own horn, nobody would ever know how good I was or what I had done that I felt deserved recognition. I remember one time, after several years in sales, I was not getting the acknowledgment I believed I deserved from a client for helping him solve a serious problem. When I asked the client why he hadn't thanked me, he gave me the classic answer, which has stayed with me for years: "That's your job, to help me solve my problems. Why do I need to thank you?" My first reaction was to say, "Yes, that's true, but a simple thank-you would be nice." I didn't say it, but I learned a valuable lesson. If you want to get any recognition, sooner or later you are going to have to learn to self-promote. The most successful people I know today are great at self-promotion. Cassius Clay (Muhammad Ali) famously remarked, "I am the greatest." He said that before he was. How about the politicians in the United States? Most—right or wrong, good or bad—are great self-promoters.

Good Versus Bad

So what are some of the bad things that could affect your career success, and what are some of the good things that can help you build on your success? Let's look at the bad stuff:

- Making a sale too early in your career and coming to the conclusion that this is really easy. Thinking, "I don't have to learn the skills or develop the right attitude. Man, this career is a snap."
- Doing anything negative or misleading (even lying) to make a sale.
- Refusing to grow and learn.
- Arrogance: thinking you are better than others because you may be selling more. You may be more successful, but that doesn't make you better than anyone.

There's more, but I don't want you to think I am too negative. Let's turn to the good stuff:

- Helping a customer solve a problem.
- Contributing to the success of your company.
- Offering support to a fellow salesperson so he or she can make a sale.
- Getting recognized for a major accomplishment.
- Winning a sales contest.
- Exceeding your quota.
- Making more money than you thought possible.

Again, there are lots more of the positives as well. See how many you can think of.

Keeping a Personal Success Journal

What is a personal success journal? It is not a diary. It is a tool to help you achieve greater success and remember what you have achieved in your career and life. Your journal can be as simple as a three-ring binder or a fancy perfect-bound journal that you purchase in a gift shop or bookstore. The point is that it doesn't matter what you use as long as you do the following:

- Get in the habit of writing in it every day.
- Record your achievements no matter how trivial they might seem.
- Use it to keep track of your progress reaching your goals.
- Keep it positive and upbeat.
- Don't editorialize as you write (you can be the only one who ever reads it).
- Don't leave anything out.
- Start today.

> *Think About It*
> Count your blessings every day. Gratitude is the secret to more in life.

I have been keeping a journal for more than thirty years. My only mistake was not starting earlier in my career. It is so easy to forget all of the things we have learned, shared, and accomplished in our lives if we don't have a system for recording them. Here are a few things I keep in my journal:

- lessons learned
- goals I have set
- goals I have accomplished
- special recognition I have earned
- special quotations I have run across
- books I have read
- books I want to read
- places I have visited
- places I want to visit
- new skills I have developed
- new people I have met
- people who have helped me and how
- career milestones
- special events in my life

I am sure you get the picture: Anything that makes you feel good about yourself and your past goes in the journal.

Why keep a journal, anyway? Why go to all of the trouble? That was what I thought years ago, and I didn't take early advice from a mentor that I keep a journal. Well, I can only tell you that my journal has helped me through more than one setback or failure in my life. When life gets difficult, and you are not sure if it (whatever it is) is worth the continued effort, struggle, or commitment, referring back to your journal will give you the confidence and patience to persevere. My journal reminds me of how far I have come and how good I am, not compared with anyone else, but compared with how good I was five, ten, even twenty years ago. Don't wait: Start your personal success journal today.

Creating a "Good Stuff" Wall or Jar

I know what you are thinking. A "good stuff" jar? What's that, anyway? Several years ago I started a "good stuff" jar and a "good stuff" wall.

The "good stuff" jar: it is just what it sounds like—a large jar that sits on my desk. Anytime I accomplish anything worthwhile or want to put something in the jar that reminds me of some special time in my life, I write it down and put it in the jar. Today as I write I can see it on my desk, crammed full of stuff. What's in my jar?

- a copy of the check I received from the publisher as an advance for this book
- a testimonial I received from a special client
- a wonderful birthday card I received from my son on my fifty-eighth birthday
- a note from a friend thanking me for special consideration
- a copy of a check for the biggest sale I have made in my career
- a picture my granddaughter made for me when she was visiting one summer
- a photo I took while on vacation in Spain
- a copy of an e-mail I received from a customer who purchased one of my books
- a copy of a royalty check from the publisher of my first book, *Soft Sell*

What's the value of a "good stuff" jar? Well, it is very similar to my success journal. Whenever I feel a little discouraged, down, or as if I might like to quit, I just reach in the jar, pull out a handful, and reflect on the contents. You would be amazed at what this can do to melt away your frustration, anxiety, or sense of loss or discouragement. Try it for a few months. Put anything and everything in it that has special meaning for you, and, I will bet, before you know it you will need a second jar.

Take some time to reflect on what you read in this chapter as well as what you are going to do with it.

CHAPTER 8

TRAITS OF SALES SUPERSTARS

No matter how good you are, you can always reach a higher level. Often each next step takes a little more effort to ascend than the previous one did. But read on: The more you know about what it takes to continue your rise to stardom, the easier it will be to reach the top.

GOING TO THE NEXT LEVEL

I have observed thousands of salespeople during my years of sales training. I have found that there are twenty-three ways in which pros are quantum leaps ahead of their competition. Want to move to the next level in sales? Then adopt the principles that appear on the following pages as your guiding philosophy.

Sales Leaders Have Passion

They are more passionate about their opportunity to be of service, to learn, and to improve their status and their lifestyles. They are more passionate about their organizations' products and services. They are more passionate about developing their sales and relationship skills. Sales leaders are more passionate about life. They see life as an adventure, not as the "same stuff, different day." If you want to be a sales leader, you must be passionate about your job and your future.

In addition, they are passionate about solving their clients' problems. And they are passionate about learning everything they can about their customers' businesses. For them, passion comes from within; it is not something they have to force. There is a fire inside them, and it is reflected in their eyes. Do you have the passion to make your clients' and customers' wants and needs your first priority?

> *Think About It*
> It is what you do today that will make you a star in the future.

Sales Leaders Go the Extra Mile

In an age when organizations are handing their salespeople a great deal to do—sell, market, service, administer, promote, solve, and so on—it is no wonder that poor salespeople have less time to sell and learn. Successful salespeople promise a lot and deliver even more than they promise. But to accomplish this, they must manage their time, activities, and resources with precision. Going the extra mile means doing more for a customer than the customer expects, demands, or pays for. This philosophy helps successful salespeople build solid relationships that are not impervious to competition, but are certainly stronger than those based on lower prices and empty promises.

Sales Leaders Are a Resource

Poor salespeople sell products, services, features, benefits, solutions, price, and any number of other commodities. The pros who put distance between themselves and their nearest competitors sell themselves as resources for their clients. As resources, sales leaders are asked for their advice, counsel, and opinions on many issues. They regularly bring creative ideas and information to their customers. Their clients look forward to their visits and telephone calls because they know the salespeople will bring value to them rather than simply trying to sell another service or new product.

Sales leaders are more passionate about life. They see life as an adventure, not as the "same stuff, different day."

Sales Leaders Are Creative

Every day, you could find thousands of people who would tell you that there's nothing new under the sun. They're wrong. These people are living either in fantasyland or on some island that's removed from civilization. Every day, thousands of new inventions, new kinds of technology, new approaches—whatever you can think of—are being created. Salespeople who keep the business once they get it know that they must also keep vigil for new, creative ideas that can help their customers compete better and succeed more. To keep up with the tremendous flow of new ideas, they constantly seek out information and publications, like this one, that keep them abreast of changes that might affect their current or future clients.

Sales Leaders Invest in Themselves

The key to success in the coming years is personal growth. The pros who are outdistancing their nearest competitors are doing so because they have better skills, greater understanding, and increased awareness—and they integrate this information into their daily sales activity. Personal growth means many different things to different people. What I am referring to here is the consistent pursuit of knowledge that will allow you to compete and win in the marketplace of tomorrow. It takes time, money, and commitment to devote yourself to a path of self-improvement. But these pros know that the payoff will far exceed the cost.

Sales Leaders Are Authentic

Vulnerability and humility are valuable traits. People who act their way through life must constantly expend a great deal of energy to maintain their facades. People who behave as they really are, in contrast, can focus on being. The pros are consistent in their behavior because that behavior comes from a set of core values, beliefs, and attitudes. They are comfortable with who they are and are not looking for approval or acceptance of their behavior. In the truest sense, they are real. When you meet them, you can see this in their actions and decisions. They live with an inner integrity. They are not trying to be anything or anyone else, and they are inner-directed, not outer-directed.

> *Think About It*
> What defines real superstars is not what they take from life but rather what they give in life.

Sales Leaders Love What They Are Doing

People who live with inner acceptance, peace, and harmony also live spontaneously. Successful and happy people spend their time in the present. With this philosophy, they enjoy and live life to the fullest. In other words, they have fun. They are fun to be with. They don't take life or themselves too seriously. They win some and lose some, but they know that when they lose, they can also grow, and that when they win, they gain new opportunities. Their definition of winning is beating their own personal best, not beating other people.

Sales Leaders Focus on Service

Ineffective salespeople focus on what they get, while the pros focus on what the customer gets. Their sole purpose is to serve. And they know that in this service, they build reputations and lifestyles that testify to this philosophy. They believe that if their clients ever lose or perceive that they have lost, they lose as well. For these salespeople, service is the foundation of everything they do. Sales leaders' financial success rests on being there first, being there last, and being there anytime they are needed.

Sales Leaders Cultivate Support

Successful salespeople know that they can't always get the answers their customers need or solve their clients' problems without the support of other people, both inside and outside their organizations. They are the customers' ambassadors inside their organizations. Sales leaders build bridges of support to customer service reps, executives, and anyone else they need to help serve their customers in a satisfactory way. They are firm and unyielding yet friendly and compassionate when dealing with other people. They build bridges of understanding and cooperation.

> *Sales leaders build bridges of support to customer service reps, executives, and anyone else they need to help serve their customers in a satisfactory way.*

Sales Leaders Go to Bed Late and Get Up Early

They work hard. They know that their customers' needs, desires, and problems are the central reason that they are in these relationships. They have heard about working smart, but they know it is not a substitute for effort. They don't even consider what they do to be work. They don't follow the clock or the calendar. They love the holidays, all 365 of them. They love it all, even the parts they don't really like. They have learned to love to do the things they don't like to do.

Sales Leaders Believe

They believe in themselves, their mission, their organizations, their products and services, their management, and the free marketplace that permits them to help others while they help themselves. Their self-belief is a fiber that is woven into everything they do. They have high expectations of themselves, their organizations' ability to perform, and their clients' willingness to give them business. They build strong relationships that, even though they may be tested from time to time, can withstand the miscommunications and errors that will inevitably occur.

Sales Leaders Are Focused

They know that it is critical to maintain focus. Every day, in every activity, every sales call, and every working moment, they are aiming at a specific target. They believe that to be effective they must do one thing at a time. They will have multiple projects going on simultaneously, but moment by moment they are only working on one. They know the tremendous power of singularity of purpose.

Sales Leaders Break the Rules

Effective salespeople don't follow conventional wisdom. They have learned that conventional wisdom is more often wrong than right. Sales leaders push the limits in all areas of their life. They are never satisfied with the status quo. Their motto is "It can be better. I can be better. I can do it better."

> Sales leaders push the limits in all areas of their life. They are never satisfied with the status quo.

Sales Leaders Are Here, There, and Everywhere

To succeed in today's world, exposure is critical. These salespeople know that their customers are their competitors' best prospects. They network, they collect business cards, and they attend meetings and seminars looking for new contacts who will contribute to their careers. They appear to be everywhere. They don't waste their time, but they target their exposure. They ensure that each exposure keeps them on the right track. They are not looking to simply add names to their database but to build relationships that can aid their careers.

Sales Leaders Are Macro Thinkers

They see the big picture. They know that they must handle the details, but their creative thought patterns focus on the macro issues. They don't get bogged down in petty, negative, or small thinking. They pay attention to the terrain immediately in front of them while at the same time seeing the mountain on the horizon. They are big dreamers. They know that they won't always reach their goals on schedule, but they always shoot further and higher than they or even the world thinks is possible. Their attitude is "Why not? What have I got to lose?" They focus on the ends rather than the means.

Sales Leaders Study Their Clients' Businesses

They are walking encyclopedias of information about their customers. They know their objectives, histories, problems, frustrations, expectations, style of doing business, needs, dreams, and their people. Their customers' employees perceive them as colleagues, not adversaries. They are on the lookout for methods, tools, ideas, and information that they can bring to their clients to help them improve performance, income, market penetration, growth, and longevity.

Sales Leaders Study Their Competitors

They are not surprised when they don't get business. They know the weaknesses as well as the strengths of their competition. They know their competitors' philosophies, people, attitudes, and vulnerabilities. They freely recommend another firm if they believe that to do so is in the best long-term interests of their prospect. They know that when the prospect does business with a competitor they have recommended, they may have lost a sale, but they have not lost a potential client. And they understand the difference. They are playing the long game.

Sales Leaders Keep in Touch

Out of sight, out of mind. Successful salespeople who put distance between themselves and their less successful counterparts know the value of staying in touch with their clients. They do this in a variety of ways. They inform them regularly about new organizational policies or procedures, new products or services, success stories, and market conditions in other industries that might affect the customers. They pass along any number of bits of information that are of potential value to clients. They do this using newsletters, e-mails, letters, telephone calls, meetings, and special forums. They do not waste their clients' time with such useless lines as "I was in the area, so I thought I would drop by."

> *Think About It*
> Life is not about who wins but who keeps at it even in the face of failure.

Sales Leaders Are Detectives

The pros spend the bulk of their time getting, not giving, information. They know that client, competitor, and market information is power. They may not have an immediate use for all the information they get from these sources, but they know that someday, in some way, the information they get will have value. They devour newsletters, trade periodicals, audiobooks, literature, and generally anything they can get their hands on that gives them potentially valuable information.

Pros know that they need a stable full of satisfied clients who will gladly provide positive references.

Sales Leaders Cultivate References

People like to buy from people they trust. No salesperson can know everyone who influences a buying decision. Pros know that they need a stable full of satisfied clients who will gladly provide positive references. They cultivate these sources. They know that even though they may not be able to get more business from them, customers who are full of praise can be worth their weight in gold.

Sales Leaders Ask for, and Get, Referrals

The best source of new business is from present clients. When I say present, I mean anyone you have ever done business with. They may not be active clients, but they are always present clients. It costs more energy, time, money, resources, stress, and effort to get a new client than it does to keep one. Pros work as hard to keep the business as they did to get it. Once they have a client, they keep the relationship alive and positive through service, attention, and interest. They might not get more business from these clients, but they know that a qualified referral from a present client is well worth the time and energy required to keep the client. Always nurture and maintain your existing relationships, and those clients will become your allies in cultivating new business.

Sales Leaders Use Customer Profiles

It is impossible to see every possible prospect. Ineffective salespeople have the philosophy "If they will see me, I will see them." Pros know that some prospects are better than others. They also know that every customer is also a prospect. The customer profile is a template. It is a system they use to determine who is the best-qualified prospect they can see now. Poor salespeople try to turn poor prospects into customers. The pros don't have time for this kind of activity. They want to spend their limited sales time only with well-qualified prospects.

Sales Leaders Believe in Win-Win Negotiation

In a win-win negotiation, both sides get something they want or need. Poor salespeople sell or negotiate on price alone. The pros who are winning in the marketplace know that although price is a concern for today's buyer, it is not, in the long term, the most important issue. Poor salespeople are always on the defensive. They are reducing prices, giving away more than they need to. Pros know that when you win with a dime, you will lose by a dime.

In a win-win negotiation, both sides get something they want or need.

Well, there they are. The twenty-three concepts used by professional sales-people who are each day putting more and more distance between themselves and their closest rivals. How are you doing? Which areas should you pay some attention to if you are to compete successfully in the marketplace of tomorrow?

KEEPING YOUR FOCUS IN A DOWN SALES CYCLE

We discussed earlier the concept of a sales slump. The causes of these slow periods include the following:

1. poor training
2. poor product knowledge
3. poor attitude management
4. poor sales records
5. poor organization reputation
6. poor product quality, distribution, or organization support
7. an organization-focused, rather than customer-focused, sales strategy
8. sales compensation that rewards results only and is not focused on activity
9. excessive administrative responsibilities
10. poor territory potential
11. unsupportive management
12. a sales management team with poor coaching skills
13. an organizational culture that encourages avoiding honest communication
14. a lack of clear purpose, goals, and focus
15. poor organization and time and territory management

If you are on the sales side, I encourage you to examine each of these areas in detail to determine where you and your organization need to improve so that you can prevent future slumps. If you are in management, I recommend that you evaluate each area for which you are responsible, including training approaches, corporate policies, procedures, philosophy, communication patterns, sales reporting, management style, compensation programs, product or service quality, distribution, and billing, for issues that may contribute to poor sales performance.

PREVENTING SALES SLUMPS

Of course, the best policy is simply to avoid sales slumps. This isn't entirely a matter of luck; you just need to know how to stay out of slumps. What can you do to prevent a sales slump, or snap out of one if you are already there? Here are several ideas:

1. Conduct a careful, honest self-evaluation of your sales process's strengths and weaknesses.
2. Keep a log of your successes as well as your weaknesses in the areas of skill and attitude development. When you feel discouraged, you can review all your wins. You will be amazed at how reviewing your successes quickly can reverse a negative cycle.
3. Learn to keep detailed records of sales activity and your results. I am not talking here about your call reports. Even the best and most sophisticated call reports I have seen do not give adequate information about the critical sales ratios and trends that determine your future.
4. Spend a minimum of an hour a day listening to motivational lectures.
5. Plan your year, month, week, and day in advance.
6. Review your progress toward your goals daily. Look for areas in which you have made commitments but have not followed through.
7. Be ruthlessly honest with yourself. Don't let yourself off the hook when you have failed to do what you said you would.
8. When you succeed, reward yourself. It doesn't have to be a two-week vacation. It could be a new tie or pair of earrings.
9. At the end of each day, form the habit of reviewing your day, its gains and losses.

10. Don't beat yourself up because you didn't reach a goal, close a sale, or succeed. Learn that as long as you are learning and getting better, that is enough. Be patient with yourself, but be honest as well. Remember, you are either getting better or you are falling behind, but you can't be standing still.

11. Ask a family member or associate to be your partner in accountability. Share your successes and your failures with him or her. Ask for an objective opinion of your program and progress.

12. Don't compare yourself with other salespeople. You are on your own path.

IMPROVING YOUR KNOWLEDGE

I don't have to tell you—I am sure you've figured it out for yourself—that the world is changing every day before your very eyes. New technology, new laws, new policies, new medicines: in every area of life, you'll find something new. In sales, maintaining an edge in your product knowledge is vital for your long-term career success. I guarantee that within the past six months or year, your organization has changed something: a product, a service, a policy, a distribution method, a marketing plan, or some other aspect of the business. Your clients expect you to have the latest. You can't expect to keep using the phrases "I don't know," "I'll have to find out," "I'll look into it," etc. If people are going to trust you (and we have covered the importance of trust in a successful sales relationship numerous times), they have to believe you and think that you know more than they do about your product or service and the competition. The Internet is making it more difficult to stay ahead of your customers when it comes to product knowledge. I can only advise you: Find a way to know more than they do if you don't want to eventually be embarrassed by a prospect or customer.

Here are a few things to keep up to date on:

- the latest applications for your product or service
- how different clients are using (and benefiting from) your product or service
- your competition's latest technology, features, and benefits

- who is getting into your business and who is leaving
- why a newer product is better than a previous version

If people are going to trust you, they have to believe you and think that you know more than they do about your product or service and the competition.

RAISING THE BAR TAKES TIME, PRACTICE, AND EFFORT

To raise the bar in your career, you must first remember that there is no such thing as a natural-born salesperson, any more than there is a natural-born pilot, athlete, or physician. There has been a myth circulating for years that people who are successful in sales have innate skills or attitudes that set them apart.

I have been teaching people to sell for more than thirty years, and it is my opinion that selling is just like any other profession in that it requires learned skills and attitudes. I emphasize the word "learned." Show me an athlete who has "natural" ability, and I will show you an athlete who tends not to practice as hard as someone who has to work at developing the same skills and abilities.

What are these so-called natural skills and attitudes that people believe contribute to this innate ability to sell successfully?

- an outgoing personality
- a friendly demeanor
- the natural ability to persuade people to buy
- an aggressive, money-driven philosophy
- a social orientation
- a big ego

What does it really take to be successful in sales? The essential qualities include:

- the ability to adapt to others
- the willingness to serve and help others
- the ability to control your ego
- the desire to control your destiny
- effective communication skills
- the willingness to continue to learn and grow personally and professionally
- a customer-driven rather than a product- or company-driven sales approach

> **Think About It**
> You won't win them all and you won't lose them all. So just enjoy the ride.

These are not natural tendencies, none of them. People who are willing to adapt, grow, and learn achieve success with effort, time, commitment, and persistence. These traits can be in a person's genes, but people can also cultivate them over time. When they do, they incorporate them into all areas of their lives, not just sales.

So, does Michael Jordan have natural ability, or did he spend hours on the gym floor practicing? All successful athletes practice for thousands of hours, developing both their inner strength and outer skills. Sales is no different. If you want to achieve excellence in sales, practice, study, implement, create, try, ask, grow, and persist.

DISTINGUISHING YOURSELF

Success in an ever-changing business climate requires that you distinguish yourself and your organization from your competitors. Many products and services appear, superficially, to be identical. Printers all use ink, paper, and equipment. Staffing companies all have similar pools of employees, conduct similar interviews, and carry out the same evaluation of candidates. Many computers are the same color, have the same hardware, and use the same software. So how can you create, in the minds of your prospects and clients, distance between you and your competitors in the marketplace? You have to do it with the quality of your skills, the uniqueness of your attitudes, and the professionalism of your approach: These intangibles will increase your perceived value. If you start comparing apples to apples, you may end up representing your products as commodities, and therefore you will be competing on price alone.

> **Think About It**
> Live as if you are going to die tomorrow and work as if you are going to live forever.

There is only one way to establish your product's difference in the market—by discovering the unique features of your offerings *and* your sales ability. For example, most salespeople talk too much. They launch into a "feature dump," unloading information on the prospect early in the sales process. Every salesperson who sells this way is lumped by the prospect into the category of people who are interested only in selling rather than helping the clients solve their problems. On the other hand, if your approach is to ask lots of effective, pertinent, and well-timed questions before you begin to throw information at the prospect, you will send the message that you are different, you are a professional, and you are really interested in helping rather than simply making the sale. To differentiate yourself, you need to establish, from a business perspective, what it is that actually makes *you* unique.

I strongly recommend that you spend some time creating a list of traits, attitudes, skills, experiences, and techniques that make you truly distinct. Once you complete the list, see if you can develop a strategy to use these differences to position yourself in the marketplace so your prospects don't think of you as being just like everyone else.

CHAPTER 9

THE SALES PROCESS

One of the biggest problems for many salespeople is that they do not understand that selling is a process, not an event. To sell effectively, you cannot merely close the sale, carry out better prospecting, or make more effective sales presentations—although each of these is important in its own way. Effective sales today involves blending these together in such a way that your prospects trust, believe, and respect you and your organization and need your product or service to help improve the quality of their lives and business enterprises.

For many years, traditional sales training focused on the close of the sale as the most important element of the sales process. Then the 1970s and 1980s rolled around, and the hot topics were prospecting, qualifying, and getting to the key decision makers. The 1990s brought "consultative" selling. What will the future bring? Who knows? What we do know now is that selling successfully is only half of the task: The other half is keeping the business. Organizations spend millions of dollars annually to attract and sell new business. They then lose it for any number of reasons and must replace it. The saga continues.

Sales, as a career, is about finding good prospects who can benefit from your products or services, persuading them to buy from you, and then maintaining positive relationships with them to ensure repeat business, as well as referrals and good references. Are you focusing solely on one aspect of the sales process as you sell? Are you weak in any particular part?

> **Think About It**
> To be successful, you must adjust your selling style to accommodate your prospect's buying style.

Each element of the process is inextricably related to the others. For example, consider prospecting. If you have a poor prospect, you will find it difficult to give a solid sales presentation. You will not be able to overcome the prospect's objections to the sale, and as for closing the sale—forget it.

How about the issue of attitude in the sales process? Let's say you lack confidence in the quality of your products. That will affect your willingness to find new prospects. If you do find some, your lack of confidence will affect your ability to give a confident sales presentation.

Let's say you have a fear of rejection. This will have an impact on your willingness to ask questions to qualify your prospects and discuss issues that they might perceive as less than ideal. And asking for the order? Well, not in this lifetime.

I am sure you see my point. If you are going to sell successfully, you can't just improve one aspect of the sales process. You can't compensate for poor prospecting with tricky closes. You can't cover up your lack of knowledge of the product with fancy footwork.

GETTING READY TO SELL

Selling today is easier, in many ways, than it was in the past, but in other ways it is more difficult.

It is easier because of the Internet, globalization, improved customer education and sophistication, better-quality products and services, improved organizational management, and increased training in sales skills.

At the same time, it is more difficult because of the Internet, globalization, improved customer education and sophistication, increased consumer choices, organizational downsizing or restructuring, company turnover, and shorter product life cycles.

How, then, are you to survive, succeed, and excel in the sales environment of today? You should take multiple actions:

1. Develop positive sales rituals.
2. Develop emotional and psychological anchors that keep you focused.
3. Read some self-help material every day.
4. Study the competition.
5. Know your own products and services better than anyone.
6. Manage your time and territory effectively.
7. Maintain balance in your life.
8. Maintain your sales training either through your organization or on your own.
9. Develop career advocates.
10. Become a positive resource for your prospects and clients.
11. Keep asking yourself how you can improve.
12. Have clear, focused, and specific career goals.
13. Network with people who can help you.
14. Listen to self-help CDs in the car to and from work or on the way to appointments.
15. Develop strategic alliances with people who can advance your career.
16. Subscribe to publications that serve your industry or that of your clients and prospects.
17. Develop daily, weekly, monthly, and yearly affirmations that motivate you to take action.
18. Learn to relax, flow, and be rather than push, manipulate, and control.
19. Become a solution creator for your clients rather than just a problem solver.
20. Cultivate your ability to communicate: Improve your vocabulary, learn to speak in front of groups, and write effective letters and articles.

WHY PEOPLE DON'T BUY

People buy for individual reasons, not for the reasons the salesperson's (or the organization's) marketing department thinks that they should. You cannot turn a poor prospect into a customer with a great product or a persuasive sales appeal. The key to increasing sales is to identify why people buy and what causes them not to buy. People don't buy for any number of the following reasons:

1. They can't afford what they want.
2. They don't really know what they want.
3. They have a generally poor history with salespeople.
4. They don't want the product or service.
5. They don't need the product or service.
6. They have not been convinced that the value equals the price.
7. They are concerned with what others will think of their purchase.
8. They don't trust the salesperson.
9. They don't trust the organization.
10. They don't like the product or service.
11. The timing isn't right for them to make the purchase.
12. They are indecisive buyers.
13. They don't trust the salesperson (repeated intentionally).

When a prospect doesn't buy, do everything possible to determine what prevented the purchase, especially if this was a well-qualified prospect.

When a prospect doesn't buy, do everything possible to determine what prevented the purchase, especially if this was a well-qualified prospect. This can be done with a visit after you make the sales call, via a telephone call, a letter, an e-mail, or a fax. Once you learn why many of your prospects are not buying, then, and only then, can you disarm these points of resistance.

Most ineffective salespeople give more information than they get. They talk too much. You learn nothing while you are talking. You can learn a great deal if you can get the prospect talking. After every failed sales attempt, make it a regular practice to ask the prospect, "What was it about our product or service that prevented you from making a favorable decision?"

You will learn a great deal that can help future sales results if you consistently determine why people don't buy from you.

Competition for Thought

Let's say that you sell widgets. Your prospect can use more or better widgets. On Monday, you present the features and benefits of your widgets to a new prospect. The prospect tells you he will consider purchasing them from you but needs some time to consider your proposal.

On Tuesday, another salesperson who sells a totally unrelated product gives your prospect a presentation on the advantages of a new communication network for his organization. No competition, right? Wrong! Although both of you are selling completely different products, you are both trying to get a share of the dollars that the prospect has available to spend this year on a variety of products and services. The prospect calls you back on Friday and says that he has decided to purchase the communication program and can't order your widgets until next year. Lost sale. A direct competitor? No. The prospect wanted your widgets and the communication program both, but he couldn't afford both now. An indirect competitor? Yes.

Apparently, the communication salesperson did a better job of convincing the prospect that he needed to buy the communication system more than he needed to buy your widgets. He might not even have known the prospect was considering buying widgets, and you might not have known he was considering buying the communication system.

WHO ARE YOUR COMPETITORS?

Salespeople tend to think of their competition only as organizations that sell the same products or services that they do. I would like you to see this issue from another perspective. To sell successfully, you need to be better than every other salesperson who is trying to get at your prospect's available cash—even if you don't know exactly who your competition is or what they are trying to sell. Tough job? Not really. All you have to do is master your basic sales skills, which means letting go of the attitude that your only competitors are companies that sell exactly what you sell.

CLERK (ORDER TAKER) OR PRO?

What is the difference between a sales clerk (an order taker) and a professional salesperson? What follows is an easy way to make this distinction: You go into a tire store to buy new tires, and an employee takes your credit card and puts on the new tires. Order taker. You venture into a retail establishment, and you purchase a new dress or suit, and the clerk takes your check and puts your merchandise in a bag. Clerk. Not all tire-store or retail salespeople are clerks; this is only an illustration. Essentially, clerks take your money and put stuff in a bag.

How about a pro? You go into the same tire store or retail store and want to buy a new set of tires or suit. The salesperson asks you several questions to ensure that what you are buying will satisfy not only the demands of your budget but also your long-term expectations. Pros are more interested in solving your problems than selling you stuff. I don't care if you are selling $10 million airplanes or Amway soap. The criteria are the same.

Clerks generally make a modest wage. The pros can make a fortune. And it doesn't matter what you sell, so don't sit there thinking, "I only sell a low-price consumable" (or a seasonal item or whatever).

SALES CYCLES

Many products and services have different sales cycles, measured from the first time the salesperson meets the prospect to the close of the sale. Some cycles can last several months to a few years. Some can last only a few days.

Qualities of Successful Salespeople

As discussed throughout this book, successful salespeople have many attitudes and characteristics that contribute to their success. Effective salespeople also

- get more information than they give;
- promise a lot and deliver more;

- are interested in their customers' satisfaction, happiness, concerns, and other issues;
- are more interested in how customers benefit than what they get in the form of compensation;
- are really good listeners;
- have the ability to ask good questions;
- care;
- want a long-term relationship;
- sell value, not price;
- give outstanding service;
- are an ongoing resource for their customers;
- survive for the long term.

Can you add any? Go ahead: See if you can expand this list. Remember, a pro is not defined by what he or she sells, but by how the sale is conducted.

Many salespeople believe that they are not in control of the sales cycle. They put the buying control into the hands of the prospect. Of course, you cannot sell something to someone before he or she is ready to buy, but you *can* discover how intense the client's sense of urgency is, or even create a sense of urgency that will compel the client to make a deal.

Keep in mind that people buy when they are ready to buy, not when you need to sell.

Let's focus on sales cycles. First of all, remember that you do not change the prospects' buying needs, timetable, readiness, or urgency; you "discover" it for them. If your prospect has just signed a three-year contract with a competitor, guess what? This is not a prospect for you until the time when he or she begins to consider renewing or changing suppliers.

Most sales cycles are not etched in stone. They are a function of your ability to get to the real issues, needs, pain, and problems. If you fail to identify these accurately, you will most likely never develop the interest or desire necessary to make a prospect decide to buy your product or service. However, if you are adept enough at questioning and can quickly cut to the chase to figure out the prospect's primary emotional buying motive, and you respond to that motive well, you can most likely move the sales process along more quickly.

Don't get yourself into the mind-set that your sales cycle always has to be eight weeks, six months, seven days, or whatever. To those of you who believe that your normal buying cycle is, let's say, six months, I'll bet that you have closed sales in less time than that. The point is that the cycle is not a predetermined period of time. It is a function of your ability to identify critical prospect issues and then show the prospect how you can satisfy these issues in a way that the prospect can accept.

> *Think About It*
> The role of the salesperson is to sell the prospect, then educate the customer.

The same is true of budgets. Budgets are not—or at least should not—be entirely inflexible. If the prospect has a pressing need or challenge that your product or service solves, trust me, he or she will find the money to pay for it. There's a game I love to play when I hear budget as an issue: "Let's find the money. It has to be somewhere!"

Resist the tendency to fall into the budget trap, where the prospect claims to need the product or service but doesn't have the money. If the prospect really can't find the money, he or she probably does not need what you're selling that badly. So find another prospect. Next.

OBSERVING THE FIVE LEVELS OF PROSPECT TENSION

One of the most basic premises of effective selling is tension management. As a salesperson, you not only have to be in tune with your prospects' fluctuating levels of tension but you also have to adjust your selling process and your questioning tactics to manage their tension to suit your needs. The bottom line is, pay attention to tension.

Are people resistant to change? The obvious answer is yes. However, if this were true all the time and of all people, would we ever date, try a new restaurant, get married, have kids, start a new job, move to a new location, buy a house, buy a new car, or upgrade our computer operating system?

Change is the central activity of the human experience. Change is also at the heart of every relationship and the purpose of every job. Isn't the profession of selling based around getting prospects and clients to change?

So when do people change something in their life, career, or business? When they want something better, newer, or easier.

Why do people change? Every change has to do with control. People don't change if everything is under control, and they do change when they feel out of control.

So when you think about it, aren't all salespeople "control agents"? Selling is really all about helping the prospect discover where they are out of control and showing how your products will give them back the control they need.

Let me ask you, if a prospect doesn't feel out of control, what will he or she do? Probably nothing.

Control equals value. Most salespeople believe they are selling only features and benefits, and yes, in a way we are—but if the prospect doesn't feel out of control, it doesn't matter how good our products are.

Pay attention to tension.

At any given moment, a prospect can be on one of five levels of tension. They are Stress, Power Stress, Power, Power Apathy, and Apathy.

Let's review. People change when their need for control increases, that is to say, when their tension is high. Consequently, it is critical that a salesperson understand where the prospect's tension is and what is causing it.

The first level of tension is Stress. It is pretty easy to identify prospects in Stress; their decision making is reactive, their body language is almost hyper, they pace or move around a lot, their voices sound strained, and they communicate in streams of thought. Prospects in this state of tension know they need to do something, but they don't know what to do. Often they just want someone else to tell them what to do. Emotionally, prospects in Stress are dominated by anger, grief, or fear.

The next level of tension is Power Stress. This level is the most productive for humans to be on at any given time. Prospects in Power Stress know they need to do something, they know exactly what they need to do, and their plan is to do it now. Even though their resources may be limited, their decision making is active.

Then there is Power. People in Power are generally productive, but they are also in search mode. They know they need to do something—but they haven't yet decided what to do. Essentially, they are shopping for options. Often prospects in the state of Power will delay making a decision but find ways to justify this delay. They can be resourceful, but their reasoning ability is mixed. It's almost as if these people are waiting for something to push them into Power Stress.

The next state of tension is related to Power Stress—Power Apathy. This state is dominated by people wanting to delegate responsibility for action. They know they need to do something—but they just want someone else to do it. Even if they have abundant resources, prospects in this state are passive decision makers. They generally feel ambivalent and complacent, and their emotional state can best be described as mixed.

The last tension level of the five is Apathy. This can be described as almost being in a daze or emotional coma. These people's attitude is, "Do something? I don't need to do anything. Everything is just fine the way it is." Prospects in a state of Apathy tend to be unresourceful and completely unwilling to make a decision. People in Apathy have more resources than they could ever imagine, but they still are unproductive and often have the illusion of control.

This concludes our brief description of the five levels of emotional tension. The important thing to remember is that you can use these different levels of tension to your advantage—for example, if my prospect is operating on the Power level of tension, by taking away some resources I can move him or her up to either Power Stress or even Stress. It's a delicate balance, but if you understand the levels of tension and use them to your advantage, you can go far.

MAINTAIN CONTROL

One of the biggest mistakes that ineffective salespeople make is that they lose control of the sales process. This happens in one of many ways. Following are a few for your consideration:

1. They quote price only because the prospect has asked (before they have had a chance to build value).
2. They don't ask enough questions early in the sales process. They just ramble on.
3. They send out literature when asked, without first verifying that the prospect is a good one.
4. They deliver proposals to the prospect's door and wait for an answer. To buy or not to buy, that is the question.
5. They fail to set appointments that are convenient for them, always bowing to the customer.
6. They lug equipment to demonstrate in the prospect's office rather than getting the prospect to visit them.
7. They don't get deposits, but hope that the prospect will pay someday.
8. They leave "will calls" when telephoning a prospect.

I could go on, but I am sure you get my drift.

Control is one of the key elements of success in sales. Successful salespeople understand that control is not manipulation, but is in the ultimate best interests of the prospect or client. I bet you have a prospect right now, as you are reading this, with whom you have lost control. You are waiting for this prospect to respond to your offer, appeal, or whatever. I know because I teach this stuff, and I am guilty, from time to time, of making the same mistake. How do you get and keep control? It is simple, but it is not easy. The best time to get control of the sales process is in the early stages of the relationship. It is very difficult, if not impossible, to get it back later if you don't get it early. One of the best strategies is to get information before you give it. Questions should always come before your presentation, pricing, and literature.

Successful salespeople determine not only the buying habits and payment

philosophy of the prospects and clients
they have but also the respect they receive
and the manner in which they are treated
by these prospects and clients. I have some
great clients. Their behavior makes me

> *Think About It*
> Control of the sales process is the critical skill for ultimate sales success.

want to do an even better job for them. I also have a few difficult clients. Guess what? Their behavior in the beginning told me they were going to be difficult. Some of you may have some clients you wish you didn't have. Right? Pay attention to early signals and remember—you and I have what our prospects need: solutions to their problems. So keep control of the buying process.

SALES QUESTIONS

Accurate and timely information is the key to success in sales. One of the biggest mistakes ineffective salespeople make is that they give information before they get it. If you practice this approach, you are going to make one or both of the following mistakes: You will give too much information (more than is necessary to make the sale), or you will give the wrong information (based on an incomplete understanding of the prospect's needs, wants, desires, or problems).

Traditional sales training, for many years, has stressed the importance of either the presentation—delivering your sales message—or closing the sale and getting the order. Unfortunately, these two elements are equally unimportant if you are not in the presence of a qualified prospect. Remember, your prospects will tell you what you need to tell them to sell them.

Preparation, Preparation, Preparation

It is essential to develop a long list of questions that can be asked at various times during the sales process. This mental list of questions can help you do the following:

1. Gain control of the sales process. The person who asks the questions controls the conversation; the person who talks the most dominates it.

2. Capture and maintain the prospect's attention.

3. Build a positive rapport.

4. Save time.

5. Avoid rejection.

6. Determine how cooperative the prospect will be.

7. Uncover potential sales resistance.

8. Prevent youself from talking too much.

9. Determine the prospect's dominant emotional buying motive.

10. Determine the prospect's personality type and how to approach and work with it.

Keep in mind that information is power. I recommend that you spend more time planning the *questions* you are going to ask during your next sales visit than the *information* you are going to give.

Avoiding the Setup

I guarantee that you have been set up at least once in your career, and I'll bet you're getting set up more frequently and don't even recognize it anymore.

The setup is when a client or prospect has no intention of buying from you now or in the near future, but leads you down that lonesome, discouraging sales path for any number of reasons. Here are some classic setup scenarios:

1. Your prospect is willing to see you after you inform him of your services or products. You ask a variety of probing questions, and his answers seem logical—it seems like he has a need and a desire to do business (the setup continues). After you give your presentation and explain various features and benefits, the prospect asks you for a written proposal. You go to work and do the due diligence in order to provide this. You then meet with him to discuss your proposal, and he tells you that he will need to consider it. You ask what his decision process is, and he says he will give you an answer in a few

weeks. You call after the allotted time and get a stall. You call again in another week and get another stall. You call yet again and he is in a meeting and you leave a message. He doesn't return your call. Get the picture? Finally you learn that he has decided to renew his contract with his current vendor. His intention all along? Using you just to test the market and the integrity of his current vendor. It happens all the time. You wasted time, energy, and resources for what? The setup.

2. Your prospect says she is very interested in your products or services. She likes what she sees and is going to make a decision soon. She asks you to send additional materials, samples, brochures. You comply. You follow up and she asks for more evidence, materials, etc. You comply. This process goes on for weeks and you keep complying. Why? I haven't got a clue—you're being set up!

What can you do to prevent getting caught in the setup? There are hundreds of these scenarios, but they usually end the same: wasted time, effort, energy, and materials and lots and lots of false hope.

Consider for a moment. When do you think many of these prospects set you up? When you made your first appointment with them, after your initial meeting, after they heard your price or terms, after they spoke with references? Who knows. The question is, When did they decide they were not going to do business with you—after your presentation? After your first follow-up? All I can tell you is that when you have experienced enough setups and decide that your time is more valuable than their empty promises, you will finally change your approach.

The key to avoiding the trap of the setup is to uncover the prospect's true intention as early in the sales process as possible—and the only way to do this is to ask enough of the right questions, and to stand your ground, refusing to go on to the next step until you are confident the prospect is being honest about his or her needs, wants, and answers to your questions. I'll guarantee that if you look back at the times you were set up, you'll find that it's because you didn't ask enough of the right questions or you believed some of the answers even though they were suspect.

The Skill of Asking Good Questions

Positive sales outcomes—for both the salesperson and the client—depend entirely on the accuracy, amount, and timeliness of the information.

It is difficult to give an effective sales presentation if you lack enough information on the prospect's wants, needs, concerns, issues, problems, or interests. It is difficult to close a poor prospect. Poor prospects tend to make more objections than well-qualified prospects do.

The most important sales skill that you need to master (to improve your sales results as well as customer satisfaction and loyalty) is the ability to ask well-thought-out questions in an effective manner.

There are several types of questions, but the two we will address are open- and closed-ended questions. Open-ended questions ask for feelings, opinions, interests, attitudes, history, awareness, or anything that gives you information. Open-ended questions tend to encourage more dialogue. Closed-ended questions ask for specific information, or a yes or a no. Closed-ended questions tend to shut the dialogue down.

In every sales presentation, you need to ask closed-ended questions as well as open-ended ones. Here is a strategy that I recommend. Start the presentation with open ones to get the prospect comfortable talking. When you ask a closed-ended question, follow it with an open-ended one to get the conversation moving again.

> *In every sales presentation, you need to ask closed-ended questions as well as open-ended ones.*

Here is the opening question I have been using for more than thirty years. If it works for you, use it: "I don't know how I can be of service to you. The only way for me to determine that is if I can ask you a few questions. Is that OK?"

ELEVATOR QUESTIONS, ELEVATOR STATEMENTS, AND DEFINING STATEMENTS

Let me ask you a question: If you were told by a prospect that you had sixty seconds to sell him, what would you do? Would you condense your sales message into a one-minute presentation or talk about your organization and its strengths and history?

Would you ask a few thought-provoking questions or sit or stand there dumbfounded, wondering what to do or what to say?

Elevator Questions

I recently met a man on a hotel elevator. He looked like he was a businessperson, so I asked him, "What do you do for a living?" He responded, "I am in the insurance industry." My follow-up question was, "What do you do in the insurance business?" He said he was the president. (Keep in mind, I don't have a lot of time here; we are on an elevator.)

My follow-up question was, "Are you aware of what your lost sales are costing you every year?" (EQ: elevator question.)

He responded, "What do you do for a living?"

I said, "I am in the lost-sale-prevention business." (ES: elevator statement.)

Needless to say, we continued the discussion in the lobby, and we left that initial meeting with an exchange of business cards and a commitment to discuss his challenges and my services later in the week by phone.

An elevator question is any question that cuts to the heart of your prospect's challenges, concerns, or fears and makes him think. It also implies that you or your organization may have a solution for his problems.

Elevator questions are designed to encourage more dialogue between you and your prospect. At this point, you are not selling; you are probing. Remember, there is a time to sell, and there is a time to prospect. Riding on an elevator is not the time to sell. However, judging from the other person's reply and emotional reaction to your question, you will begin to determine whether this prospect is worth more of your time, energy, and resources.

I am constantly amazed at salespeople who jump too quickly from the probing and qualifying phase of the sales process to the presentation phase. And then they wonder why they are not closing more sales.

In the profession of medicine, we call a diagnosis without proper information malpractice. In selling, you may not get sued, but you will certainly blow another sale.

If you can master the skill of elevator questions, you will be astonished at the results you will achieve with them.

Remember that elevator questions are not used only on elevators. They can be used in social settings, while selling on the telephone, or at any point during the sales process.

All of the great salespeople I have ever met or had the privilege of having in my audiences are masters of elevator questions.

How about you? Do you have any? Do you use them regularly? Do they work?

The Purpose

Your sales efforts can have one of two outcomes: a sale or no sale. That's it. Yes, in theory you can close a sale that was postponed or delayed because of some internal or external circumstance. But at the end of the day, you either sell now or you don't.

The purpose of elevator questions is to peel away the layers of excuses, stalls, and lies (yes, people lie) that prospects use to sabotage a sale. The key is to get to the bottom of what they want and need. One way you know you are getting the truth from a prospect is when the answers to your various questions are consistent. Elevator questions, when designed and delivered properly, will ensure that you don't get any surprises later in the sales process after having invested your time and resources. Their main purpose, however, is to help the prospect "self-discover" his or her real issues, needs, problems, desires, or challenges, and to do it in a way that makes you look like you understand. Elevator questions should do the following:

- create or uncover a sense of urgency in the prospect
- come from the prospect's perspective, not yours
- be easy to understand
- be thought provoking
- make you look knowledgeable
- create a desire for more information from you
- position you as a professional rather than just another salesperson
- build trust
- create a desire for a solution

The Process

Selling is a process, not a transaction. Selling is about developing relationships and building trust. Neither of these comes easily or quickly, but with patience, the right focus, unfailing integrity, and a willingness to serve, they will come to you in the end. The process for developing elevator questions is simple:

1. You need to know what your prospect's greatest needs, desires, problems, or challenges are.
2. You have to have the courage to ask difficult and thought-provoking questions.
3. You need to phrase the questions in a way that implies you have an answer or a solution.
4. They should be brief and not complicated.
5. They should ask for only one piece of information in the other person's answer.
6. They should be free of technical or industry lingo.
7. They should be open-ended questions.
8. They should make the other person think about the answer and want to resolve the question further.
9. You should be prepared with follow-up elevator questions to probe even deeper.

Ingredients

Effective EQs share one or more of the following attributes:

1. **They create a sense of urgency on the prospect's part.** Urgency means that the other person wants the problem solved now rather than later.
2. **They come from the prospect's perspective, not yours.** These questions should not be about what you or your company does, but should focus on the prospect.
3. **They are easy to understand.** They should use simple, common words (eighth-grade level) and should be free of industry jargon.
4. **They make the prospect think.** They provoke thought in a way that creates a little unrest around the problem.
5. **They make you look knowledgeable.** When delivered with confidence, they should send a message loud and clear: You are different.
6. **They create a desire for more information from you.** They imply that further conversation with you will be a wise investment, not a waste of time.
7. **They position you as a professional rather than just another salesperson.** They set you apart in the profession because you demonstrate that you are not there to waste the prospect's time.
8. **They build trust.** One of the best ways to build trust is to be interested in others' needs and problems.
9. **They create a desire for a solution.** If you have a problem, when do you want it solved—now or later?

Samples

Here are some sample elevator questions:

How are your competitors dealing with _____?

What would be the biggest negative consequence of your waiting to take action on _____?

What is preventing you from addressing this problem now?

What do you feel are the critical factors for success in your industry [or business]?

How do you define quality, organization effectiveness, or _____?

How do you feel that your present strategy [or approach] is preparing you for the future?

What are the three critical factors for success in your business, industry, or _____?

What is one lesson you have learned about _____ that has made a significant difference in your success?

If you could do one thing better than all of your competitors, what would it be?

What does the loss of a good employee, customer, or supplier cost you?

Where do you see your business in five years? Ten years?

If you could improve one area of your business that would increase your profits, effectiveness, etc., what would that be?

Elevator Statements

A Definition

Most salespeople talk too much and say too little. These people believe that what a prospect wants to hear is everything the salesperson knows. If this were true, every prospect would want to participate in all of your in-house sales-training programs.

Your prospects actually want answers to just a few questions:

- Can you solve my problem?
- Can you do it better than my current supplier?
- Can you do it cheaper than my current supplier?
- Why should I do business with you?
- Can I trust and believe you?

Elevator questions are designed to get your prospects thinking, to create a sense of urgency, and to convince them that they need to hear what you have to say. Once you have piqued their interest with the elevator question, the elevator statement drives your point home. Elevator statements are concise, simple, easy to understand, general yet precise, and are positioned so that prospects can relate to them from the perspective of their needs, problems, or desires.

Elevator statements are not feature based, but prospect based, and are not long definitions, but short ideas that convey precisely how prospects will benefit from your product or service and how they will benefit now.

Elevator statements are only miniature sales-presentation statements. They are not intended to move prospects from not buying to buying. Their purpose is not to thoroughly educate them on a particular feature or benefit, and they are not meant to replace your normal presentation message or approach.

Defining Statements

A defining statement is a very specific and precise elevator statement. It combines all of the necessary ingredients so that when prospects walk away from an elevator conversation with you, they know who you are, what you do, and how they will benefit by doing business with you.

A defining statement should have all of the following qualities:

1. *It must use common one- or two-syllable words that are easy to understand.* If you stick to the language an eighth grader would grasp (and I am not referring here to slang), you are in good shape.
2. *It must be conversational.* It is not an advertising theme or slogan; it is a conversational answer to "What do you do?"
3. *It must create some attraction on the part of the other person.* It should make people want to talk with you, be with you, learn from you.
4. *It must have a dream focus.* If it helps the prospect see the future as better than the present in any way, you have a dream focus.
5. *It must contain the what and the who.* It defines outcomes and who would be served by working with you or buying from you.
6. *It must have a dual focus.* Create a two-part statement that has two outcomes and you will thereby appeal to a wider audience. (See my defining statement below.)
7. *It must have repeatability.* This may be the hardest one to accomplish, but if you can get other people to want to repeat it, you will watch your referrals soar.

Here are a few tips to consider:

1. Use the phrase "work with."
2. Use the word "want."
3. Use one "and" in your statement.
4. Use three- to five-word outcomes.

Here are a few ways to use a defining statement:

1. Introduce yourself with it when appropriate.
2. Use it in your telemarketing efforts.
3. Turn it into a headline for a brochure.
4. Use it on the home page of your website.
5. Use it on your voice-mail greeting.
6. Put it in your e-mail signature.
7. Write articles built around it.
8. Order promotional gifts and giveaways printed or engraved with it.

I thought I would wrap up this section with my own defining statement: "I own an international business that works with large and small organizations worldwide that want to increase their sales and improve their management focus."

Take your time developing a defining statement. This one took me several hours over a period of a few weeks. But once you have it, let it get a hold over you—believe it, memorize it, practice it, use it, and watch it galvanize the people with whom you interact.

The Purpose

Elevator statements are not miniature sales presentations. They are not a discussion of a feature and its benefits. They, by themselves, will not sell or educate your prospect; however, if carefully designed and executed, they will ensure that your prospect will want to hear more.

If you can tell me everything your product or service does in fifteen words or less and leave me totally understanding how I will benefit from doing business with you, you are a genius; I should be reading *your* book. However, if you can tell me in the same fifteen words or less how a particular problem or challenge of mine will be solved or a desire answered, I will give you more of my time. The main objective of elevator statements is to buy little blocks of the prospect's time, one block at a time.

Ask a prospect if he or she has twenty minutes or all day for you to sell to her, and don't be surprised with the answer. Ask if you can have one minute to see if you can show the prospect how to make more money, save more time, have more fun, have better relationships, and so on, and most people will give you that minute. Of course, it's up to you to perform flawlessly during that minute.

The sequence: an elevator question followed by an elevator statement. Total time, less than sixty seconds—not counting the prospect's answer.

Elevator statements are only miniature sales-presentation statements. They are not intended to move prospects from not buying to buying. Their purpose is not to thoroughly educate them on a particular feature or benefit, and they are not meant to replace your normal presentation message or approach.

The Process

A series of elevator statements should paraphrase key elements of your product or service to help your prospects clearly understand what your product or service can do for them.

The process of developing elevator statements is as follows:

1. Develop a list of the major problems or concerns that the typical prospect has when it comes to your product or service.
2. Prioritize this list in terms of their importance to the prospect.
3. Now take each item on your list and develop a statement that clearly explains how you, your product, or your organization will address this issue.

Ingredients

Effective elevator statements have one or more of the following attributes:

1. **They use pronouns such as "we," "you," and "us" rather than "me" or "I."** (Use these sparingly if you must.) These include the other person in your discussion.
2. **They focus on how the customer benefits.** Prospects care primarily about what they want or need, not about what you have to sell.
3. **They are limited to one major topic.** If you cover two concepts or benefits in one sentence, it will be too long or too complicated.
4. **They are action oriented.** If the statement does not imply an action that one of you will take, then you will need to follow it up with a question. This defeats the purpose of the single elevator statement.
5. **They use little or no jargon or slang.** Assume that your prospect knows nothing about your product or service. Using jargon sets up the communication for confusion and misunderstanding.
6. **They relate the statement to your defining statement.** Every elevator statement should reinforce or relate to your defining statement in some way.
7. **They use very little technical language.** If the prospect has little background knowledge of your product, tech talk invites confusion.
8. **They use simple and straightforward language.** KISS: keep it simple, stupid.

Samples

Here are some sample elevator statements:

- Let's demonstrate our competency so you can make a better-informed decision.
- There is a risk/reward ratio in everything, and we want to help you keep your reward high and your risk low.
- We always promise a lot and deliver more by exceeding your expectations.
- If anything happens during our relationship that might disappoint you, I will take personal responsibility for making it right.
- When you achieve the results you want by using our product or service, you will be glad you decided to invest in this program.
- If this program is important enough to start, by working together we can ensure its success.
- You will significantly reduce your overhead by investing in our product [or service].
- This feature will guarantee that you save valuable time once you begin using it.

THE SALES QUESTION MATRIX

All right, so you've figured out that using effective questions in the right order is one of the most important skills you can master. So what's next? The critical next step is to develop a questioning strategy, or what I call the Question Matrix. There are six phases of the Question Matrix:

- greeting/introduction
- rapport building
- trust building
- relationship building
- qualifying
- action/decision

One of the things separating me from most of the other sales trainers in the world today is that I focus on asking questions as *the* critical skill for sustained success in sales. The text that follows conveniently lists the steps for developing a powerful and effective series of questions that will propel you through the sales process.

The Why, *or the Purpose of Your Questioning Strategy*

You are asking questions in order to accomplish the following:

- Get the prospects talking—and keep them talking.
- Get accurate and timely information.
- Validate their concerns.
- Eliminate poor prospects.
- Verify prospect intentions.
- Build trust.
- Manage the prospects' levels of tension.
- Create a rapport.
- Find common ground.
- Identify the personality types of your prospects.
- Appear smart and engaged.
- Discover their real intent—that is to say, their buying motives and needs and desires.
- Disarm potential future sales resistance.
- Keep their attention focused.
- Determine timing/urgency.
- Find a rationale for their needs, desires, or pain.
- Create leverage.
- Build credibility.
- Determine what your strategy should be for the next phase of the process (the presentation).

The Who, *or Creating a Target Profile*

Before reaching out to your prospects, you must establish several things:

- the traits of an ideal customer
- the typical needs and desires of clients drawn to your product or service
- the common problems and challenges facing your prospects
- their buying process
- their potential volume
- their relationship concerns or needs
- the circumstances of their current vendor relationships
- their sense of urgency—how desperately do their needs, wants, or problems need to be satisfied?
- their timing

The How, *or Getting Information Before You Give It*

When you are initially probing your targets for information, it is crucial to remember these principles:

- There are no absolutes.
- You can never make assumptions.
- Your prospects will tell you what you need to tell them to sell them.
- The information you don't get early will hurt you later in the sales process.
- Questions determine the ongoing interest and qualification of the prospects.
- A questioning approach makes you stand out and look more professional.
- You always need a walk-away strategy.

The When, *or Why Your Question Timing Might Be Off*

Following are some classic examples of prospecting challenges:

- You are too busy with current clients.
- You don't have a working sales-question approach or strategy.

- You can't seem to get in to see the most important people.
- You don't even have the confidence to *try* to see the most important people.
- You're spending too much time at the bottom of the food chain.
- You don't have a clear target-customer profile.
- You move from getting information to giving information too soon.
- You don't prove to your prospects how much their inaction is costing them.

The What, *or the Elements That Make a Questioning Strategy Work—and Work Well*

These rules are critical to effective questioning:

- Always take notes—your prospects may unwittingly reveal to you the key to a sale.
- Listen actively. Why ask questions if you're not going to pay attention to the answers?
- Keep an open mind.
- Don't repeat questions. It seems unprofessional and disorganized.
- Don't rush the process. Your questions are meant to open your prospects up, to earn their trust. This takes time.
- Ask questions in the right order. It's important to be as clear and logical as possible.
- Don't skip critical questions.
- Constantly ask yourself, Which questions are working? Which aren't? Which could be improved?
- Eliminate ambiguity in your questions. Use clear, straightforward language. You never want your prospects to think that you have something to hide.
- Ask one question at a time.
- Address questions to everyone in group presentations.
- Use plural words as often as possible—this helps everyone feel included and engaged in the sales process. The key is to keep the process interactive.

- Don't let the prospects control the presentation.
- Prepare follow-up questions.
- Use transition phrases like "you said," "you mentioned," and "please clarify" to let prospects know that you are listening and genuinely interested in what they are saying.
- Have a stockpile of planned answers that you have tested and that work.
- Pay attention to when you use open-ended and when you use closed-ended questions.
- Come up with questions that will let you transition smoothly from one phase of the sales process to the next.

Now that you understand the why, the who, the how, the when, and the what of the Question Matrix, it is time to apply these guidelines to the different categories of questions (greeting/introduction, rapport building, trust building, relationship building, qualifying, action/decision). Below are some sample questions that apply to each.

Greeting/Introduction

The purpose of my visit is to determine how we can contribute to your improved effectiveness in [relevant business or industry]. The best way for me to determine that is if I can ask you a few questions. Is that OK?

Rapport Building

Some of our customers tell us they are concerned about [relevant problem]. What are some of the challenges that you feel may be getting in the way of your organization's effectiveness?

Trust Building

It sounds like [relevant challenge, concern, or desire] is having a profound effect on your company. How and why did this problem start?

Relationship Building

How would you see your firm and us working together?
Would you please share with me your [background, major objectives, etc.]?

Could you bring me up to date on what has led to your belief that it may
be time for you to consider [relevant product or service]?

Please tell me how you see our products or services contributing to your
effectiveness in [relevant industry].

Qualifying

Could you please elaborate further on [relevant detail]?

Have you ever considered other alternatives?

How do you typically budget for these types of expenditures?

Action/Decision

What do you see as our next step?

If we could [suggest service or solution], would you be willing to consider it?

If we could [suggest service or solution], when would you be in a position
to start?

INCREASING REFERRALS

One of the most difficult questions for beginning salespeople to ask comes near
the end of the sales process—and although this question sometimes seems
tricky, it is in fact the easiest and most effective way to increase your sales success. I am of course talking about asking for a referral.

It is easier, less stressful, less costly, and less time consuming to sell to
qualified referrals than to any other prospects. It is amazing how many salespeople fail to make asking for referrals a regular part of their selling behavior.
Getting referrals is not rocket science. Although there are several ways to generate referral business, the best way I know of is to just ask. I have surveyed
my sales audiences for more than twenty years by asking how many of them
would like to have more referrals. I always get a unanimous show of hands.
My next question is, "Why don't you have them?" And the answer is always, "I
don't ask." Referrals can come from anywhere: from customers, noncompeting salespeople or suppliers, friends, your banker, your neighbors, and even
your relatives.

Referrals can come from anywhere: from customers, noncompeting salespeople or suppliers, friends, your banker, your neighbors, and even your relatives.

There is no wrong time to ask for referrals. Many salespeople feel that to ask for referrals from customers, they must have first provided the service or product in a satisfactory way. Why wait to ask? Every minute you are not creating referral awareness in the minds of your customers or other sources, your competitors might be one step ahead of you.

Timing is important in selling. Every moment you lose in discovering new prospects who will benefit from your product or service brings you closer to missing out on additional business.

Don't wait. There are several ways to generate referrals. You can call customers, write them, e-mail them, or visit them for the sole purpose of asking for referrals.

INGREDIENTS OF POSITIVE SALES PRESENTATIONS

The attention span of the average adult is twelve to fourteen seconds. If your sales presentation lasts more than one minute, don't flatter yourself thinking that most prospects hear or remember what you say.

In a recent sales survey, it was discovered that most salespeople cover five to seven features during their presentations. So when the prospects were asked what they remembered twenty-four hours later, they mentioned only one of the features. Guess which one? Not the first one or the last one, but the one that related to their needs, wants, problems, desires, or concerns.

People buy for their reasons, not yours.

So what is the key to an effective sales presentation? Cover only the features and corresponding benefits that are of interest to the prospect. People buy for their reasons, not yours. People buy based on emotions and then justify their buying decisions logically. Therefore, a powerful presentation

- comes from the prospect's perspective
- is interactive
- is a conversation with an agenda
- balances emotional appeal and logic
- is brief
- lets the prospect tell you what he or she wants and needs
- qualifies interest in the features as you move along
- tests the prospect's interest along the way with trial closing questions
- adjusts to the prospect's personality type
- is tailored to each prospect

Most salespeople go into what I call a "feature dump." Are you giving more information than you are getting? Most good prospects are ready to buy before they tell you. Just give them a chance, and they will help you sell them.

Really, you should be "eavesdropping" on any conversations that your prospects might be having with themselves—look to them for cues (verbal and nonverbal) about what it is they want, need, or fear.

My fundamental philosophy of selling is that we don't *sell* anything to anyone. We don't coerce, manipulate, or force people into making decisions that are not in their best interests. If people are going to buy from you, they obviously have to have a want or a need—but more than that, they have a sense of urgency and believe that your products or services are the best solution for them now. Thus, you aren't really "selling"—you just help people come to good decisions about the purchase of your products or services.

While you are selling, and often even before you begin the sales process, a conversation has begun in the prospect's mind: *Should I or shouldn't I? Now, or should I wait? Can I afford it? Can I afford to wait? What will be the consequences if I do buy? Don't? What's the best source of products or services available to me?*

The problem is, this conversation that is going on in the prospect's mind is silent—and not one you can participate in directly. But this brings me back to the idea of eavesdropping. No, you can't eavesdrop on propsects' actual thoughts, but you can observe the subtle signals that give away their mind-set. Observe their level of tension or stress. This is often your first clue that there is some sense of urgency in their internal conversation.

In addition to watching and interpreting your prospects' verbal and nonverbal cues, you should also "eavesdrop" by asking a lot of probing questions. As I have said many times (to the point where you may think I'm ranting!), most salespeople make two significant mistakes when selling:

1. They move too quickly from the information *gathering* stage of the sales process to the information *giving* phase.
2. They just talk too much.

If you're not asking smart, probing questions of your prospects, you'll have trouble finding their exact sense of urgency, and you will most likely have to default to a "Sales 101" generic presentation. Needless to say, this is never a wise move on your part. When you give everyone the same presentation—"Here are the features, here are the benefits"—you are assuming that everyone buys for the same reason. Wrong!

So if you want to know what your prospect is thinking at every stage of the buying (or not-buying) process, keep asking questions. It will help you avoid the most disappointing sales conclusions of all: "No," "Maybe," "We'll think about it," and "We're really happy with the way things are."

THE FIRST FIFTEEN MINUTES

Was it a comedy? A tragedy? A monologue or a dialogue? A hit? Or was the show canceled? We are not talking about the latest effort from Hollywood or New York, but your last sales presentation.

There are three ways to evaluate the success of any sales presentation. Let's continue for a moment with our movie example. Before the reel finds its way to your local movie theater, there are hours of planning, preparation, and execution before the actual filming takes place.

The sales process is a series of relationships: not just personal relationships, but the relationships between the elements of the process.

In every profession there are these same three steps, whether carried out by a doctor performing surgery, a builder building a house, or a parent making the next meal. There is always some degree of planning, preparation, and execution. The success of the outcome depends on the effectiveness of all three. The sales process is no exception.

The planning is the precall research, investigation, and general information gathering. The preparation is deciding the strategy for the call: not the information that will be delivered but rather the sequence of events. The execution is what you say and do once you are in the prospect's domain. The focus of this section is on the execution. However, it is necessary to cover some of the key points that should be addressed in the first two steps if the actual execution is to be successful.

The sales process is a series of relationships: not just personal relationships, but the relationships between the elements of the process. The first element consists of your attitudes about and perceptions of the sales process itself, which in turn influence every other aspect of the process. This element, more than any other, will determine your success or failure in selling. The next element is prospecting, when you get information, followed by the sales presentation, when you give information and answer sales resistance. Then comes the close and, finally, repeat business.

The success of the sales presentation is a function of your effectiveness in managing your attitudes and of the timeliness and accuracy of the information you receive. We are going to assume that you have what you believe is a good prospect, and you are now in the prospect's office ready to begin. It's showtime.

Fifteen Minutes to Shine

"You have fifteen minutes to convince me that I should give you any more of my valuable time." Ever heard that? Well, you will. And if your prospects don't say it, you can bet they are thinking it. You have these objectives in the first fifteen minutes:

- Build a positive rapport.
- Establish an atmosphere of trust and respect.
- Gain control of the sales process.
- Fill in the gaps of specific prospect information that you have not learned up to this point.
- Confirm the accuracy of previous information gained.
- Uncover prospect prejudices, needs, desires, attitudes, opinions, problems, and potential resistance.
- Discover the dominant emotional buying motive.
- Determine the prospect's urgency and the willingness to proceed now.
- Determine whether you are in the presence of the decision maker. If not, discover who else should be involved.

A lot in only fifteen minutes, yes, but there is one selling skill than can accomplish all of this in the time allotted: the ability to ask the right questions in the right way at the right time.

As I said earlier, there are two basic types of questions that you want to use in the early stages of the sales process. They are open- and closed-ended questions. Closed-ended questions are used to verify specific attitudes and find out specific information. For example, "What equipment are you currently using?

Who is your present supplier?" Open-ended questions are used to query the prospect's feelings, attitudes, opinions, prejudices, and judgments. For example, "How do you feel about the service you are getting from your current supplier?" Or, "What has been your experience with our type of product [or service]?" Remember, closed-ended questions cut off dialogue, and open-ended questions encourage dialogue.

Information is power. Questions help you prevent lost sales by getting you important information about your prospect before you deliver your sales message. They will help you focus on only those features that are of interest to the buyer.

Generally speaking, you want to use more open-ended questions in the early portion of the sales process. If you use a closed-ended question early, follow it immediately with an open-ended question. You want to get the prospect to talk—and keep talking.

Remember that the person who asks the questions controls the conversation, and the person who talks the most dominates it. Which do you think is the most effective strategy?

This strategy accomplishes three critical things in the early part of the presentation. First, it gets you in control of the sales process and gives you permission to get as much information as you can. Remember that the person who asks the questions controls the conversation, and the person who talks the most dominates it. Which do you think is the most effective strategy?

Remember, your prospects are constantly asking themselves, Why should I give this salesperson more time? Questions keep the focus on their needs, problems, and concerns, and off of your products, features, and selling style.

Second, asking questions shows prospects that you are more interested in them than you are in merely selling something, anything, to them. Being more interested in your clients than you are in yourself is one of the best ways to build trust in any relationship.

Third, questioning helps grab and maintain their attention by breaking through their preoccupation with the many other issues they are dealing with at the same time.

There are a few concepts that you should consider, however, before you continue with your presentation:

Never discuss price until you have built value. Price will always seem high if value is perceived as low. The way you build value is to relate the features and benefits of your products or services to the specific needs, desires, or problems of the prospect. You must first know what these needs, desires, and problems are before you can build value. If you introduce price too soon, you will end up in a price-alone battle. An early request for a price is a signal that you have a poor prospect or one who will decide to buy based solely on price. The way to disarm a premature price request is to say something like, "I am sure price is a concern for you. Are you only interested in price, or are service, quality, and reputation also important to you?"

Don't deal in "maybes." I would rather leave early in the process with a no than go through the entire process and get a maybe. When a prospect says no, I know where I stand. With a maybe, I have only false hope. And after so many years in sales, I have concluded that most maybes end up being noes. If you cut an appointment short, be sure to leave behind a prospect, not an enemy. One way to accomplish this is to say, "Mr. Prospect, your answers to my questions have indicated that this is not a good time to be discussing our product [or service]. Allow me to get back to you in six months to see how your circumstances have changed."

Timing is everything in sales. Remember, people buy when they are ready to buy, not when you need to sell. Attempting to force a prospect to buy when you need to sell is what we commonly call the hard sell. There must be a sense of urgency, or you must create one.

Now, back to the presentation.

Your opening question and your follow-ups will determine how much more time your prospect will allow you. Ask poor questions, and you'll be out of there. Ask good questions, and you can stay as long as you must to decide whether you have a prospect who is worth more of your time. The critical thing to remember is that you are not selling your product or service in this early stage. You are earning the right to take more of your prospect's time later. Let's relate this entire scenario to one that isn't as different as it might sound: visiting your doctor because you are having stomach problems. If the doctor prescribes a medication right after you describe your symptoms, I doubt you will take that advice. Doctors need information, and they get it from patient history, exams, X-rays, and so on. Once they feel confident that they see the big picture, it's time to make the diagnosis—and you will be more receptive to that diagnosis, too. What if you arrive in the office and are told that the doctor is willing to spend only fifteen minutes to decide your medical fate? I bet you will find another doctor. What if the doctor spends the entire time telling you about his or her education, experience, successes, personal philosophy, and other matters unrelated to your problem? You aren't there to hear that information. By the same token, this is not why the prospect is there. You are there to obtain information, not to give it. You'll have time for that in the second segment of the sales process.

Let's summarize with a few basic sales rules:

1. Your prospects will tell you what you need to tell them to make the sale.
2. The information you don't learn soon enough will hurt you later in the process.
3. Just because the prospect agrees to see you doesn't mean that he or she is a good prospect now.
4. People buy from people they trust, not people they like.
5. Your role is to sell the prospect and then educate your customer, not educate the prospect and sell your customer.

6. You will never close a sale on a poor prospect with a good product, good sales presentation, or tricky close; however, well-qualified prospects will help you sell them.

Delivering the first fifteen minutes of a sales presentation is like building the foundation of a house. Get the foundation right, and the rest of the construction will be successful.

CHAPTER 10

BIGGEST SALES MISTAKES

This chapter is not meant to make you nervous, and it's not meant to frighten you. Just like chapter 6, "The Greatest Challenges in Sales," this chapter should serve only as a warning and make you aware of problems that might arise as you start your new career. I certainly have fallen into more than one of these traps. But knowing about the most common mistakes that salespeople make—and knowing about them *from day one*—is sure to set you apart from the competition.

MISTAKE 1: NOT MANAGING YOUR EXPECTATIONS

One of the biggest causes of frustration and disappointment in life is unrealized expectations—especially expectations you have of other people. Why won't my kids, spouse, employees, friends, and so on act the way I think they should? They never will, so relax and let it go. You'll never be content if your happiness is attached to your expectations of other people, no matter who they are.

I am not implying here that you should never have expectations, or that you should never count on other people. I'm just saying that sooner or later people in your life, be they friends, parents, spouses, kids, bosses, customers, or even faithful old Aunt Sally, will let you down.

To manage your expectations means that you understand that other people are all doing the best they can, at any given moment, with what they have learned thus far in life. We are all learning every day, either by accident or design. Keep in mind that few people in life set out deliberately to disappoint you. They may not always act as we would have, or think they should have, but guess what? That's OK.

MISTAKE 2: NOT HAVING FUN

Most people take life far too seriously. In my book *The Road to Happiness Is Full of Potholes,* I stress that one of the key traits of truly happy people is their ability to have fun. Laughter is medicine for the soul. It helps you reduce the negative impact of the stressors in your life as well as see the problems you may be facing for what they really are—temporary teachers on the path of life.

What does having fun mean to you? When was the last time you played hooky and just spent the day doing what you wanted to do, not what you had to do?

I have a great many heroes. As I was recently considering their impact on my life, I realized that most of them make me laugh. There is Will Rogers and Mark Twain, George Burns and Red Skelton. There is Groucho Marx and Steve Allen. I could go on, but the point is we all need to laugh more, smile more, and enjoy the gift of life more.

Few people on their deathbed will say they should have worked harder, attended more meetings, or made more money. Many, however, will say they should have laughed and smiled more.

Have some fun today. It doesn't matter how you define fun. Just have some. You will be better able to face the struggles, problems, challenges, and trials that life throws your way. While you are at it, why not brighten someone else's day as well? Do something to bring a smile to another person's face or just have some fun. You both will feel better.

MISTAKE 3: NOT READING ENOUGH

What if someone spent a lifetime learning about what works and what doesn't work in building a successful career, financial wealth, a profitable business, or positive and successful relationships and then wrote a book about this knowledge—about what works and what doesn't, what to do, and what to avoid. The book costs only $20. Imagine being able to save years or thousands of dollars by learning what the author shared. Wouldn't it make sense to rush to the bookstore and buy the book and devour its contents as quickly as possible? Makes sense to me.

We are fortunate that there are bookstores filled with ideas on every conceivable topic. Libraries are filled with volumes by authors spanning centuries. I recently read a survey that found that many Americans read less than a book a year. And I'll wager that many of these same people spend a great deal of time and energy complaining about the quality of their life.

The answers to most of life's issues and challenges can be found on a shelf somewhere. However, you do have to look for the book, buy it or check it out of the library (this is the easy part), and then read it.

Read to have fun, to learn, to unlearn, to challenge your perceptions and opinions, to grow, and to discover ideas and worlds that you may never get to visit. Reading is one of the most profitable activities you can do to accelerate your career and enrich your life. It is an investment in your future.

I suggest you devote a certain amount of money to buying books and a certain amount of time to reading the books you have purchased. There is an old saying, "Readers are leaders." Readers have more to say, can contribute more to conversations, and can help others along the path of life. Do you read enough? Do you read at all? There are no legitimate excuses for not reading more. Yes, it takes time to read, but imagine the time you could save with one solid idea gained from an author who was willing to share his or her insight and experience with you.

MISTAKE 4: NOT INVESTING IN YOURSELF

Is next year going to be better than last year? The same? Worse?

Every year thousands of salespeople start on January 1 with big goals, wonderful intentions, and executable plans. However, at the end of each year thousands of salespeople ask themselves, Where did I miss the boat? Why was this year not much better than the previous one?

Over the years, one common trait I have observed in successful salespeople is the willingness to invest in the continued improvement of their skills, attitudes, and philosophy. What did you invest in yourself last year? And no, I'm not talking about investing in your bank account, home improvements, travel, or daily maintenance. I'm not talking about what your company invested on your behalf in seminars, courses, or learning materials, either. I'm talking about all the things—tangible or otherwise—that you did on your own time, of your own initiative, to make yourself a better person. If you are excelling in this demanding career, I guarantee that you have invested more in yourself than you have in dinners out or personal entertainment.

In life, there is a very fundamental relationship between paying the price and winning the prize, between self-investment and rewards. It is never too late to begin an aggressive self-development program. There are hundreds of books to read, audiobooks to listen to, and seminars to attend. Don't wait for your organization to invest in you and your future value. Take full responsibility for the quality of your life and learning, and do it now!

MISTAKE 5: LOSING YOUR PURPOSE

When you lose faith or patience in your ability to perform effectively and successfully, you lose your purpose in sales. When you lose your purpose, you feel like no matter what you do, it will not be good enough or soon enough. Nagging questions keep popping into your consciousness.

Purpose is the single most important motivator in a salesperson's life. It keeps you keeping on when everything else is falling to pieces, when nothing seems to work, when people have abandoned you, and the world seems to have forgotten that you exist.

There is no easy way to regain your purpose. It is a function of many elements, such as will, desire, resolve, faith, and trust. Discovering (or rediscovering) your purpose takes time, effort, passion, patience, contemplation, self-evaluation, and commitment. These traits are not innate or easily acquired, but once you own them there is nothing that can stand in your way as you move into the rest of your sales career and your life.

The first step in discovering your purpose is to find what you love, what you are passionate about, and why you are in sales in the first place. Most people live their lives always hoping for something better, but they don't know how to do the work it takes to elevate themselves to that better place—they don't know how to realize their purpose. I didn't discover mine until my late thirties, after devouring dozens of sales and self-help books and contemplating hundreds of questions. After more hours than I care to admit of difficult self-appraisal, it finally came to me: I want to help people with what I have learned on my life's journey. This led to my speaking, training, and eventually my writing.

MISTAKE 6: QUITTING TOO SOON

You would be amazed at how many people quit just before they are about to achieve the success they have been working toward. They just get tired of waiting, trying, or dreaming, and they give up. Why is this?

I believe it is for one of six reasons:

1. They really didn't want what they were going after in the first place.
2. They thought it would be easier to just give up.
3. They thought what they were working toward would come sooner and were disappointed with their failed expectations.
4. They lost belief in themselves or their mission.
5. They let someone else discourage them or talk them out of wanting it.
6. They failed to realize that anything worthwhile takes time, faith, patience, and, yes, action.

Is there an area in your life today where you are wavering? Thinking about giving up?

No one can determine another person's limits of endurance or courage. No one can judge what another person is willing or not willing to do. Never let anyone talk you out of your dream, no matter how well meaning they might appear. Go for it. Keep at it. Just do it and enjoy the process. Don't expect that there will always be a crowd cheering you on. Much of success is enjoyed in quiet solitude, one moment at a time.

MISTAKE 7: BEING PESSIMISTIC

Is the glass half full or half empty? Will this product, policy, or strategy work or fail? Can I really achieve my dreams, or am I living in fantasyland? These are the questions asked every day by well-meaning and hardworking salespeople.

In his great book *Optimism: The Biology of Hope,* Lionel Tiger discusses how optimism has an impact on a person's attitudes, outlook, success, and health. He suggests that people who are less optimistic tend to get sick more frequently and often die sooner.

You can't measure optimism. You can't bottle it, regulate it, run out of it, or manufacture it, but you can learn to develop it if you only make the time and effort. Some people feel it is better to be realistic than optimistic: Why set yourself up for disappointment? Tell me, what is realistic? Look back over the past one hundred years. Where would we be if Edison, Bell, Gates, Ford, Disney, et al. had been realistic? If they had said, "It hasn't been done yet, so I guess it can't be done"?

MISTAKE 8: HAVING LOW SELF-ESTEEM

When you look in the mirror, listen to your own voice on a recording device, or see yourself in a photo or on a video screen, what is your first reaction?

- I could like myself better if _____.
- I will like myself better when _____.
- I'm really OK just the way I am.

When you fail, your first reaction is to

- blame others or your circumstances,
- take full responsibility for your own life,
- begin again, or
- never try again?

When life gives you a problem, do you

- look for an excuse or a scapegoat,
- adjust, or
- quit?

When people say unpleasant things about you, do you

- get angry at them or
- accept their view as theirs and in no way related to who you are?

When you receive a compliment, do you

- make excuses or
- say thank you?

When you succeed, do you

- pat yourself on the back or
- belittle your success?

MISTAKE 9: LACKING DISCIPLINE

In life, we either pay the price of discipline or the price of regret. We pay these prices in all areas of our lives: our careers, relationships, health, spiritual development, and financial affairs. It is unfortunate that many of us, yours truly included, fail to comprehend this simple law of life.

Let me explain. The laws that apply to all of life's issues—such as discipline, commitment, patience, integrity, practice, self-control, and focus—either help us live with freedom, peace, and harmony or heartache, failure, regret, and misfortune as we move along the path of life. Much of the latter (not all of it) could be avoided (not all of it) if we would integrate this simple truth into our lives.

The price of discipline is that daily dose of exercise, that moderation in our life affairs, our eating habits, and our relationship strategies—such as open and honest communication and managing our resources wisely. The lack of these daily little disciplines accumulates day by day and year by year until each of us inherits the consequences of these misdeeds.

I have had many experiences where my daily lack of discipline later came back to haunt me. I am discovering through these learning experiences that no one is immune to this truth. Arrogance, ignorance, or a combination of both is no excuse, and life really doesn't give a twit if you claim either. We pay one way or another. And discipline weighs ounces, while regret weighs tons.

The pain of discipline is nothing compared with the sting of regret.

MISTAKE 10: HAVING THE WRONG INTENT

Intent is important, but your success comes from your action: what you do. I believe it is important to have positive (good) intentions, but show me what a person does and I will show you what his or her *real* intent was. Does any of this sound familiar?

- I know people who consistently say, "Someday I will _____."
- I have heard hundreds of times: "I would like to start my own business, but _____."
- I have observed thousands of people say they want to lose weight but can't give up that last french fry or piece of carrot cake.
- I have received hundreds of commitments from people who said they would call me back, meet me for lunch, send me something, etc., and never heard a word or saw them.

I bet you have had many of the same experiences. The real question is, are you guilty of any of them? I have been, many times. I said for years I wanted to lose weight while I kept eating and eating myself into oblivion. Said I wanted to write a book for over five years before I wrote *Soft Sell* in 1981. By the way, its sales are now over 500,000 copies worldwide and still going strong.

A few questions for you:

1. Is your word your bond?
2. Do you make promises to pacify people?
3. Do you do what you say you will do?
4. Do you let little roadblocks keep you from taking positive action?
5. Do you vacillate on what you want to do and why?
6. Do you talk about doing things to see how other people will react?
7. Do you talk about doing something to convince yourself?

MISTAKE 11: NOT CONTROLLING YOUR STRESS

Stress in life is normal. Everything causes stress. There are positive things that cause stress, like promotions, marriage, relocation, starting a business, winning the lottery, retirement, and having a baby. There are also negative things, such as failure, getting fired, divorce, missing a deadline, having a baby, promotions, starting a business, winning the lottery, the death of a loved one, relocation, etc. Did you notice that I repeated some of the items in each list? Not a mistake, folks. It was intentional. Stress is not about what is happening, but how you respond to those things.

Stressors are not positive or negative. A relocation can be positive for one person and negative for another. A promotion can be the same, and so can all of the other life events. How can the death of a loved one be interpreted as a positive stressor? Personally, I don't know of anyone who wishes for the death of a loved one. However, I am confident that somewhere out there in this world there is someone who will be a little bit relieved when a sick relative passes away and no longer has to deal with the pain and humiliation that disease can bring.

Stress is not caused by events; if it were, everyone would have the same reaction to the same events, and we know that this isn't true. Stress can kill you or keep you alive. Stress can and will destroy your happiness if you do not learn to accept the reality of life and all of its issues, problems, and challenges. The key to successfully managing the stressors in your life is to develop some practical routines that help reduce their impact on your emotional and physical well-being—things like exercise, prayer, meditation, and making time for laughter and fun.

MISTAKE 12: SELLING BY THE NUMBERS ONLY

For years, sales managers and sales trainers have been saying that sales is a numbers game. I can recall my first sales manager telling me more than thirty-five years ago, "If you see enough people, you will make enough sales." First, what's enough sales? Second, how many are enough people? Third, is this the best approach to prospecting for new business? This is why I hate clichés—and the managers and sales trainers who quote them only because that is what they have heard for years.

If you see enough qualified people, you will make enough sales. It isn't just the number, folks; it is the quality of the prospects that matters. Now, with this concept I am not suggesting that you see fewer prospects. I am only suggesting that just focusing on the numbers alone will guarantee failure. Why? The more people you see, the more you will tend to see who are poor prospects—thus, more rejection. The average salesperson can't handle the amount of rejection that comes with this philosophy. This is why so many people become discouraged and fail or quit.

Think about it for yourself for just a minute. You see or call twenty-five prospects a week. You close one-fifth. That means you wasted time on twenty poor prospects. I know, I know: How do you know they are poor prospects until you spend time with them? What if you took the time you spent with the twenty poor prospects and spent it with more good prospects, or even cultivated the five sales you made for repeat and referral business? See where I am going with this? Maybe your closing ratio could be one-third or even one-half. Here is a real winner: Do both. See and call more prospects, and make sure they are qualified before you give them too much of your time and energy.

MISTAKE 13: ACTING LIKE YOU NEED THE BUSINESS

Sounding pathetic is one of the surest ways to ensure that your customer will lack confidence in and respect for both you and your organization. People buy when they are ready to buy, not when you need to sell. It is essential that in every sales situation you always put the prospect or customer ahead of your needs.

Begging is not attractive.

AVOID: *What time is convenient for you?*
INSTEAD TRY: *Let's see if we can arrange a mutually beneficial time.*

AVOID: *We're the best in the business.*
INSTEAD TRY: *Let's see our product [or service] solve your problem.*

AVOID: *When can you let me know your decision?*
INSTEAD TRY: *Let's set a time to discuss your decision.*

AVOID: *Can I call you in a few weeks to follow up?*
INSTEAD TRY: *I'll call you in a few weeks to discuss your questions and further interest.*

AVOID: *We can't do that. It's against company policy.*
INSTEAD TRY: *Let's see how we can accomplish this.*

There are thousands of ways to sound insecure and unprofessional. All of them send the message that you lack confidence in your credibility and your ability to perform.

MISTAKE 14: PRACTICING ON YOUR BEST PROSPECTS

How much time do you spend developing your skills? Do you test a new technique on a prospect, a fellow salesperson, or your supervisor? Do you not practice at all and just show up? Show me any athlete who achieves success, fame, or even makes a decent living, and I will show you someone who spends more time practicing than performing.

Most Olympic athletes spend in excess of three thousand hours preparing for a two-, three-, or ten-minute race. Most good golfers hit hundreds of golf balls every day to refine their swing, balance, and performance. Take baseball, basketball, or football: Teams practice for several hours three to five days a week for just a three-hour game. Are other careers different? No. Doctors, contractors, teachers, and counselors spend time in research, discovery, and experimentation. They don't wait until they get into the operating room or in front of the classroom. Yours truly spends a minimum of two to three hours preparing for every hour in front of an audience.

Show me someone who just shows up, and I will show you someone who is average at best, never makes a difference, and seldom achieves greatness. How about salespeople? What can they practice before a sales call? A telephone call?

Here are some ideas:

- new questions to ask prospects
- new ways to ask those questions
- how to cover the benefits of a product feature
- how to create a sense of urgency
- how to professionally terminate a presentation for a poor prospect
- how to increase a sale by up-selling
- how to better answer a prospect's questions

MISTAKE 15: TALKING TOO MUCH

One of the biggest mistakes poor salespeople make is *they talk too much*. The second-biggest: *they give information before they get it*. When you make these mistakes, you will tend to turn off most potential customers.

In a product- or organization-driven sales approach, the focus is on giving information rather than getting it. In a customer-driven presentation, you get more information than you give—and the information you do give is what the prospect needs or wants to hear, not what you want to convey.

The key to your success is not to deliver a rehearsed message that covers all the features that some genius in your organization has decided are important. The key to your success is to discover what your prospects' needs, concerns, problems, desires, or attitudes are. Then deliver only the information they will need to make an intelligent buying decision now. Give them the rest of the stuff later, if they want it.

If you talk too much, you will give unnecessary or wrong information. Learn to let the prospects drive the process; you are still in control, but their needs dictate the information portion. Another way of stating this is the outdated sales axiom "Plan your sales calls."

But don't plan the information you are going to give. If you have been selling your product or service for a year or more, you shouldn't need to do this. Instead, plan the information you need to get: the questions you are going to ask.

MISTAKE 16: NOT GETTING TO THE DECISION MAKER

One of the biggest time wasters in sales is when salespeople fail to get to the real decision makers and present their products or services to people who cannot say yes or who can only say no. Since many organizations are undergoing sweeping changes in management and in purchasing behavior, it is increasingly difficult to identify who is really in charge.

I am not suggesting that, at certain times in the sales process, it is inappropriate to give a presentation to someone who can only recommend your products. But keep in mind that every time you present to a non–decision maker, you lose an important ingredient in the sales process: control.

Back to decision makers. There are two prospecting strategies you can follow—bottom up or top down. In bottom-up prospecting, you start anywhere in the organization with someone who will see you. In top down, you begin with the senior person and work down. I have found that, once you have identified a prospect as qualified, the best approach is both: top down and bottom up simultaneously. The bottom-up portion is the easier of the two. It is how you gather additional pertinent information about needs, wants, current suppliers, etc. Top down is how you sell the big picture.

When I call a new prospect, I ask, "Who is the person in your organization making the buying decision about_____?" My next question is, "Who is that person's supervisor?" The next step is easy. I say thank you and call back and ask for the supervisor. It could be the president, senior VP, or CEO; it doesn't matter. I am looking for the ultimate decision maker at that location (or branch, division, or subsidiary—whatever). Without getting to the ultimate buyer, you are only logging sales calls that may never go anywhere.

MISTAKE 17: NOT USING A PROSPECT-PROFILING PROCESS

Identification is finding potential customers who have the need, desire, and money for your products or services; the willingness to see you; and the power to make the buying decision or contribute significantly to it. Qualification is the strategy used to determine which of the prospects you have identified are the best to invest your time, energy, and resources in now. In this stage you also discover the information you need to develop a sales approach that will enable you to tailor your presentation to the needs, concerns, and buying style of your prospect.

If you sell a product or service to the general consumer, the identification process can be time-consuming and difficult. Of the thousands of people you could see, you must somehow judge from only a cursory first look which ones would make it past qualification.

If you sell to the business community, health-care industry, the government, or any other major sector, the identification process is as easy as perusing a directory, a custom database, or a specific mailing list for those prospects that meet your criteria.

A system I have used successfully for over thirty years is the ideal-prospect profile. To build one, evaluate the characteristics of your best customers and then create a template that you keep in mind as you identify and qualify each prospect. Aim for prospects who match that profile as closely as possible.

MISTAKE 18: INVALIDATING THE PROSPECT

What is an invalidator? Invalidators are people who put others down, insult them (even subtly), manipulate them, disregard their opinions, negate their feelings, do not listen, or let their own egos try to control other people. How do you know if you tend to invalidate people? Answer the following questions:

1. Do you interrupt prospects while they are talking?
2. Are you an active listener regardless of who is speaking or how?
3. Is your ego (the need to be right, look good) getting in your way?
4. Are you more concerned with your need to make the sale than with the prospect's needs?

What are the consequences of being an invalidator in sales? Let me give you a couple of examples that I witnessed at actual sales presentations:

1. While a salesperson was trying to sell a product to UPS, he said, "Tell you what, I'll FedEx a sample to you so you have it tomorrow to review." Dumb? Yes. Invalidation? Yes. How? Well, he sent the subtle signal that FedEx was more reliable for shipping the sample than UPS. Whether he believed that really doesn't matter. He lost the sale.
2. During a presentation the prospect, a Pepsi-Cola distributor, asked the salesperson if she would like something to drink. Before she realized what she was saying, she blurted out, "Sure, I'd love a Coke." Dumb? Yes. Invalidation? Yes. For the same reason.

There are hundreds of ways salespeople invalidate prospects every day. Here's a simple one: "Let me repeat that"—as if the prospect were stupid.

MISTAKE 19: HAVING POOR LANGUAGE SKILLS

The tools of the professional salesperson are words. We paint word pictures, we tell stories, we describe features and benefits, we influence, we inspire, and we hope to convince people of the wisdom of doing business with us. All of this requires a command of language. It amazes me how many salespeople have a poor vocabulary. These people fail to realize that they are limiting their success and negatively affecting their destiny and lifestyle by not having the ability to use the right word at the right time.

The key is to have a good enough vocabulary that you can effectively communicate with people who have either an outstanding vocabulary or a poor one. In both cases, you need to be able to choose words that can be understood by your prospect. The ability to articulate your feelings, attitudes, needs, skills, desires, and knowledge is one of the most important ingredients for success in sales and in life.

How is your vocabulary? Do you often find you overuse certain words because you lack the ability to use synonyms? Do you ever find yourself searching for just the right word for a particular situation? Is your vocabulary getting in the way of your success? Do you tend to overuse profanity? For more ideas on improving vocabulary, see page 102.

MISTAKE 20: NOT RELATING TO THE PROSPECT

If you have been in sales for more than six months, you have most likely heard from a manager or another salesperson that you have to start every presentation with some small talk. You have to break the ice, get to know the prospects, or make them comfortable. Yes and no!

Some prospects want to get to know you; and you, them. Others just want their problems solved and their needs satisfied. Spending time in getting-to-know-you mode with prospects who do not want this is certain to cause you to fail or at least lose valuable selling momentum.

The key is to know how your prospects want you to relate to them. I recommend that you begin every presentation with a simple question, and I don't care whether you are selling Learjets or Tupperware: "Ms. Prospect, I don't know how I and my organization can best be of service to you. The only way for me to determine that is if I can ask you a few questions. Is that OK?" This approach does two very important things in the sales process:

1. It gives you control. (Remember, the person who asks the questions controls the conversation. The person who talks the most dominates it. And in a sales situation, you want to control it, not dominate it.)
2. It gets the prospect talking and keeps her talking.

In my career I have discovered that poor prospects don't want a lot of questions; they just want you to get to the price. Good prospects want you to know what their needs or wants are in order to find out if you can satisfy them.

You'll never know and they will never know if you do all of the talking.

MISTAKE 21: FEARING SALES OBJECTIONS

Objections from good prospects are not negative. They are a sign of interest, a buying signal, or a request for more information. Objections from poor prospects are their strategy for getting rid of you.

I would like you to think of sales objections as unanswered questions rather than resistance. In other words, what is the prospect really asking?

OBJECTION: *The price is too high.*
QUESTION: *Why should I pay this much?*

OBJECTION: *I am happy with our current supplier.*
QUESTION: *What are the advantages of switching to your organization?*

OBJECTION: *We are going to purchase this product from you, but we need to wait until the end of the month, next quarter, or next year.*
QUESTION: *What are the benefits of doing this now rather than later?*

OBJECTION: *We need to check with some other suppliers before we make our decision.*

QUESTION: *How is your product better than your competitors'?*

OBJECTION: *We really don't need this product.*

QUESTION: *What problem does it solve or pain does it ease?*

MISTAKE 22: NOT SEEING THE CUSTOMER AS A PROSPECT

Many salespeople treat customers as onetime sales opportunities. When they have this limited view, they fail to see additional sales opportunities with these customers. Not only are clients clients but they are also always prospects for something more.

In order to get these results, however, the salesperson must have a relationship-oriented mentality.

This is one of my favorite sales concepts: Make a sale—you will make a living and sell a relationship, and you can make a fortune.

I know what some of you may be thinking, and no, I am not a mind reader. If I were, I would not be writing this tip now. Some of you may be thinking, Tim, I am getting 100 percent of my client's business now; how can this client be a prospect for more business?

There is more than one way to get more business from clients. They can also be a source of additional business by

1. giving you referrals,
2. giving you references,
3. being willing to network for you,
4. being willing to give you third-party influence, and
5. giving you written letters of testimony.

As you can see from the above list, there are many ways clients can help you get additional business even if you have 100 percent of their business, which is often unlikely.

Don't underestimate the power of testimonials and third-party influence to help you sell more in less time, with less energy, and with fewer corporate resources.

Remember, it is easier, less stressful, less time-consuming, and often more fun to do more business with a present customer than it is to keep finding new customers.

MISTAKE 23: NOT PAYING ATTENTION TO EARLY SIGNALS

I'll bet every one of you has at least one customer you wish you didn't have. Right? If so, when did this customer reveal that he or she was going to be like this? Yep, you guessed it, early in the game. One of the mistakes salespeople make is that they fail to accurately observe early prospect and client signals. These signals are dead giveaways of how these people will behave as the relationship unfolds. For example, if you have prospects who do not return your phone calls while you are in the selling stage, do not be surprised if they fail to return your calls after they have bought from you. And if they are slow to pay in the early part of the relationship, they will be slow to pay as long as you let them.

These signals can be early warning signs that you may not want to do business with this customer. Not all customers are created equal. Some are more responsive, nicer, easier to work with, less critical, etc., than others. If you are in a position to choose who you get to do business with—and not all of us have that choice—why would you want to have an arrogant, unpleasant, or unresponsive person as a customer? I suggest you develop a few profiles: characteristics of the ideal customer, criteria you are not willing to give up in a customer, and qualities that are deal busters. These will help you stay focused largely on what you do want rather than what you don't.

Even if you decide to do business with a customer who has many of the negative traits, you will be doing it with full awareness, and you won't have a tendency to get broadsided later, wondering, "Where did this behavior come from? I never noticed it before."

People basically don't change. Yes, they can grow, learn, develop new skills and attitudes, and modify some behavior if life pushes them to do so, but the behavior you see today will generally be the behavior you will need to learn to live with as long as you are doing business with that individual or organization.

This truth applies just as much in your personal relationships as it does in your business ones. Many people in relationships who appear to have been broadsided by this new behavior were just not paying attention earlier in the relationship. Learn to pay attention to early signals. This doesn't mean the relationship is not worth pursuing—only that if you choose to pursue it, you are doing so with your eyes wide open and your awareness keenly in focus.

MISTAKE 24: PROJECTING YOUR PERSONAL PREJUDICES

The objection that you will tend to have the most difficulty answering successfully is the one that is the most consistent with your own value system. What do I mean by this?

If you are a price buyer and your prospect objects to price, you will tend to accept this objection. Or say you are the type of buyer who tends to think over decisions before making a purchase, and your prospect says to you, "We need to think this over." Again, you will tend to see this objection as rational (because that is the way you buy).

This simple act of accepting sales objections that resonate with you is nothing more than projecting your personal attitudes onto the sales process. You don't have the right to do this. Furthermore, it makes no sense to assume just because some prospects say the price is too high that they actually believe it or mean it.

People lie. People often don't know what they want or why. People often buy things that they don't need. Why? Who knows; they just do.

When you project your personal biases onto the sales process, you are assuming that everyone who buys buys like you. You are also assuming that when they don't buy for a reason that is similar to one of yours, it makes perfect sense.

This attitude is going to cost you a lot of sales.

MISTAKE 25: NOT ASKING FOR THE BUSINESS

A number of years ago *Sales & Marketing Management Magazine* did a survey showing that in 60 percent of sales closing situations, the salesperson failed to ask for the order.

People want to buy things, but often they don't want to make the decision to buy things. Why? They want a better life, a more successful business, or happier relationships, but they don't want to commit the money, time, or energy that will give them these things.

Consider this: During every sales presentation a sale is closed. Either you sell your product or service to the prospects or they sell you on why they don't need it, can't afford it, or don't need it now.

Why don't salespeople, after putting in all of the time, energy, and effort to present their products or services, ask for the business?

I have discovered that there are five main reasons:

1. They fear rejection.
2. They feel that if they have done a good job presenting, the prospect will buy.
3. They don't know how to close the sale.
4. They don't have a closing strategy.
5. They never got control of the sales process at the beginning and don't know how to get it at the end.

MISTAKE 26: ADVERTISING CONCESSIONS

Advertising your willingness to make a concession before you are asked to make one is insanity. What do I mean by this?

During the presentation you state that you can give the prospects a discount. They haven't asked for a discount and they may not need a discount. Let me ask you: What have you now set up by making that statement? Again, they are going to ask for a discount, unless of course they are asleep. And then you act surprised!

How about this: Your price list says something like "suggested retail price." Now, I ask you, are you going to be surprised when the prospect asks for a price concession at the end of the sales presentation?

Every day millions of salespeople make offhand remarks that send the message loud and clear: this price, these terms, this feature, whatever, is negotiable.

I urge you to carefully evaluate all of the statements you make while selling to see if you are advertising your willingness to make a concession later in the process. One way to do this is to look at your prospects' most frequent negotiating requests to see if there is anything you have done or said that may have set this in motion.

MISTAKE 27: LACKING A LOST-SALE-RECOVERY STRATEGY

We all lose business because of customers who decide to use a new supplier, businesses that no longer need our products or services, or any number of other valid circumstances. You cannot sell everyone and you cannot keep customers for life. The idea that you can is a myth, no matter what you may have heard or read. The key is to not lose them because of poor performance, poor quality, poor service, or poor sales skills.

Some salespeople, when they lose a sale or a customer, go into a variety of irrational emotional reactions: They blame someone or everyone, they make excuses, they sulk, they get angry, or they run and hide. Successful salespeople understand the ebb and flow of business and relationships. If you have good sales skills, a good product or service, a positive attitude, and good prospects, sooner or later you will sell them. Here are a few suggestions to use when you lose a sale:

- Follow up with a note thanking your prospects for their time.
- Follow up with an after-sales critique or evaluation.
- Follow up with additional proof sources, e.g., testimonials or articles.
- Accept the fact that things, people, and businesses change.
- Find out what your competitor did better than you to get the business.
- Don't let the lost sale negatively affect your attitude. Keep at it.

This week's lost business can be next month's sale. This month's lost customer can become next year's home run. You will win some and you will lose some. You won't win them all, and you won't lose them all. Just remember: staying power over the long haul is much more beneficial than quick short-term success.

MISTAKE 28: TRYING TO NEGOTIATE BEFORE YOU ARE FINISHED SELLING

Deft negotiating is not a substitute for effective selling skills. Many salespeople believe that they need to be better negotiators when what they really need are improved sales skills. Let's define the requirements for effective and successful selling:

1. Maintain a positive outlook and an enthusiastic and passionate demeanor.
2. Find and identify good prospects (those who have a need, desire, and sense of urgency for a solution to a problem that your product or service will provide).
3. Position your product or service in the minds of the prospects as the best-possible solution given their resources.
4. Present the features and benefits of your product or service to the prospects in such a way that they easily see how the solution will be achieved.
5. Disarm any unspoken sales objections during this process and then ask for the business. (That's called closing, folks, in case you are unfamiliar with the term.)
6. Service your clients to ensure their satisfaction and gain repeat and referral business.
7. Maintain accurate sales records.

Let's define "negotiating." Negotiating begins where selling leaves off. It is a way to resolve differences over the main points of a deal:

1. Features (what prospects can or cannot live without)
2. Delivery terms (what they need and what you can give them)
3. Financial terms (again, what they need and what you can allow)

Negotiating is finding a way to reach common ground so that you and your prospect can understand each other's circumstances and still have a win-win relationship.

MISTAKE 29: ONLY GOING FOR THE BIG SALES

Every now and then you'll hit a home run and close a big deal. When this happens, you have the right to celebrate and pat yourself on the back for your patience, persistence, and skill. No matter what you sell, most of you have the opportunity for a big one from time to time. But if you close only these big sales and nothing else in between, you will most likely starve. Successful salespeople understand the concept of hitting singles and doubles while they are working on one of those biggies. Why? Because the big deals

- can take longer to close
- generally require more work
- can leave you with a big lost-sale hangover if they don't close
- require more corporate resources
- require a higher level of skill because of who your contact is

The critical factor is maintaining balance in the mix of big deals and smaller ones. Yes, a $100,000 deal could represent 20 percent of your quota for the year, but it could also take 50 percent of your time. Five $20,000 deals will tend to close faster and get you the same outcome. What is in your pipeline? A lot of big deals? A few big deals? Just smaller ones? Again, the key is in the mix. The formula I use is ten to one: ten smaller active prospects in my pipeline for every big prospect.

The secret is to get the sales closed and then cultivate the client for more business. I would much rather have a high repeat-business ratio than a new high-sale ratio. This strategy is not meant to give you permission to skimp on generating new business. You can't upgrade current customers until you have sold them the first time.

MISTAKE 30: NOT WATCHING THE TRENDS

Are you watching the business trends so you can keep your customers informed about how new developments may affect their business in the future? Here are some of the areas of interest you should be following:

- economic trends
- market trends
- technology trends
- buyer perceptions
- product evolution
- new service needs and expectations
- buyer groups

I can tell you that over 75 percent of my business for the past twenty-five years has come from only five major industries—and I selected those industries in 1973. Was it luck? I am not that lucky. Was it brilliance? I am not that smart. No, it was research into what I believed at the time would be long-term trends. That decision years ago has permitted me to keep my business growing and my new-sales-acquisition costs to a minimum.

How did I do it? I still do it today. I read the books, articles, case studies—whatever I can get my hands on—by the futurists. Who are they? Here are a few of my favorites: Marvin Cetron, Roger Herman, Carolyn Corbin, John Naisbitt, William Strauss, Willis Harman, Paul Kennedy, Daniel Burrus, Joe Pine and Jim Gilmore, and William Bridges.

MISTAKE 31: SEEING THE SALE AS A TRANSACTION ONLY

Poor salespeople focus on just closing the sale. Successful salespeople focus on creating relationships. Which is your approach?

Selling is not simply about closing current prospects on a particular product or service that solves one of their pressing problems. It is about building a trusting relationship with them, by becoming a resource and helping them satisfy their needs and desires as they continually evolve.

MISTAKE 32: POOR FOLLOW-UP

Customers and prospects have a great deal on their plates today. They have the demands of their customers, bosses, fellow staff members, suppliers, as well as a variety of organizational, departmental, and industry issues that take a great deal of their time and energy. When salespeople call on these busy prospects or clients they must realize that what they are selling is not the most important thing in that prospect's life. Although what they are selling might be of interest and value, prospects and clients often just do not have the time to do the salesperson's work: the follow-up.

Often, when I have followed up with a prospect who has been considering my services, I have heard, "Thanks for getting back to me. I had every intention of calling you but have just been too busy. Let's get this program rolling." Why don't salespeople follow up? And what are the benefits of an effective follow-up strategy? These two issues are critical in determining the success of salespeople today. So why don't salespeople follow up?

1. They fear rejection.
2. They believe that if the prospects are really interested, they will call and help the salespeople do their jobs.
3. They are too disorganized and are not even aware that they should follow up.
4. They lack a positive attitude about their product, service, or offer.
5. They know the prospect is not going to buy.
6. They believe the prospect is too busy to talk with them or to see them.
7. They are too scattered.
8. They lack confidence in themselves or in their organizations and their services or products.
9. They believe their competitors are going to get the business anyway.
10. They don't have an effective follow-up strategy.
11. They have nothing else to say.
12. They knew they had a poor prospect anyway, so why bother?

Guilty of any of these? I have been, and I have been selling for more than thirty years. It is easy to fall into the no-follow-up trap. But it is just as easy to prospect effectively and present your product with confidence and professionalism; once you've done that, the follow-up is a natural extension of the previous step. Here are a few ideas to consider when you next follow up on a sales call:

1. Don't open with a closed-ended question like, "Have you made a decision yet?" Rather, opt for something like, "Where are you in the decision process?"

2. Don't ask, "Did you get the information I sent?" Instead say, "What is your impression of the information I sent?"

3. Don't ask, "When can we get together to discuss our next step?" Instead say, "Let's get together next Monday to _____."

4. Don't ask, "Do you have any questions about the proposal?" Instead say, "Is there anything in the proposal that would prevent us from getting this order started?"

MISTAKE 33: NOT KEEPING YOUR ENERGY LEVEL HIGH

Have you ever noticed that when you are with certain people, you can almost feel your energy level draining? How about the opposite? Ever been around a person for a few minutes and walked away feeling energized and refreshed, with a more positive outlook? If you have noticed it, and wondered why, I hope I can shed a little light on the subject in as few words as possible.

Each of us is made up of mostly space and energy. This energy is constantly being released through a number of outlets, including our eyes, posture, and facial expressions. Think of two people who are together as two energy fields interacting. Some of these energy fields are compatible, while others are not. Think for a minute about people you like to be around. If you are positive, you like to be around positive people. If you are negative, you like to be around negative people. There are several reasons that people can drain or energize us. Here are a few, but keep in mind there are many others:

1. People are unconsciously attracted to certain types of people; therefore, they feel more comfortable and positive while around them.

2. People have attachments to mental pictures of traits they like or agree with in other people. When the people they are with do not display these, they feel like the others are draining them.

3. Some people have chemistry, or electricity, with certain people. When they are with these people, they only see what they want to see and fail

to consciously observe any traits, behaviors, or attitudes that might contradict this emotional interest.

4. Each of us is attracted to certain body types, facial shapes, hairstyles, eye colors, gesture types, and facial features. When we get a match, somehow the unconscious says, "Yes," and we feel this surge of energy. We can also hear a no and feel an energy drain.

Think for a moment about someone in your life who drains you, and then think of someone who energizes you. The next thing is to determine how you can keep your energy drain to a minimum if you have to be around this person a lot—as with a spouse, parent, or supervisor. The key is to spend as much time as possible with people who add to your energy bank rather than deplete it. You know who these people are, I guarantee it. You just may need to pay more attention to how you are feeling and why when you are with these people.

CHAPTER 11

TODAY'S SALES ENVIRONMENT

Corporate consolidation and restructuring have salespeople scrambling like never before in the history of American business.

The game changes with regularity and uncertainty. Yesterday's decision makers are today's researchers. Last week's stable relationship is no longer a sure thing. Buying committees, group purchasing organizations, and senior corporate executives are making decisions that were once delegated. It is difficult, at best, to navigate in the choppy waters of today's corporate environment. Everyone seems to want lower or better prices. Many client and customer relationships are in jeopardy.

THE NEW ECONOMY BALANCING ACT

How can today's salesperson balance the drive for corporate profits and the customer's desire for lower prices and high value yet avoid sacrificing the organization's ability to maintain market share, competitive position, and long-term success? In this chapter, I address three areas related to this question:

1. What is the root cause of or catalyst for the drive for better prices?
2. What will the impact be if this better-price trend continues?
3. How can salespeople learn to be successful in this new arena?

What Is the Root Cause of and Catalyst for the Drive for Better Prices?

For the past several years, consumers have been effectively selling salespeople on the idea that price is their greatest concern. At first this attitude moved into business purchasing gradually, then accelerated to lightning speed. Purchasing agents have always been price conscious, often pitting one supplier against another to gain a lower price. This is not new behavior. But the zeal with which they are increasing this price shopping is taking a great toll on sales efforts in every industry.

Today corporate buyers are putting more pressure on salespeople to give them better prices. Often the buyers sacrifice customer satisfaction and loyalty in this drive to lower their costs. These savings are sometimes not justified if you look at the long-term market consequences. There may be short-term savings that improve the bottom line, but sooner or later the real costs will become quite evident. These future costs can be in poor customer awareness, loss of competitive market position, or turnover of key personnel, to mention only a few.

Permit me to expand this idea a little further. You can offer a consumer low price and low value or you can offer a fair price for a good value. Consumers have proven again and again that it is the most important thing.

An Unhealthy Philosophy

The recent changes in purchasing practices in the health-care industry are an excellent example of low prices equaling higher costs. The trend in this industry is to consolidate purchasing with group purchasing organizations, thereby enjoying the benefits of lower costs through improved buying power. I believe that this drive for lower prices will ultimately hurt, not benefit, the customers, or patients. Yes, it is true that many organizations need to become more efficient and prudent in their buying, as well as to rethink their profit objectives and margins, but to squeeze corporate America until it bleeds benefits no one.

Price is what you pay for a product or service, and cost is what it ultimately costs you. As a trainer and a consultant to a wide variety of organizations over the past twenty years, I have discovered that companies can always find the money to fix a problem, but they never have enough money to prevent it. Time and again, I have seen corporate buying decisions made with little thought for how cutting a marginal product or service would lead to decreased efficiency, loss of good reputation, and greater customer turnover. Making purchasing decisions in which the only focus is cutting costs is shortsighted.

What Will the Impact Be If This Better-Price Trend Continues?

In the past several years, there has been a customer backlash against corporations that practice this type of purchasing. Increasing numbers of customers are now venting their frustration and anger with these organizations that have become penny-wise and pound-foolish. And they are expressing their disapproval by taking their business elsewhere.

Organizations need to revisit their willingness to sacrifice the ultimate benefit of high value for the immediate pleasure of low price.

Another trend of these past few years, one that I've noted in various industries, is that decision making is moving higher up the corporate hierarchy. For several reasons, I believe that this trend will not last:

1. With the thinning of management levels and staff in many organizations, the people at the top have more and more responsibilities that often require their immediate attention. For this reason, they will have neither the time nor the ability to make the best overall purchasing decisions.

2. In the most successful organizations today, decision making, authority, and autonomy are moving down the ladder, not up. The 1960s, 1970s, and most of the 1980s were dominated by a top-down management mentality. The employee rebellion of the late 1980s and early 1990s has cured that malady in most of the fast-growing and successful organizations of today. However, some organizations are refusing to modify their opinions, expectations, and business style. These organizations will soon find themselves far behind their competitors, with no hope of ever regaining their lost market share.

3. The best people to evaluate a product or service and its worthiness and value are the people who must routinely use it. Often they are

the point people: those who deal directly with the customers. Shoving inappropriate, poor-quality, or outdated products down the throats of employees who must ultimately defend them to the customers causes increased stress and frustration, and fires the pilot light of discontent.

4. History shows that saving money in the short term does not always mean saving money in the long term. You can't measure everything with a calculator or a spreadsheet. Saving a dime per widget when you buy thousands per month may create a bug that in turn squeezes machine operators, customer service representatives, or repairmen. It will certainly take a toll on their attitude and morale, which will manifest when they visit a customer's office, showroom, or plant.

How Can Salespeople Learn to Be Successful in This New Arena?

A number of factors contribute to the salesperson's decision to cave to customer pressure and lower the price:

1. There is the self-esteem of the salesperson. Salespeople with low self-esteem tend to reduce prices more often than do salespeople with high self-esteem. This is because they hope to receive appreciation, approval, or recognition, all of which are psychologically necessary to them. Salespeople with high self-esteem are not looking to get approval, but to make sales and solve customer needs, problems, or wants in both the short term and the long term. They also tend to be much stronger negotiators for the same reasons.

2. If an organization is losing market share, for whatever reason, the leaders will tend to react by lowering prices, which only accelerates the company's demise. It becomes a downward spiral. Increased competition leads to lower prices, which lead to less working capital to fuel the organization's ability to compete, which results in less-satisfied customers and increased customer turnover, which means less and less working capital, and so on into oblivion. Exaggeration? Just look at the increased numbers of businesses of all sizes that have failed during the past several years.

3. According to a prevailing attitude in many organizations today, if you want to get more business, you must give away more business. I have seen hundreds of corporations whose management believes that to penetrate a new market or introduce a new product or service, they must lowball their product or service to get a foothold. I have never seen this work as a long-term strategy either for the organizations or their customers. Both lose in the end.

4. Many salespeople are numbers driven. Their mandate is to increase sales at whatever cost. They are often successful at increasing sales, but at what cost? High stress, burnout, high turnover, and often at reduced margins. Not to mention dissatisfied, disloyal customers.

5. Organizations need to price their products or services with careful consideration of the following:
   - Is the product unique in the marketplace?
   - Do customers really want what the company has available?
   - Is the product quality less than, the same as, or better than competitors' product quality?
   - Is the market right for the product, or is the organization attempting to force a segment of the market to purchase what it chooses to design and manufacture?
   - Is the organization pricing a particular product or service to make up for general corporate losses or weak items elsewhere in its line?
   - Is sales compensation unfairly or poorly pegged to force salespeople to sell certain products or services that would otherwise be losers?

Now, back to our original question. How can today's salesperson balance the drive for corporate profits with the customer's desire for lower prices and high value yet avoid sacrificing the organization's ability to maintain market share, competitive position, and long-term success?

I would like to share three simple yet proven strategies that can reduce and

> **Think About It**
> Poor prospects focus on price; good ones, on the value you can give them.

often completely disarm this price-only mentality among today's buyers. But before we get to that, let's consider some things salespeople need to have going for them to handle this price issue successfully. They must

- know a tremendous amount about their products
- know a great deal about their customers
- know the needs, fears, problems, concerns, or wants of their customers' customers
- have the skill to align their product knowledge with the needs, desires, concerns, and problems of their customers
- have a basic business understanding
- bring a great deal of practical experience and empathy to the sales process
- have high self-esteem
- have exceptional sales skills
- possess the ability to manage the emotional issues in sales
- manage rejection
- believe in the mission, objectives, and purpose of their organizations

Tall order? Yes, but the rewards can be just as big.

Now: the three strategies. For the purpose of brevity, I am going to assume that you have all of the above issues under control.

> **Think About It**
>
> People do not simply want the lowest price, even if they think they do. They want the best value for a fair price.

First strategy. If you believe that price is a major issue for your prospect or customer, you need to determine what else matters and why it matters. You can accomplish this by asking lots and lots of good questions in the right way at the right time. Do not, I repeat, do not launch into your presentation before you've figured out the prospect's dominant reason for buying, other than price. Once you have discovered this, you need to focus on how your product or service addresses this primary need. If the prospect attempts to control the sales process by bringing you back to price, you need to stand your ground and confirm whether this is his or her only consideration. Few prospects will say that price is the *only* thing factoring into their decision, which opens the door to you for negotiations.

Keep in mind that buyers buy when they are ready and not when you need to sell. Also remember that they buy for their reasons, not yours.

Second strategy. Resist the urge to quote price before building value. Price will always seem high if value is perceived as low. If you quote a price before you have attempted to establish a sense of value in the mind of the prospect, any price will seem high. You build value not by listing product features or benefits, but by highlighting specific benefits that will translate into customer benefits.

Third strategy. Don't be greedy. If you are dealing with a repeat customer who has a history of buying from you, don't jeopardize the business by being completely inflexible on some products or services. The important thing to remember is that this is your customer. This person has a history with you and is familiar with your service levels, response times, new-product development, and procedures for billing and shipping. When a customer asks you for a better price, he or she may be looking for a lot less of a decrease than you think. Don't react too quickly. Ask why a better price is necessary on that particular product. See if you can get something in return if the customer asks you to reduce a price where you are not inclined to do so. Request advance payment, a bigger deposit, or perhaps a portion of the customer's business that you are not currently getting. If you must take less than your desired margin, you should get compensated for it.

By asking for something in return, you can often prevent a price spiral. You may even get some business that you might not have been able to do otherwise.

Price is important, but every survey I have seen in the past several years has indicated that buyers want three things: low price, good service, and good quality. Which do you think, again and again, is number one? If you guessed service, you are right. Which is number two? If you guessed quality, you are right again. That leaves price as number three. Price is important, but in the minds of most buyers it is not the biggest factor. They would like to convince you that it is—and they often do—but never forget most consumers and business buyers do not want to sacrifice service and quality for low price. They just want you to think that they will.

THE COST-PRICE-VALUE ISSUE

If I were to ask a room of a thousand salespeople (I have done it) to name the number-one thing consumers want today, what do you think their answer would be? You guessed it: lower price. And second? Quality? Right again. And third? Service. Bingo. Now, let's switch scenes for a moment. I now have a thousand consumers or business buyers in my audience, and I ask them the same question. What answers do you think I would hear?

One of the most frequent answers I get is first, service; second, quality; third, lower price. Well, folks, we seem to have a perceptible difference between what people want and what they tell salespeople they want. How can you account for that difference?

I believe it is a matter of definition. Price is defined as what we pay for something. We write a check, use cash, or swipe a credit card, and our account is debited. Cost is how we pay for what we have bought over time. In other words, buy a cheap car, and you will have bigger service bills and greater inconvenience. Your cost over time is higher than the price you paid.

What do most consumers say they want, in your opinion? Yes, low price. But what do you think they really want? Yes again: low cost. Therefore, it seems to me, we only need to question prospects better on what they really want and define the difference for them in terms of our products or services. What we are talking about here is value for the customer. And value is always perceived value. Every prospect interprets value in his or her own terms. Our job in sales is not to always lower the price (when that is often not the real issue), but to try to better understand and influence what the perceived value is for each prospect.

The only way to accomplish this is by constantly asking professional, probing questions and then positioning your product or service appropriately in the mind of the prospect.

> *Think About It*
> Sell the business on price and you rent the business. Sell it on value and you own it.

People don't want cheap. They want value. People don't really want things that rust, break, are inconvenient, or are difficult to understand. They want life to be less complicated, less stressful, happier, and more fun. Show them how your product or service can do all of these, and I guarantee price will never be an issue.

AN EFFECTIVE CLOSING STRATEGY

People don't like to make decisions. The main reason is that they don't want to make a poor or wrong decision. In traditional closing strategies, the salesperson asks the customer to make a decision. For example, "Do you want it in green or red?" (alternative choice); "Do you want to use your pen or mine?" (action close); "Can we write up an order now?" (direct close). These closing techniques, even though they do work, have two fundamental problems. First, they ask the prospect to make a decision. Second, the average salesperson is uncomfortable using them.

Because people don't like to make decisions, I suggest you stop asking them to. Here is a simple close that I have been using for more than thirty years. Make the buying decision for the prospect and ask him or her to agree with the decision you have made. It goes like this: Let's do this; is that OK? Let's arrange for delivery on the fifteenth; is that OK? Let's get together on Thursday at 10 a.m., all right?

This close works for three reasons. First, it gets a decision made, but the prospect doesn't have to make it. By agreeing with you, the prospect in essence makes the decision. I have found that people want to get decisions made but don't want to make them. Second, it is common language. I guarantee that in the next two to three days you will either say to someone or hear from someone, "Let's go to a movie, OK?" Or, "Let's go out to dinner tonight, OK?" Third, the language is easy to remember and use, and it gets the job done.

When you use this close, the prospects have only three options. First, they go along with both your decision for them and your recommendation. Second, they go along with your decision but don't like your recommendation. In both cases, you have a close. Third, they go along with neither your decision nor your recommendation. No sale. Keep in mind, though, that using this with a qualified prospect gives you a two-to-one chance of closing.

This is the only close I have used for decades. Why? It works. Try it and find out for yourself. The same strategy can be used in any stage of the sales process, from getting appointments to confirming sales.

REACTIVATING PAST CLIENTS

Lost business does not necessarily mean that you have lost the client forever. Many salespeople neglect this lucrative source of new business. I say "new" because if you treat these past customers as new prospects, you may in fact regain the business.

Customers leave you for many reasons:

1. They no longer need the products or services that you sell.
2. They were wooed away by a competitor offering better prices, better service, or some other promise.
3. Management in the organization has changed, and the newcomers are not aware of the strengths of your services or products. Most likely their predecessors did not pass this information on to them.
4. Your organization has outgrown an interest in them for any number of reasons, and they chose to begin again with a new supplier.
5. You or your organization failed to deliver as promised.
6. You or your organization let trust or respect erode in the relationship.
7. They have outgrown your capacity and need a bigger supplier.
8. There is some hidden agenda: They have a relative in the business, have lost buying authority, or are leaving their organization for another position—some factor that you would have no way of knowing about.

There are others, but most will fall under these eight. What can you do to regain this business?

First you must learn the real reason the customer left. You and your organization must be willing to modify what you do, how you do it, or when you do it to convince the customer that it is in his or her best interests to rekindle the relationship. Consider these tips:

1. You have to be willing to begin again.
2. Work harder. It is important to remember that you need to work as hard to keep the business as you did to get it.
3. You must reassess where you went wrong. Was it a pricing issue, a service issue, a quality issue, a distribution issue, arrogance, ignorance, a

lack of interest in keeping the business, or some other major or minor mistake?

4. You must keep in touch with previous customers. You have many choices of how to do this: sending newsletters, direct mail, or e-mail or conducting a lost-business critique.

THE VALUE OF GOOD RECORDS

Have you ever experienced a sales slump? Or just not achieved the results that you thought you should have? Probably. Most salespeople have.

Successful selling requires many skills, attitudes, and personal values. When a salesperson experiences a down cycle, it is impossible to pinpoint the problem to one specific area. For example, if you are having trouble closing sales, is it because you have poor closing skills, or could it be that you may be trying to close poor prospects? Determining where the problem is, whether you're in a big slump or just a poor month, requires information. That information is about sales ratios, trends, and comparisons—and, of course, actual numbers. It is difficult to take corrective action if you are not aware of what the cause of the problem is. Just working harder or longer hours calling on poor prospects is not going to have a significant impact on your overall results. You will only experience more of the same problems.

> *Think About It*
> Salespeople who can't help but fail can't tell you why. Successful salespeople can tell you exactly why they succeed.

One of the common denominators (there are many) among top salespeople is their ruthless evaluation of their activities, behaviors, results, and progress toward goals. Most ineffective salespeople don't take the time to keep accurate records. Many sales organizations require call reports, but those reports are, in many cases, no more than busywork. They provide little, if any, valuable information for the salesperson or the sales manager about current or potential sales problems and their causes. Generally call reports only list whom you saw and what you sold. This is not enough information if you are going to reach the stars as a salesperson.

In my best-selling book *Soft Sell,* the last chapter is devoted to which records to keep, how to evaluate them, and how to forecast the future based on the type and amount of your previous and current activity. If you are failing or doing poorly, do you know why? If you are consistently beating your goals, I bet you have formed the habit of keeping good numbers and evaluating them on a regular basis to determine where you need to change your behavior or acquire new skills.

CHAPTER 12

SELLING THROUGH THE HIGH TIMES AND THE LOW

In sales, as in every profession and industry, there are high times and there are low. Too many salespeople work themselves up into an emotional and financial frenzy when the tough times hit. But even in the most uncertain economic climate, when customers reduce orders, prospects cancel sales, and suppliers can't perform up to your standards, every salesperson has three choices:

1. Relax and try to learn as much as you can from these challenges.
2. Rant, rave, and work yourself up into an anxiety attack worrying about all of the negative consequences that could arise (canceled orders, etc).
3. Think clearly and rationally about what you can do now to improve or reverse the situation—think beyond *why* it happened, and start to figure out *how* it can end.

I am neither insensitive nor impervious to the effects of canceled orders or lower customer sales. I know the disappointment of a sale gone wrong or a business relationship that has soured. But I also have learned that for every lost sale, there is another potential one around the next corner. One has to keep walking, looking, and discovering to find it.

Some salespeople today can't seem to rise above the self-pity, discouragement, and anger they feel over conditions they can't control. What's the point? Instead, you should be preparing yourself for the next boom time. It's coming; it always does. But if you are not prepared, you'll find yourself languishing in the dust left behind by your intelligent peers, who have chosen to use this downtime to get better, wiser, faster, and stronger.

THE PYGMALION EFFECT

Many years ago there was a study done at a major university. The researchers wanted to determine if there was a relationship between expectations and outcomes. The result was called the Pygmalion Effect. In essence, the study found that what you believe will come to pass will eventually become a reality. How does this relate to you and your burgeoning sales career? Let's use a practical business example to explain. Take yourself back to the late 1980s and imagine the economic and social landscape of the time:

- Housing starts were declining.
- Interest rates were rising.
- Layoffs were beginning.
- Unemployment was rising.
- Businesses were cutting back.
- The media were focused on the negatives rather than the positives.
- Negative word-of-mouth was increasing.

And surprise! We talked ourselves into a full-blown recession. Why? How? The Pygmalion Effect was in full swing.

Expecting negative outcomes changes your attitudes, actions, and behavior. Your outcomes match your expectations, no matter how dire, because you focus on what's wrong and what you can't do rather than on what you can, and you talk about what's not working rather than what is. This can have debilitating effects on your sales career.

But can it all be avoided? Is there anything you can do as a salesperson to stop the downward spiral? The answer is *yes*. The economy has been ebbing and flowing (down and up) for more than a hundred years. In these down periods, some people survive, some fail, and some prosper. What explains the difference in these outcomes when everyone is operating in the same economic climate? The answer is what people focus on, expect, talk about, and do.

Regardless of what is going on out there in the marketplace, you and I can control what is going on in here—in our own minds—through our attitudes, our beliefs, our expectations, and our goals. If business is slow you may have to do the following:

- think differently
- act more creatively
- sell more aggressively
- work smarter
- think faster
- work harder
- get up earlier
- go to bed later
- react sooner

In the end, because you have been proactive, you will always beat out the competition. And what's the alternative? Resigning yourself to believe that

- there is nothing you can do;
- it is out of your control;
- the situation is inevitable;
- you'll just have to wait it out, hoping you make it through.

How about you? How are you handling the current economic challenges?

TWELVE STRATEGIES FOR SUSTAINED SALES SUCCESS

In chapter 2 we discussed the personal traits any beginning salesperson should cultivate in order to be successful. In chapter 8 we discussed the special traits that set salespeople apart and propel the best ones to sales superstardom. Now I would like to offer one final variation on these two roundups: the Twelve Strategies for Sustained Sales Success. Read this list carefully and take it to heart. It will serve you during high economic times as well as low, in your sales career and in your daily life.

1. Control Your Thoughts

The most important thing you can do that will guarantee your success and happiness is to learn to control your thoughts. At first glance, this might seem an easy task, but just think of how many times today your thoughts and attention were controlled by someone or something else. Good thought control is a trait of all happy and successful people—whether they are professional athletes or business leaders, artists or musicians.

Most people live their lives in a perpetual feedback loop. They recycle old thoughts and old information over and over again, dwelling on past joy and pain, successes and failures, without focusing on new experiences.

Real thought control lets you push out these old, stale memories. It lets you take charge of your own subconscious, deciding which memories you will save and which you will throw away—and it will give you the time and mental energy to focus on what lies ahead. Most people think about what they don't want, can't have, won't become, or would like to change. Successful people, on the other hand, understand how to use their own minds as a positive tool. They focus on productive "now" moments and don't waste time dwelling on negativity.

Sometimes negative thoughts do creep in while you are not looking, but successful thought controllers know how to dispose of them quickly without working themselves into a lather. What thoughts are filling your mind today? Happy ones? Sad ones? Positive ones? Negative ones? Destructive ones?

James Allen sums up these ideas best in his book *As a Man Thinketh,* which is as resonant today as when it was written over a century ago:

> All that a man achieves and all that he fails to achieve is the direct result of his own thoughts. He who has conquered doubt and fear has conquered failure. Men do not attract that which they want, but that which they are. Their whims, fancies, and ambitions are thwarted at every step, but their inmost thoughts and desires are fed with their own food, be it foul or clean.

As a being of Power, Intelligence, and Love, and the lord of his own thoughts, man holds the key to every situation, and contains within himself that transforming and regenerative agency by which he may make himself what he wills.

Generations later, Napoleon Hill reiterated Allen's point in *Think and Grow Rich:* "What the mind of man can conceive and believe, it can achieve." Control how you think, and you take control both of what you earn and what you become.

2. Promote Yourself Relentlessly

Have you ever heard of any of these people?

Dale Earnhardt
Dr. Phil
Martha Stewart
Donald Trump
Madonna
Billy Graham

Regardless of their chosen profession, these people have one thing in common: They are or were relentless self-promoters.

What exactly is self-promotion? Is it self-confidence? No. There are many people with great self-confidence who are not comfortable self-promoters. Is it talent? No. Many very talented people have never been successful or publicly recognized.

The best self-promoters know exactly how to get themselves noticed—but more than that, they know how to get themselves noticed by the audience that they wish to be recognized by. For example, Madonna wasn't concerned about being a household name with NASCAR fans, and I guarantee Billy Graham wasn't particularly concerned if Dr. Phil's followers didn't tune into his Sunday broadcasts. Self-promotion is the willingness, desire, and ability to gain large numbers of followers. It is the ability to put yourself out there without coming

across as arrogant or self-serving. Self-promoters have as their strongest characteristics things like courage, belief, self-acceptance, high self-esteem, and persistence. Yes, these are common traits among successful people in general, but
those who are both successful *and* famous have them in abundance. Of course, I
don't mean to imply that fame is or should be important to everyone, or that
people who are not famous are not contributing as much to society.

Has anyone who was *not* a super self-promoter been supersuccessful at
bringing their ideas, products, or talent to the rest of the world? I can't think of
anyone. Maybe you can, but I'll bet that most of the people who have achieved
enduring and satisfying success have had self-promotion high on their list of priorities.

Now, don't get me wrong here. I am not saying that fame or fortune equals
success. I am only saying that self-promotion is a recurring trait among successful people. Let me illustrate this with some familiar examples.

Is Donald Trump smarter than all other corporate executives? Is Oprah
Winfrey better looking than all other media people? Was Sam Walton (the
founder of Wal-Mart) better educated than you or I?

Obviously, education is important. Talent is important. Effort is important.
Timing is important. The right contacts are important. But even if you have all
of these, you can still never achieve greatness or sustained success without the
willingness and ability to be a relentless self-promoter.

3. Believe with Conviction

Do you believe in, trust, and accept yourself? Consistently? Steadfastly? This is
one of the keys to enduring success, peace, happiness, and a worthwhile life.

Believing in yourself with conviction is knowing that no matter what
crosses your path, you can handle it. No matter how hard you fall, how long you
are down, or who is kicking you while you're there, this too shall pass, and you
can always learn from the experience.

There are two types of people in any given situation: those who whine and
those who act. Those who believe in a better tomorrow and those who don't.
Those who blame and those who take responsibility. Those who resist change
and those who flow with it. Those who understand that they—through hard

work, perseverance, and ingenuity—can get through anything, and those who throw in the towel. As a salesperson, you should never doubt your capabilities or your competence. Believe in yourself with conviction, and when you face rejection, instead of retreating into yourself, think about the ways in which the experience can improve you. Always believe that you have nowhere to go but up, and soon your sales record will be proof of your constant growth.

What is your approach to adversity, trouble, failure, problems, challenges, or any negative circumstances? Do you have a *Yes, I can* or a *No, I can't* in your heart?

4. Know Your Purpose

Webster's defines purpose as "the reason for which something exists or is done or made. An intended or desired result, aim, or goal. To intend or resolve." But I will go beyond Webster's literal definition and say that purpose is *the* determining factor of objectives. If a person lacks a clear purpose in his or her life, career, or business, then it is difficult to set and achieve meaningful goals. Without purpose, people easily lose their motivation when life throws them a curve. Without purpose it is difficult to derive any satisfaction from doing something positive. And without purpose, you will change direction in life whenever the going gets rough.

Purpose is similar to a personal mission statement. Recall that for more than three decades my personal mission statement has been "to learn as much as I can as I move through life and to share what I have learned with others who cross my path." This mission statement has become the foundation for my speaking goals, writing goals, and publishing efforts.

When I don't feel like writing, or would rather stay home than travel ten thousand miles to speak, or am not in the mood to work on another book, my purpose—my mission statement—kicks in. The thought that often comes up in my mind is, Either change your mission or purpose, or get on with it.

What are you striving for today? Do you have a major purpose in life? Do you have a personal mission statement? Have you converted your purpose or mission statement into practical, rewarding, and meaningful goals? If not, what are you waiting for?

5. Maintain Your Passion

Passion is the great equalizer. It can make up for a lack of experience or knowledge. Of course, this does not mean that you can give up on developing your knowledge or experience, because these traits will only enhance and further empower your passion. By improving your passion—your strong belief in yourself, your ability, your mission, and your purpose—you better yourself.

Passion is different from enthusiasm, and in my opinion it is more fulfilling. There's an old saying that goes, "Act enthusiastic and you will become enthusiastic." I have never subscribed to this cliché—it suggests that by simply contriving enthusiasm, you can deal with any situation. But what happens when things go badly? Acting like everything is OK is not going to immediately solve your problems.

Passion is not an act. It is a fundamental belief in what you are doing. You should be far more than "enthusiastic" about who you are, who you are becoming, where you are, where you are going, and what you believe in, stand for, and would die for. Your passion is ingrained in your psyche, and it should be visible to those around you. Who are the people you know who are passionate about something? You can see it in their eyes, hear it in their voice, and sense it in their behavior. What are you passionate about—how are you doing? Are you in love with where you are, where you are going, who you are becoming, and what you are contributing? Or are you living the way much of the population does, with the attitude "same stuff, different day."

If you have lost or are losing your passion for life, your career, or a relationship, it is crucial that you remember this one key guideline:

Do what you love, not what you must do.

6. Make Time Your Ally

Obviously, there are many different factors that affect our successes and our failures—ranging from education and gender to status and wealth. But there is one thing that we all have in common, regardless of those factors: We all get twenty-four hours each day to accomplish our goals.

Successful people understand that there are only so many hours in the day and that they can't get more time. They know they have to use the time they do have more effectively if they want to achieve success.

Time passes. When you are doing what you like or are with people you enjoy, time seems to speed by. When you are doing things you hate or are with people you don't like, time seems to creep by very slowly. The rate of time does not change. Your perception of time passing does. "Time management" is a misnomer—no one can manage time. *Effective use of time* is different from time management; by effectively using your time, you recognize and accept that there are only so many hours in a day, and you chart out the best way to achieve your goals in that time frame. Effective time use is a function of many skills, prejudices, habits, and personal philosophies. The keys to improving time use are to

1. know yourself
2. know your tendencies
3. know your strengths
4. know your weaknesses
5. know your goals
6. identify your common time wasters
7. establish regular planning times
8. be relentless with your self-discipline
9. balance multiple demands, job requirements, personal needs and desires, routine activities, and family roles

7. Overcome Adversity

Adversity gives us the opportunity to do a number of things as we move through our lives: reevaluate old patterns that are not working; see ourselves more clearly as contributors; develop new attitudes about life, relationships, money, people, or work; or observe how we handle the lessons we are given.

8. Develop a Spirit of Optimism

There are only two ways to look at life: with a YES or a NO in your heart and mind. If you begin every task, relationship, or activity with a NO outlook, you are doomed to live a life filled with disappointment, frustration, and anxiety. If you begin with a YES outlook, you have a greater chance of achieving your desires. There is no guarantee that with optimism you will achieve success, but the chances are in your favor.

It is a medical fact that people who are positive and optimistic get sick less often and live longer than people who are negative and pessimistic. I am not referring here to blind optimism or an "anything and everything is possible" mentality; we all know it's just not that kind of world. However, if your outlook tends to be "I can, I deserve, I will," then circumstances will often work in your favor. Some call it synchronicity. Psychologist Martin Seligman calls it opportunity. Others call it fate; still others, luck. I choose to call it the consequences of life working in your favor.

In reality, there is a lot of negativity in our world. The thing to remember is that judging a thing to be negative or positive is not about the thing itself. It is about us and our perceptions. Life is a neutral process that gives each of us the opportunity to *decide* whether a situation is going to be negative or positive within the context of our own lives. We don't always get to choose the circumstances of our lives, but we can always choose our attitudes about them.

9. Be Persistent

It is an unfortunate fact, but many people quit just before all of their effort, patience, commitment, and belief have time to pay off. Why is this? Why do people fail to stick with things?

Conversely, how is it that some people seem so good at sticking to their guns? I would like to share with you why these people successfully stay with relationships, projects, careers, businesses, or simple activities and hobbies. People often persist for these reasons:

1. They believe in themselves.
2. They perceive failure as an opportunity to do better.
3. They interpret problems as hurdles, not roadblocks.
4. They understand that failure is not final, only a circumstance.
5. Their self-esteem is too high to permit giving up.
6. Their dreams are too important to them to settle for less.

7. They do not accept the views or judgments of others that would limit their potential and ability.
8. They know that their legacies are in their hands alone.
9. They see rejection as the other person's issue, not theirs.
10. Their egos are not in control of their lives.
11. They believe in their mission in life.
12. They believe that the specific gifts they have been given are to be used for the benefit of others.
13. They know their time is limited, so they need to get on with it—now.

This is a long list, I know, but I wanted to make sure to include all the factors that make persistent people who they are. Do you fall under any of these categories?

10. Focus on What You Can Do Now

When it comes to focus, you can take one of two approaches. You can focus on either what is not working or what is, what you don't have or what you do, what you want or don't want, or what you believe in or don't. One of my favorite quotations is from Arthur Ashe. He said, "True greatness is starting where you are, using what you have, and doing what you can."

Most winners in life are grateful for their blessings, and they focus on what they want, have, and can do. By the same token, most losers focus on what is missing, where they are not, and what they can't do. Winners learn to work with what they have. They improvise, innovate, adjust, or compromise—whatever it takes to get the job done with the tools at hand.

You have three options in any situation: Change it, accept it, or leave it.

A key trait in all successful people is focus. What is your focus today? Is it on what you can or cannot do? Have or don't have? Be aware that you can't focus on both. You can't focus on what is and on what isn't at the same time. It is simply impossible.

11. Cultivate Integrity and Character

Adversity is normal in life. It can develop character, strength, courage, self-confidence, and self-belief.

For years I have had an ongoing debate with several people about the value and importance of letting people fail, not helping them at every turn of life's wheel, and not giving them whatever they think they need to succeed or even just survive. Now, don't get me wrong: I believe in providing a safety net at those critical times in people's lives when they really need it. It can often mean the difference between overwhelming discouragement and making it through another day. I also believe, however, that the more you help some people, the less you help them in the long run.

I ask you: If you help people every time they are in need or have a perceived need, what do they learn? They learn that their life is always in someone else's hands. They learn that whenever they are in trouble, they can pick up the cell phone and call for help. They develop the attitude that just because they are here, they deserve everything. The problem is that these people never learn self-reliance or self-confidence.

I am reminded of Tom Hanks's role in *Cast Away.* Would his character have survived better or reached safety sooner with help? Maybe, maybe not. But would he have developed the same inner strength, courage, self-belief, and self-reliance in the process? I doubt it.

Integrity and trust go hand in hand with success. It is not possible to have one without the other. If you trust someone, it is most likely because he or she is trustworthy and has ethics, integrity, and character. People who lack any one of the three generally will lack them all. So what is integrity? Integrity is behaving in such a way that if all your actions, words, deeds, and thoughts—yes, your thoughts, too—were posted on the company bulletin board or on the Internet for all to see, you wouldn't be caught in a scandal.

When we do something wrong, disingenuous, or immoral, sooner or later we all get caught. We may not get caught in the way we were anticipating, but there is a law of cause and effect in place that has been operating for millions of years. Break the rules and pay the price—no matter where—in your health, relationships, or even career. Which is why every time we consider doing something morally ambiguous, we must ask ourselves the following questions:

1. What will I lose or gain?
2. Who will this affect other than me?
3. Is it easy for me to shade the truth, and do I do it often? Why?

4. If I deal only in the truth—all the time—what will that do for me?

5. Can I handle getting caught? Is the gain worth it?

Yes, there are many wealthy and powerful people who have virtually no ethics, integrity, or character—you've seen them in the media. You might be thinking, "But they achieved wealth and fame." Well, I'll leave you with one parting thought: Were these people successful? And is that a version of success that *you* want to have any part in?

12. Be Grateful

Have you ever noticed that some people seem to have more fun, friends, success, money, stuff, influence, achievements, wisdom, peace, harmony, and freedom than others do? Why is this? Over the years I have observed people from all walks of life. As a speaker, I am privileged to meet thousands of people each year worldwide through my programs. One thing I have seen is a wide range of attitudes, feelings, and beliefs about life and what it should be like. It is interesting to note that the people I have met who have the greatest degree of peace, joy, harmony, life balance, and success are people who live with a great deal of *gratitude*.

Some of you might believe that you have nothing to be grateful for. Here are just a few things we have that we often take for granted:

1. Air to breathe

2. Food to eat

3. Hearts that pump 2.5 million times a month

4. Minds that can think

5. Work that is satisfying or challenging or that contributes to our growth

6. The right to believe what we want

7. The ability to control what we feel and think

8. The ability to feel

9. The ability to express love and receive it

10. The ability to share with others

Obviously, there are many more. Each of us, regardless of our social status, education, or circumstances, has much to be grateful for.

I would like you to take a few minutes and count your blessings. Think of everything you are or have been thankful for:

in your relationships
in your finances
in your health
in your social life
in your spiritual life
in your career or business
with your friends
in your education, wisdom, and knowledge
with your family

Successful people focus on what they can do, not what they can't; what they have, not what has been taken from them; and where they are, not where they think they would like to be.

CHAPTER 13

ANSWERS TO REMEMBER

To summarize what I've said throughout this book, I'll end by sharing with you some of the questions I have frequently been asked by audience members during my thirty-five-year sales training career. The answers are short, since most of these questions are addressed in the book's previous chapters. What I do here is give you a few brief ideas to consider.

I have arranged the questions by topic: attitudes, prospecting, sales presentations, time and territory management, sales objections, closing the sale, after-sales service, sales records, and administrative matters.

Take time to read through the following and figure out how you can apply these principles to your specific position. Remember these situations, answers, suggestions, and actions. Review them from time to time to make sure you continue to apply them in your career.

ATTITUDES

QUESTION: How do I stay motivated in a down economy?

ANSWER: Motivation—real motivation—is inside out, not outside in. When you turn over the responsibility for your motivation to the economy, your boss, the weather, or any other outside influence, you give up control of your most valuable tool: your mind. The best way to stay motivated inside is to have specific goals and keep track of your progress. Another thing I do is keep a "good stuff" jar. Anytime something good happens in my life or career, I write about it and put the piece of paper in my jar. When things go sour, or when I need a lift, I grab a few of the scraps in the jar and read or reflect on them. Trust me, it works. But it can only work if you put the stuff in when things are going well.

The best way to stay motivated inside is to have specific goals and keep track of your progress.

QUESTION: How can I overcome a negative supervisor?

ANSWER: No one is perfect. Sooner or later you will have to deal with negative people: prospects, customers, fellow salespeople, your boss, or a friend or family member. Just keep remembering that you are the only person in charge of your attitudes, success, motivation, and feelings. Other people can't make you feel anything unless you allow them to do so. If you have a negative boss, you might try meeting with him and reminding him of how far you have come, how well you are doing, how much you have learned, and other positive aspects of your performances. You have to learn to toot your own horn.

QUESTION: What is the best way to ensure I reach my goals?

ANSWER: There are four essential elements to reaching any goal:

1. Know why your goals are important to you. Just setting goals is not enough. You have to know why you want something.
2. Write them down. Keeping your goals in your head is a sure recipe for failure. You need to be able to see them, change them, understand them, believe in them, and feel good when you achieve them. It is hard to do all that when they are only in your head.
3. Give yourself deadlines. Don't give yourself forever to accomplish

something. But remember, some goals require a lot more time to come to fruition than others.

4. Reward yourself when you achieve a goal. Celebrate your success.

Reward yourself when you achieve a goal. Celebrate your success.

QUESTION: Why are attitudes so important to my sales success?

ANSWER: Attitudes in life are everything. You do what you do, don't do what you don't, believe what you do, and don't believe what you don't because of your attitudes. Your attitudes are yours and only yours. When you let other people control your attitudes, you let them control your life. Attitudes come from feelings. Feelings are the result of habits. Habits are created because of values and beliefs. So what you believe will eventually come to pass in your life because your outer reality will become a reflection of your inner state of mind.

PROSPECTING

QUESTION: What is the best way to get past a gatekeeper?

ANSWER: You need to keep multiple factors in mind: confidence, belief, communication, and desire. Be confident in yourself. Believe in your products and services and how they will benefit the prospect. Communicate clearly and truly with your prospect. And desire, above all, to succeed. The role of the gatekeeper is not to keep you out but to shelter your prospects against people who will waste their time—that is to say, people who don't have confidence, belief, communication, and desire. The best way to get past these gatekeepers (whether on the phone or in person) is to have the leverage of a referral or strategic alliance. These people can make it easier for you to get through to your prospect.

Think About It
Most good prospects are ready to buy before they tell you so.

QUESTION: How can I get to important decision makers?

ANSWER: Decision makers' time is very valuable. They don't want to waste it on poor or incompetent salespeople who have nothing of value to say or to offer. The best way to get through to a decision maker is through a recommendation from someone they respect. Work at creating these types of relationships. It will take time, but in the long run it will save you time by ensuring that you have solid rapport with the ultimate decision makers.

QUESTION: How can I get more referrals?

ANSWER: The best way to get more referrals is to ask for them. This is not rocket science. But you first need to know what to ask for. Referrals can come from anywhere: vendors, prospects, clients, personal relationships, previous customers, and even good old Aunt Sally. The main thing is to understand what a good prospect is for you, then ensure that the referrals you get closely match that profile. In the end, though, the key to success with referrals is to ask more often.

QUESTION: Is cold-calling the most effective way to prospect?

ANSWER: In my opinion, cold-calling is the least valuable use of your time. Yes, yes, I know that many companies want their salespeople to spend endless hours cold-calling. The reason is that they don't know how to teach them how to prospect more effectively. That being said, though, I do acknowledge that you have to have someone to sell to. When you begin your career, if you don't have referrals or other alliances and are not yet effective at networking, then guess what—it's time to hit the streets. But, please, after you have been selling for several months, stop spending your valuable sales time shooting in the dark—it is an ineffective method.

Good prospects are everywhere. You just have to know where to look.

QUESTION: How do I know when I have a good prospect?

ANSWER: Good prospects are everywhere. You just have to know where to look. The key to knowing whether you have a good prospect is to answer the following: Is there a sense of urgency to the person's need? Does he or she match your ideal-customer profile? Is the timing right? Can you get an appointment? Does the company have a positive relationship with your competitor? Can you get to the final decision maker? Does this prospect really need, or will he or she benefit from, your product or service? Is the money there?

SALES PRESENTATIONS

QUESTION: How long should a good presentation be?

ANSWER: As long as it takes to ensure that you have effectively gained your prospect's trust, confidence, and respect and established a willingness to buy. It also should be no longer than necessary. Most salespeople spend too much time trying to talk the prospect into buying. People buy when they are ready. The purpose of the presentation is to give them enough information so that they will make a purchase. Then your job is to educate them on everything else you didn't cover. Some presentations can be as short as fifteen minutes, while others can take several meetings that may last a few hours each.

QUESTION: What should I do if there is more than one person at the presentation?

ANSWER: This answer could fill an entire book. But here are a few things to consider. Don't play to any one individual. Don't ignore anyone. When you ask questions, look at each person for a response. Don't make assumptions about who is the decision maker. Encourage everyone to participate. Make sure everyone can see you clearly. Position yourself so no one can look at a fellow member of the group without you being able to see his or her expression.

> *Think About It*
> The critical factor in the sales process is control. Get it early, keep it, and don't ever give it up.

QUESTION: What should I do if the prospect tries to rush me?

ANSWER: Poor prospects want you to get to the end of the sales presentation quickly so that they can be rid of you. Good prospects want to engage you so that you have the knowledge to help them with their problems, challenges, or issues. Poor prospects are concerned only about price, not value. If the prospect tries to rush you, ask a simple question: "You seem to be rushed. Should we reschedule this appointment for when you will have more time?" If that doesn't work, and you still feel you are being rushed, you might want to consider terminating the appointment. Here's how I do it: "Mr. Prospect, after hearing some of your answers to my questions, I feel this is not the best time for us to be considering doing business together. Permit me to get back to you next week [or month or year] to see how your circumstances have changed." But I'm outta there. The important thing to remember in this situation is that you should always leave behind a prospect, not an enemy.

QUESTION: How many presentations should I give before I give up on a prospect?

ANSWER: The mind of a prospect must go through four stages: attention, interest, desire, and action. My feeling is that it shouldn't take more than one presentation (or appointment) for each of the four stages. So my limit is four.

TIME AND TERRITORY MANAGEMENT

QUESTION: How should I decide which new prospects to see in my territory?

ANSWER: This depends on a number of factors. How big is your territory? What is the mix of A, B, and C prospects? How many active customers do you have? How much time can you allocate to field time? How many maintenance customers do you have? How much service time do you need to serve existing customers? How complicated is your product or service? What is the typical sales cycle of a new prospect, from the first visit to a closed sale? Do you need field support from other employees? How do you travel through your territory: car, air, or some other form of transport? Does your territory include more than one time zone? I know, I have answered your question with a lot of other questions, but deciding how many prospects to see is no simple matter. As a general rule, you should make this decision with three factors in mind. First, make sure you spend adequate time with your best customers and prospects. Second, travel during non–sales time when possible. Third, don't spend too much time with poor or small prospects. It is the smaller, more demanding prospects and customers who steal your valuable time.

QUESTION: How do I handle a customer or a prospect who takes too much of my time?

ANSWER: Every prospect or customer makes unique demands on your time, requiring information, after-sales service, and some hand-holding. Some believe they need more of your time than is really necessary, while others say, "Don't call me unless there is a new product, service, or solution that I need to be aware of." These people still deserve your attention. (Remember, it is the smaller, more demanding prospects and customers who steal your valuable time.) The best way to handle this is to set up a regular time (not that frequent) to visit with them. Or you can handle them strictly on the telephone or via e-mail.

SALES OBJECTIONS

QUESTION: How do I overcome price objection?

ANSWER: Price is never the only issue. People usually object to price when the product's perceived value is low. The strategy here should be to discover why they perceive lower value and why they cannot justify your price in their own minds. There are two things you can do here. First, determine if it is really a price issue by asking how much it is worth to them to get their problem solved or need satisfied. Second, get back to selling value—what the product or service means to them. Recognize that there is a difference between price (what you pay for something) and cost (what it costs you to do it wrong, not at all, too little, or too late). Most prospects say they want a low price when what they really want most of the time is a low cost. The key is to get their focus off of price and onto cost. Avoid the tendency to reduce price at the first sign of price resistance.

> *Think About It*
> When you encounter price resistance, it is best to sell value first, before you reduce your price or relax your terms.

QUESTION: How do I overcome the objection that there is no rush to buy?

ANSWER: A sense of urgency on the part of prospects is often a critical aspect of a successful sales outcome. This need will often reduce their desire for a low price, or their concerns about inadequate features, delivery issues, or other factors. If a prospect does not have a sense of urgency, you need to create it in a professional way. The way to do this is to focus on prospects' problems or needs. By keeping their attention on the concern and not on the product or service, you can greatly enhance their sense of urgency.

QUESTION: How do I overcome the "satisfied with my current supplier" objection?

ANSWER: The key here is to find a need or desire the prospect has that the current supplier cannot satisfy. You accomplish this with a targeted question such as, "If we could do one thing better than your current supplier that would improve your satisfaction, what would that be?" Or, "If we could offer you one feature or service that would be important to you that your current supplier does not offer, what would that be?" Avoid saying anything negative about a competitor. When you do, you indirectly invalidate the previous decision. Your prospect made what he or she felt was a sound decision to do business with a competitor.

> *Think About It*
> You must know your competition: their strengths, weaknesses, goals, policies, and strategies.

CLOSING THE SALE

QUESTION: How early in the presentation should I attempt to ask for the order?

ANSWER: You are not a professional visitor. You are there to sell. If the prospects think your purpose is to educate them on the latest technology, choices, or whatever, then you have created the wrong environment. You and I both earn the same income on the sales we don't make: nothing, zilch, nada. You are there to help them solve a problem or take advantage of an opportunity, and you deserve the business if you can do either. The time to start closing is in the first minute. I don't mean you should ask for the order in the first sixty seconds—only that your attitude should be "I am here to do business." The best time to formally start the closing sequence is when the prospect asks for the price, gives you a buying signal, or asks questions like, "How long will it take to get it? How long will it take to get the process started? What is the next step?"

> *Think About It*
> Tailored, brief sales presentations are far more effective than feature-based, overloaded, and lengthy ones.

QUESTION: What is the best way to close the sale?

ANSWER: The best close is when the customer buys. Problem is, if you wait for the customer you will most likely make very few sales. People like to buy things, but they don't like to make the decision to buy things. The key is to have them believe that they are buying when you are really selling. This is a professional and effective way to handle the close of the sale. You do not force, push, or in any way coerce prospects into buying before they are ready, but once they are ready, you need to take control of the buying process. I show you how to do this very effectively in chapter 9, so I won't waste paper here repeating myself.

QUESTION: What do I do when customers cancel orders on sales I just made?

ANSWER: Get back with them in person immediately. Start with questions. You need to discover why they bought in the first place and what has changed since they made the buying decision. Has there been some negative outside influence from their supervisors? Are there some politics going on that you don't know about? Go back over the benefits that led to each initial purchase: what each customer liked, how it solved a problem, answered a need, and improved anything else you'd discussed.

AFTER-SALES SERVICE

QUESTION: How much time should I spend serving my customers?

ANSWER: Time with customers depends on the situation. How much of their business are you currently getting? How much more business is there to get? Is a competitor beating on their door for the business? Do they give you lots of referrals? Are they good references for you? Is it a new customer? Is it your biggest customer? Your smallest? Your most difficult? The answers to these questions should determine how much time you spend on after-sales service with each individual customer.

QUESTION: How do I tell small customers they are using too much of my time?

ANSWER: Tell them to buzz off! Seriously, your time is the only asset you have. It is the one common denominator among all people, successful or otherwise. If you have customers who waste your time, the best technique is to schedule appointments with them late on Friday afternoons or early Monday mornings. Why do you think these are the two best times to see these people? Tell them before you begin that you have a conference call scheduled in ten minutes, or that you have to get back to the office soon for an important meeting with your boss.

If you have customers who waste your time, the best technique is to schedule appointments with them late on Friday afternoons or early Monday mornings.

QUESTION: What is the best way to serve a new customer for repeat business?

ANSWER: Deliver on your promises. One of the biggest weaknesses of poor salespeople is that they can sometimes do a good job of selling, but then they drop the ball when it comes to delivering on what they promised.

SALES RECORDS

QUESTION: Why are sales records important?

ANSWER: They can help you spot potential weaknesses. They can improve your sales results. They can help you accurately track your sales time and activities. They can help you identify your strengths and the factors that contribute to your success. They can give you benchmarks. They will help you increase your income.

QUESTION: Shouldn't my manager's sales-call report be enough information to keep?

ANSWER: No. The typical call report required by management is designed to ensure that you are working, not necessarily that you are effective. Success is far too important to leave up to a few basic sales statistics. If your call report is more thorough than average, so be it. But I would bet that it doesn't ask for a fraction of the information I list in the answer below.

QUESTION: What sales records should I keep?

ANSWER: There is no simple answer to this, but here's a list of a few of the important items. There are many more, but these will get you started:

- average income per sale
- ratio of telephone calls to appointments
- ratio of appointments to closed sales
- average length of your sales cycle
- average number of referrals per customer
- average sales volume
- average number of sales per week, month, and quarter
- percentage of business from current customers versus new customers
- source of your best prospects
- average length of a successful appointment
- average number of appointments to get a closed sale
- average volume of your first sale to a new customer
- number of new prospects you need per year to reach your desired sales results

See how many more you can add to this list.

ADMINISTRATIVE MATTERS

QUESTION: How do I tell my boss that paperwork is wasting too much of my time?

ANSWER: I wouldn't make an issue out of it if you are really new or not doing well. This can be a touchy one, depending on the attitude of your boss, how new you are, and how successful you have been to date. You need to get leverage if you want to break some of the rules. The best way to get leverage is through success. So get some sales under your belt. Hit a few home runs. Beat your quota, sell more than anyone else in the company, and then have a chat with your boss.

Beat your quota, sell more than anyone else in the company, and then have a chat with your boss.

QUESTION: How do I avoid meetings that waste my time?

ANSWER: Well, it depends on who is holding them. If it is a meeting with your boss or your best client or prospect, good luck. If it is a meeting with another department or a fellow salesperson, you can always be busy somewhere else. Use a little creativity and finesse. Just tell the people who want the meeting that you can do it whenever. When is whenever? It is when you want to see them and when is most convenient for you.

QUESTION: When is the best time to do paperwork?

ANSWER: Prioritize. As I mentioned earlier in this book, you must break your time into two major areas: Prime Time and Prime Time Plus. Prime Time is when you are at your best: early morning, late in the afternoon. Your Prime Time Plus is the time when you are at your best *and* your prospects can see you. Paperwork and administrative responsibilities should be done anytime other than Prime Time and Prime Time Plus.

APPENDIX 1: ACT NOW!

The key to sustained motivation in life and sales is the ownership and mastery of basic skills and attitudes. With a guiding philosophy of learning, testing, integrating, applying, and reevaluating skills, you are assured success as you pass through the stages of your life. With this approach, you will also have the ability to use these techniques and maintain these attitudes with confidence, regardless of what new circumstances present themselves as you move through the natural ups and downs, successes and failures, and wins and losses in your career and life.

These assignments are designed to help you master the critical attitude and skill areas necessary for sales success. Whether this is your first sales position or you have been selling for a few years, it is critical that you practice, integrate, and apply the lessons you learn. The following assignments will facilitate that learning process.

The assignments are in no particular order of importance. Each assignment, when completed, can have a dramatic impact on your overall motivation, confidence, and sales success. Give each exercise the time, effort, and commitment it deserves. Don't shortchange your success by thinking that one exercise is less important than another. Once you have completed all of the exercises, I guarantee that you will see a tremendous improvement in your ability to sell more and enjoy greater success and a fuller lifestyle.

I recommend taking one to two weeks for each assignment, but you should give each what you feel is necessary to ensure mastery, continued application, and ultimate success. It is likely that in less than one year you will have completed all of the exercises. This is a strategic programmed approach to your skill and attitude development rather than a hit-or-miss, slipshod philosophy that would only add to your frustration, lack of success, and possible failure. Don't risk it. There is one investment you must make to bring these assignments to life. Purchase a three-ring binder, a tab for each assignment, and a ream of lined paper (cost: under $15) at your local office supply store.

I also recommend that you not complete any of the assignments until you have read the entire text portion of the book. This information will allow you to get the most out of the exercises.

Good luck!

Attitude Management

Attitude in life is everything.

Make a list of five regular customers, associates, friends, relatives, and suppliers. Ask each of them to describe your sales attitudes, positive and negative. List these twenty-five people in the Attitude tab of your binder and leave room next to their names for their comments. After you have completed the interviews and recorded their feedback, review it and look for similarities, incongruities, areas for possible improvement, areas where you have blind spots, and areas where your self-perception is the same as others' opinions.

Purpose

All success is the result of a definite purpose in life. You won't achieve all of your goals (unless you set your goals very low), but it is still important to constantly reach for new heights. Purpose drives you forward regardless of the setbacks, problems, disappointments, and failures in your life.

1. Define your driving purpose in life in twenty-five words or less.
2. Determine where you tend to give up easily or early.

3. If someone wrote a book about your life, what would the title be? What would the title of the current chapter be? The next chapter?

4. How do you want the book to end?

Start a Journal

A journal will become one of your most valuable possessions as you travel through the days and years of your life. A journal is a record of your successes, defeats, personal development, philosophy, goals accomplished, and goals abandoned. It is a written record of your life's peaks and valleys, lessons learned, and lessons under way.

Start a journal today. You already have a head start: You can use your binder as your journal. Just add sections to it as you move through the various stages of the rest of your life.

Control Your Thoughts

There is one trait that separates humans from every other species: the ability to control thoughts. It is interesting, however, how few people effectively exercise this ability. Most let circumstances, other people, fears, and any number of outside issues influence and even control their thoughts day in and day out, moment in and moment out.

1. Keep a journal of the recurring dominant thoughts that fill your mind when you are upset, happy, frustrated, afraid, and confident.

2. At the end of each week, for two weeks, summarize those thoughts that kept popping up, whether positive or negative.

3. Develop a mantra or sentence that you can repeat over and over again when certain negative thoughts fill your mind.

Desire and Belief

Desire is the beginning of all success. Purpose, plans, goals, and actions are consequences of desire. What you vividly desire and believe the future holds will one day be a reality. Belief is the second cousin of desire. If you can imagine it, if you can believe it is possible, and if you can create a burning desire for it, all that is required for success is consistent and purposeful action.

1. What is your single driving desire—the one thing that you want more than anything else?
2. Write it out as a statement as if it were already true.
3. Reread that statement until you can say it from memory. Etch it on your very being, believe you deserve it, and watch the world help you move toward it.

Manage Adversity

Everyone faces adversity in his or her life. No one escapes without some type of disappointment, failure, or significant life or career challenge. Each of us can determine if and how we respond to these trials. We can whine, complain, quit, try again, find a different approach, or respond in any number of other positive and negative ways. Adversity has value only if we use it to get better, smarter, stronger, or more humble.

1. List all of the major kinds of adversity you have had in your life to date.
2. Write down your reactions to them.
3. Do you see any patterns or recurring themes?
4. How would you like to learn to respond?
5. What is standing in your way of responding the way you wish—your belief system, expectations, values, self-esteem, attitudes?

Motivators and Demotivators

Some things motivate; others do the opposite.

In tab one of your binder, create two subsections:

1. Things, people, and circumstances that motivate you to act.
2. People, things, circumstances, etc., that demotivate your actions.

Now turn to each subsection and create the following four columns:

1. Event/person/circumstance, date, your reaction, and hindsight.
2. Add to the first three columns daily for at least two weeks.
3. Each week review your notes and complete the last column, hindsight (what you learned).

Now create a third subsection:

List what you need to do/how you need to think or feel differently to improve your success. Spend time and put down some ideas on this subject.

Resonance

Each of us transmits to the world a reflection of our values, beliefs, expectations, attitudes, fears, needs, and much more. With our words, tone, and demeanor, we say to the world: I like me/I don't like me; I like my job/I don't like my job; I am glad to be able to help you/I wish it were Friday and I were off work. There are many more examples I could give.

1. Ask a coworker whom you trust and respect to give you feedback on your attitudes, actions, and communication for two weeks. Give your colleague permission to be honest; make assurances that you won't get defensive.
2. Record your side of telephone conversations with customers and ask a different coworker to give you feedback on your tone and attitude.
3. Get a mirror and observe your facial expressions for one week while on the phone.

Focus

Listen to your inner-self talk. People bring into their lives more of what they already focus on. This inner-self talk, depending on whether it is positive or negative, will contribute to your behavior as you travel through life. We can focus on what is working in our lives or what isn't, what we have or lack, and what we can or can't do.

1. For one week, record your self-talk in your binder in the tab marked Focus. Keep an accurate record of those topic areas where you tend to spend time and energy thinking either positive or negative thoughts about yourself, customers, fellow employees, life, or other people and things.

2. At the end of the week, summarize those common areas and see if you can determine how the thought pattern or focus is influencing the quality of your life, your unresolved issues, and anything else.

Old Baggage

Identify yours, deal with it, and move forward. Everyone has unresolved emotional baggage from the past. This old baggage, if not dealt with, can negatively affect your success in several ways. Thus, you need to confront it.

1. Create a list of emotional slights and other things that people have said or done to you, as well as things they have not said or done that you feel they should have.

2. Identify which ones are causing you continued stress, frustration, or emotional pain.

3. See if you can identify your expectations, feelings, or reasons why you still carry this baggage.

4. Identify which customers have the ability to push your buttons and cause you to respond negatively because of past attitudes or future expectations.

It is also important to remember not to let other people's emotional baggage become our destiny.

Personal Development

Continuing your personal development is a must if you are to succeed in your career in sales as well as life.

1. Spend a day in the library or your local bookstore. Find three books

you feel will help your career, motivation, or success. Check them out or buy them.

2. Spend one hour a day for the next two weeks with the self-help books or audiobooks you selected. Don't just read or listen. Get in the habit of making notes as you read or listen. Put the notes in your binder in the tab for this assignment. Continue this habit after the two weeks have ended.

3. Spend five minutes every day thinking about how your personal development will contribute to your career success.

Overcome Your Fears

Confront your fears and you will overcome them. Avoid them and they will continue to control your thoughts, actions, and outcomes. We all have fears at some point in our lives: fears of heights, snakes, death, failure, success—yes, even success.

1. List all of your fears.
2. Organize them from greatest to least.
3. See if you can determine what you are really afraid of.
4. Ask yourself, What is the worst thing that can happen if I fail or confront my fear?

Dream Big Dreams

Anyone who has ever accomplished anything of value has had a dream. Dreams are the stuff of hope, desire, and challenge. They pull us forward as they help us overcome obstacles and the negative people in our lives who try to discourage us.

1. Ask yourself, What would I try if it were impossible to fail, if my success were assured?
2. Write down all of the dreams that you would like to realize during the rest of your life (not goals—dreams are bigger).
3. Have you given up on any dreams because of age, health, or other people?
4. Why?

Take Risks

No one can get out of this life without taking a few risks. To live life to the fullest requires "going for it" every once in a while—whether it is picking up a new hobby, beginning a new career, or just going on vacation without making reservations. (I know, I know. Some of you just cringe at the thought.)

1. Create a list of all of your fears (private and public, major, and minor).
2. Now rank them, putting the smallest ones at the top of your list and the biggest ones at the bottom.
3. For each one on the list, ask yourself, What am I afraid of?
4. Start with the smallest one at the top and just go for it.
5. Continue down the list (no matter how long it takes), going for it and building confidence and self-belief.

Build Your Self-Esteem

Self-esteem and a healthy self-image are a must. Do you like you? Do you accept you and your life as valuable? Do you feel worthwhile? Or do you only feel good when you are accomplishing, getting positive feedback from others, or succeeding? A healthy self-image is one of the most critical factors for success and happiness.

1. Create a list of everything you like about yourself.
2. Now expand on the items. Write a paragraph about why you like each specific trait or attitude.
3. Create a list of all of your accomplishments. Go as far back in your life as you can.
4. Ask people who know you well and like you to describe all of your positive attributes.

Manage Your Stressors

Stress is normal. Every day there are positive and negative stressors in your career. The ultimate impact of stress is determined by how you manage it from the inside out. The consequences of not managing stress in a positive way can be anything from physical illness to emotional withdrawal.

1. Start a stress log.
2. For two weeks, every time you feel your body sending you stress messages—nervousness, anxiety, frustration, negative self-talk, loss of energy, etc.—record the date and time, the symptoms, what you believe is the cause, and your reaction.
3. At the end of the two weeks, spend some time looking for common causes, consistent reactions, and similar outcomes: How did these affect your life?
4. Create a list of all of the customers (or types of customers) you interact with who cause you the most stress. Ask yourself, What is it about these people or these relationships that is causing me stress?

Planning

The key to life is to make plans—and then embrace the unexpected. There are few things more satisfying and calming than watching the events, activities, and projects you have planned come to fruition. But at the same time, not all of your plans will work out, and you have to be prepared for things you *didn't* plan for. That's life.

1. Develop a planning template that you can use in your personal life and career. What should be included? Time frames, expected outcomes, available resources, possible obstacles, goals, and short-term action steps. Can you add any?
2. Apply this template to any current project or activity.
3. Follow the steps and record both successes and failures.
4. Reevaluate your template and make modifications where necessary to ensure success next time.

Time Management

You can't manage time. You can only manage a variety of elements in your life as time passes.

1. Create a list of your common personal time wasters (activities that may be sabotaging your success).

2. Evaluate/estimate how much time you actually spend on each of these activities in a week. Record this information in your binder's Time Management tab.

3. For two weeks, keep a daily log in half-hour intervals. Log how you spent that time: driving, reading the paper, solving problems, etc. At the end of the week, total the time in all of the major categories. Now the fun part: evaluate where you are wasting time and determine which habits must be changed.

Territory Management

There are only so many hours in the day during which you can sell. Spending time with poor prospects or traveling during peak selling time is a certain career killer.

1. Take the number of miles you drive in any given week and divide it by the number of sales calls you make. That number is your call effectiveness. See if you can lower that number with better call scheduling.

2. Now evaluate your per-call success (closed sales, average sales volume, or income) in that same week.

3. How can you increase that success? Better prospecting? Less wasted time with poor prospects? Better sales results with higher sales-close ratios? Spend time evaluating how, where, and why you are not achieving the success in your territory you feel you are capable of. Then develop some new approaches to see more or better prospects with less wasted time and energy.

Effective Networking

It isn't whom you know, but who knows you. If you are not currently involved in groups that can increase your contacts and accelerate your career, what are you waiting for?

1. Make a list of everyone you know who can contribute to either your personal growth or your success. Call them and ask for their help. (It will be helpful to know what you want from them before you call.)

2. During the next two weeks, go out of your way to make at least one new contact a day.

3. Create a list of your top twenty-five advocates (people who are interested in your success). Update this list regularly.

Be a Resource

Competitor-proof your client relationships by becoming a better resource. This is also the best way to take prospects from a competitor.

1. Call your top fifteen clients and ask them how you can be a better resource for them.

2. Call your top fifteen prospects and ask them the same question.

3. Talk to at least ten salespeople you know and ask them how they are a resource for their customers.

4. By now you should have a fairly extensive list of actions you can take to become a better resource. Select those areas where you have the time, expertise, and resources and create an action plan to begin.

Effective Communication

There are many ways we communicate, and good communication is more than the sharing of words or gestures: it is shared understanding, though not necessarily agreement. How you communicate on the phone and in person says a great deal about your self-image, confidence, attitudes, and ability to express yourself accurately.

1. Make a list of your favorite words and then record how often you use them.

2. Learn a new word every day for the next two weeks.

3. Make a list of words that people use that you do not know the meaning of, and then look them up in the dictionary.

Listening Skills

Not listening to a customer is one of the best ways I know to invalidate a customer. Most people don't listen well. I am not referring to hearing problems. Listening takes place on a mental level, while hearing is a physical act. Learn to be a great listener.

1. The next several times you talk with customers, ask them to paraphrase the thoughts you communicated to them.
2. In every conversation you have with customers for the next week, focus on their intent or meaning, not just the words used.
3. For every conversation you have over the next few days, write no more than a three-sentence summary of each conversation. Pay particular attention to assumptions made, expectations not verbalized, or words or ideas that caused your mind to wander.

Common Customer Complaints

"Perfect" doesn't exist in the real world. Sooner or later you or your organization will disappoint a customer, perhaps even your best one. This doesn't mean you shouldn't try to give exceptional service every day, every time, to every customer.

1. List the most frequent customer complaints you hear about your organization, products or services, policies, and procedures.
2. Now prioritize the list. What are the most frequent ones?
3. Which ones do you have the responsibility or authority to address?
4. Which ones need to be addressed higher up in the organization?
5. Take both lists to your supervisor and have a discussion about them.

Conflict and Perceptions

Life is a perceptual experience. People look at everything through their own unique experiences, expectations, and feelings. No one is ever wrong—other people just see things differently than we do. Most conflict in relationships comes from these varying perspectives.

1. What are some common perceptions your customers have of your products or services, organization, and industry?
2. What are the biggest sources of conflict between your customers and your organization?
3. The next time you have a conflict with a customer, see if you can see the issue through your customer's eyes.
4. In hindsight, what could you have done differently to defuse the conflict?

What Customers Want

Customers want many things: freedom from inconvenience, fair prices, effective follow-up, employees who care, quick response time, solutions to their problems—to mention just a few. Most customers, however, will settle for just three and continue to do business with you. They primarily want to be cared about, listened to and understood, and respected. Satisfy all of their needs and desires and you will own them forever.

1. Create a list of those services, benefits, and attitudes that you believe your customers want more than anything else.
2. Now create a list of all of the services and benefits that you deliver most of the time.
3. Is there a disparity between the two lists? If so, what can you do about it?

Develop Strategic Alliances

Let other people help you sell. From clients and friends to other salespeople who are in a position to help you accelerate the sales process and your results, there are numerous connections for you to use.

1. Make a list of the top fifty people you know who could in some way contribute to your success.

2. Meet with each of them as time and logistics permit and ask for help, such as with names, resources, information about clients or prospects, etc.

3. Cultivate an active working relationship with as many of them as possible.

Go the Extra Mile

Successful salespeople promise a lot and deliver more. Poor salespeople promise a little and deliver less. Going the extra mile means doing more for your customers than they expect, want, pay for, or need.

> Create a list of activities and services you can provide your customers to help them. This is not about helping them so they will buy more from you, but helping them build their businesses and their careers. In other words, what can you give them—in terms of ideas, information, and services—that will contribute to their overall success?

Study the Competition

Product knowledge is vital for your success. It is also critical that you know everything possible about your competitors.

1. Go to your binder and make a list of all of your competitors.

2. Arrange them in the order in which you compete with them.

3. Now put each of your top competitors (those who are either aggressively after your business or whose business you want to get) at the top of a page. List everything you know about them. Also list those areas where your information is weak, inconclusive, or sparse.

4. Develop a strategy to discover what you don't know and to effectively and professionally use what you do know.

Keep Better Sales Records

If you don't know where you are going, it is difficult to get there. If you don't know where you have been, you are prone to repeat mistakes and failures. Effective records are a must for your success. They will reveal your strengths and bring weaknesses to the surface.

1. Create a list of every sales data point you can think of: number of telephone calls, presentations, close attempts, new prospects, referrals, etc. (There are at least thirty different types of information you can collect.)
2. Decide which of these is the most critical for your career or your product or service.
3. Design a form to keep track of this information, and enter information into it for two weeks.
4. Evaluate ratios between different types of information. For example, how many appointments do you need to make a sale?

Develop a Closing Strategy

Closing is not just a skill. It's also an attitude. The close of the sale is a natural conclusion to everything you have done up to that point. Most salespeople who are poor closers can trace that condition to one of two causes: poor prospects or no closing strategy.

1. Write out your closing strategy (winging it doesn't count). If you don't have one, then create one.
2. Memorize it.
3. Try it out on some of your fellow salespeople, your friends who are in sales, or your mother. But try it out before you use it on your best prospects.

Evaluate Customers and Prospects

Time is money. Spending enough time with your best clients and prospects is one of the best ways to succeed in sales. Spending too much time with poor prospects and clients who can't give you much more business can be a momentum killer.

1. Develop a list of criteria that you can use as a template to determine whether a prospect is worth your time and resources.

2. Now rank A, B, and C prospects according to how well they fit the template. The better the match, the higher the rating.

3. Take your template and measure each active prospect and client against it, noting how much time you're spending with each. This will tell you whether you are spending too little or too much time with certain clients and prospects.

Referrals

Referrals are "easier money." It is easier to do business with referrals than with any other new prospects. Referrals can come from anywhere, but the best sources tend to be current satisfied *customers.*

1. Ask every customer for at least three referrals.
2. Develop a referral awareness. Learn to ask for referrals just as if it were ingrained in your consciousness.
3. Start a referral page in your binder. Every time you get one, list the source, the referral, and the result.

Develop Better Questions

Accurate information is the key to your sales success. Asking good questions is a vital skill in selling. Most salespeople talk too much. They give information before they get it.

1. Create a list of everything you need to know before you can accurately evaluate whether you have a good prospect.
2. Prioritize the list. Some information may be vital, while other information may be insignificant.
3. Now develop questions to get this information.
4. Test the questions. If you get what you ask for, great. If not, go back to the drawing board and redesign the questions.
5. Once you have a set of questions that gets you all the critical information you need to make the sale, memorize the questions.

Tailor the Presentation

Each customer is unique. People buy according to their needs and wants, not according to yours. They buy when they are ready to buy, not when you need to sell. Avoid a feature dump. Tailor the message to the prospect's dominant emotional buying motive and to his or her buying style.

1. Evaluate your selling style. Do you talk too much? Too little? Expect people to buy for your reasons? Do you project your buying prejudices onto the sales process?
2. Get a book on behavior styles.
3. Develop a strategy to effectively sell to each of the different styles.

Letters of Testimony

Ask every customer for a written letter of testimony—short and sweet, yet one of the most valuable exercises.

Service

Effective after-sales service is the glue in all sales relationships. It is when you deliver on promises you made on behalf of your organization. Service either builds more trust and strengthens the relationship, or it sabotages the relationship when it is not present, satisfactory, or consistent.

1. List all the ways you provide service (both you personally and your organization) for your customers.
2. Call or write all of your clients and ask them to comment on your service (again, you and the organization).
3. Ask them how you could do a better job with after-sales service.

By now you're familiar with the many traits that turn beginning salespeople into sales superstars. Below is a list of some of the most important characteristics that will contribute to your continued success.

This list is supposed to be a handy reference; don't be overwhelmed by how long it is. Just try to focus on one skill per week. Some topics might require more time and effort than others; it's up to you to develop strategies that will help you achieve each of your weekly goals.

1. Read something positive every day. Learn to fill your mind with inspirational thoughts.
2. Have fun. Smile and look like you are enjoying yourself.
3. Spend at least one to two hours each week planning your activities. Make planning a routine.
4. Set weekly, monthly, and yearly goals, and write them down. Direction is a critical factor in life.
5. Spend time with people who are successful. Have lunch once a week with someone you respect.
6. Commit. To be successful you must lock the back door once you begin something new.

7. Learn from everyone. Study success and successful people with purpose and passion.

8. Get a mentor. Mentors can save you time, money, and effort; prevent you from making poor decisions; and more.

9. Stay focused. Focus is the vital trait that all successful people have in common.

10. Become other-centered rather than self-centered. It's not all about you.

11. Join or start a Mastermind Group. When like minds share ideas, the results can be incredible.

12. Spend routine time in self-evaluation. If you don't know what you are doing wrong, it is hard to improve.

13. Develop a do-it-now attitude. Overcome procrastination. Learn to do the difficult things first.

14. Learn to handle your fears. Fear prevents people from happiness and success more than anything else.

15. Get a personal coach. A coach will ensure that you stick to your goals and purpose.

16. Do what you love. Live without regrets. Regrets weigh tons. Discipline weighs ounces.

17. Maintain balance. Your life is always either moving toward balance or away from it.

18. Listen to positive messages at least two or three times a week. Repetition is the key to understanding.

19. Manage your stress. Stress is your inside-out reaction to outside-in circumstances, events, or people.

20. Deal only in the truth.

21. Say thank you every day for all of your blessings.

22. Keep a "good stuff" jar. This is a storehouse of everything that is good about your life.

23. Know your real intent. This is a "whatever it takes" attitude about goals, projects, and challenges.

24. Don't ever lose your passion and desire. Dream big dreams and don't let anyone talk you out of them.

25. Keep a journal. This is a compilation of lessons learned, goals achieved, and much more.

26. Improve one area of your life every month. This approach can cut years off the journey to success.

27. Make decisions. Don't try to make right decisions. Make decisions and then make them turn out right.

28. Keep things simple. When things get too complicated, people get confused and tentative.

29. Be an early person. Get to meetings, work, and everything early, then read while you are waiting.

30. Listen better. You will learn far more about everything and everyone by listening rather than talking.

31. Take responsibility for your life. No one owes you a thing. You have and get what you deserve.

32. Never give up. Persistence is the key to long-term success. Stick with it, try again, and keep trying.

33. Invest in yourself regularly. Invest at least 10 percent of your income and 10 percent of your time in personal growth every year.

34. Control your thoughts. Don't let someone else's mental baggage become your destiny.

35. Let go of old baggage. Letting go of slights and disappointments will help you live longer.

36. Share what you have with others. Try giving yourself away more often.

37. Forgive yourself and others. Not forgiving yourself for your mistakes and failures is unforgivable.

38. Live in the present moment. It is the only one you have. The future isn't here yet, and the past is gone.

39. Detach from outcomes. You can't control the future. All outcomes are subject to outside influences.

40. Manage your expectations. Most of life's disappointments are the result of unrealistic expectations.

41. Now put some effort into it. Success requires work: You can't just sit there all day and hope.

42. Save 10 percent of everything you earn. The key to wealth is an effective savings and investment plan.

43. Believe in abundance and prosperity. Abundance is everywhere; all you have to do is look.

44. Develop your character. Character is the congruence between your behavior in public and private.

45. Practice being happy. Happiness is not an address or a bank balance. It is inside you, not outside.

46. Take risks. What would you try if you knew failure was impossible?

47. See problems, adversity, and failure as tools. Problems and failure in themselves are neither positive nor negative.

48. Eliminate your limitations. The only thing that holds you back in life is yourself.

Success is never easy or fast. Many people lack the courage, commitment, belief, and persistence to make these strategies a part of their everyday lives. But if you do, your first year in sales will be a guaranteed success!

Books

Advanced Selling Strategies
Brian Tracy
Fireside

Anatomy of a Successful Salesman
Arthur Mortell
Farnsworth Publishing

The Ancient Scrolls
Tim Connor
Connor Resource Group

Consultative Selling
Mack Hanan
AMACOM

The Experience Economy
B. Joseph Pine, James H.
Gilmore, B. Joseph Pine II
Harvard Business School Press

Full Price
Thomas Winninger
Dearborn Trade

The Greatest Salesman in the World
Og Mandino
Bantam Books

Growing Your Business
Mark LeBlanc
Expert Publishing

How to Sell More in Less Time
Tim Connor
Connor Resource Group

*How to Sell More in Less Time,
   with No Rejection, Using
   Common Sense*
Art Sobczak
Business by Phone

Jonathan Livingston Seagull
Richard Bach
MacMillan Publishing

Life Is Tremendous
Charles E. Jones
Executive Books

Niche Selling
William T. Brooks
McGraw-Hill Professional
    Publishing

No Bull Selling
Hank Trisler
Fell's

The Perfect Sales Presentation
Robert Shook
Bantam Books-Audio

The Platinum Rule
Anthony Allesandra
Warner Books

Please Understand Me
David Keirsey, Marilyn Bates
Prometheus Nemesis Book Co.

Price Wars
Tom Winninger
St. Thomas Press

Sales Mastery
Tim Connor
Connor Resource Group

Sales Questions That Close the Sale
Charles D. Brennan Jr.
AMACOM

Selling Leverage
William Exton Jr.
Prentice Hall

Soft Sell
Tim Connor
Sourcebooks

Spin Selling
Neil Rackham
McGraw-Hill

Telephone Tips That Sell
Art Sobczak
Business by Phone

Ten Greatest Salespersons
Robert Shook

Think and Grow Rich
Napoleon Hill
Fawcett Books

Recommended Websites

Executive Books Website for Books
(20 to 90 percent discounts)
www.executivebooks.com

Just Sell
www.justsell.com

INDEX

prices, 90, 96, 239–46,
270–71
costs and, 239
value and, 208, 242, 243,
244, 245–46, 270
problems, 29, 124, 131, 132
product knowledge, 45–46
improving, 168–69
professionalism, 3–5, 6. 13, 64
professional salesperson
versus sales clerk, 177
promoting yourself, 254–55
prospecting, 172, 173,
266–68
slumps in, 43, 44
prospects, 45, 220, 248
customer profiles and, 165,
198, 223–24
early signals from, 228–29
evaluating, 291–92
objections from, 226–27,
229, 270–71
practicing on, 89, 221
reasons for not buying,
174–76
relating to, 225–26
seeing customers as, 227–28
tension management and,
179–81
psychological debt, 25–26
punching your own ticket,
148
purpose, 214–15, 256,
278–79
Pygmalion Effect, 251–52

quality, 244, 245
questions and answers,
264–75
quick start, 2–3, 66
quitting too soon, 215, 259

raising the bar, 169–70
reading, 212–13
realism, 8, 67, 216
recognition, 147–49, 152, 241
record-keeping, 42, 248–49,
273–74, 290–91

rediscovery, 75–76
references, 164–65, 173
referrals, 90–91, 165, 172,
201–2, 267, 292
regaining lost business,
247–48
reinvention attitudes, xxiv
rejection, 23, 62, 173
managing, 27–29, 128–30
relationships, 40
with clients, see sales
relationships
with fellow salespeople,
32–33, 60–61, 92
skills and attitudes for,
32–33
repeat business, 90
resilience, 6
resonance, 281
resource, acting as, 158, 287
resource guide, 299–300
rewards, 149
risk-taking, 284
Road to Happiness Is Full of
Potholes, The (Connor),
212
Rogers, Will, 111, 212
rule-breaking, 162

sacrifice, xxviii, 134–35
sales-acquisition costs, 95
Sales & Marketing Manage-
ment Magazine, 229
sales cycles, 177–79
sales leaders, traits of, 157–66
sales presentations, 172, 173,
183, 186, 188, 202–10,
268–69
asking questions in, 209
elevator statements and,
192, 193, 194
length of, 268, 272
more than one person at,
268
tailoring to prospects, 293
sales process, 172–210
and acting like you need
the business, 220–21

advertising concessions in,
230–31
asking questions in, 10–12,
185, 186, 187–91,
196–201, 206–8
closing in, see closing
competitors and, 176
control in, 180, 182–83,
222, 226
decision making in, 246,
272
defining statements in,
192–93
elevator questions in,
187–91, 194
elevator statements in,
187, 191–96
information in, 23, 164,
171, 175, 182, 183–84,
198, 203, 222, 292
negotiation in, 165–66,
232, 241
objections from prospects
in, 226–27, 229,
270–71
personal prejudices in,
229
presentations in, see sales
presentations
prospecting in, see
prospecting
question matrix in,
196–201
referrals in, 90–91, 165,
172, 201–2
setups and, 184–85
reasons for not buying,
174–76
tension management in,
179–81
sales profession:
basics of, xiii–xv
boundaries and limits of,
70–72
changes in, xi–xii,
xviii–xix, 19, 173
defining, xi–xiii, 3–5
fads in, xiii

ABOUT THE AUTHOR

Tim Connor, CSP, is a world-renowned speaker, trainer, and best-selling author.

Tim is the president and CEO of Connor Resource Group and Peak Performance Institute. He has been a full-time professional speaker, trainer, coach, and consultant, as well as a best-selling author, for more than thirty-five years. Since 1973 he has given more than four thousand presentations to a wide variety of audiences in twenty-one countries around the world.

Each year more than 85 percent of his presentations are return engagements; he covers such topics as peak-performance management, effective leadership, customer-focused sales strategies, personal motivation, value-driven customer service, and building positive business and personal relationships.

Each year he also facilitates a number of strategic-planning events and meetings for many of his clients, and he offers several public boot camps. He is a results-oriented business coach and consultant, working with a few select clients each year to help them improve their individual and organizational performance.

Tim has been a member of the National Speakers Association for over twenty-five years, and he is one of only four hundred Certified Speaking Professionals in the world, a designation given by the National Speakers Association since 1979.

He is the best-selling author of more than sixty-five books, including several international best sellers: *Soft Sell* (the number-one best-selling sales book in the world, now in twenty-one languages), *81 Challenges Smart Managers Face, 91 Mistakes Smart Salespeople Make, Life Is Short,* and *Above Ground.*

Tim's international clients range in sales from $5 million to more than $50 billion a year and come from a wide variety of industries, including food manufacturing and distribution; housing and construction; financial services; hospitality; technology and communications; and personal and professional services.

His presentations are filled with insightful and contemporary ideas and are delivered in a riveting and entertaining style.

To discuss hiring Tim for your organization, contact him at 704-895-1230 (voice), 704-895-1231 (fax), tim@timconnor.com (e-mail), or www.timconnor .com (website). www.corporatedisconnect.com.